CW00538280

Business Development

A Practical Handbook for Lawyers

Consulting Editor **Stephen Revell**
on behalf of the International Bar Association

Consulting editor
Stephen Revell
On behalf of the International Bar Association

Managing director
Sian O'Neill

Business Development: A Practical Handbook for Lawyers
is published by
Globe Law and Business Ltd
3 Mylor Close
Horsell
Woking
Surrey GU21 4DD
Tel: +44 20 3745 4770
www.globelawandbusiness.com

Print and bound by CPI Antony Rowe

Business Development: A Practical Handbook for Lawyers
ISBN 9781911078005

Mixed Sources
Product group from well-managed
forests and other controlled sources
www.fsc.org Cert no. SGS-COC-002953
© 1996 Forest Stewardship Council
FSC

Table of contents

Introduction

Stephen Revell
Freshfields Bruckhaus Deringer

In today's legal market, good business development is central to differentiation and success for both individual lawyers and law firms. To succeed, you need to develop and nurture properly existing relationships with clients, as well as proactively look for and attract new clients. As Murray Coffey and Emily Cunningham Rushing discuss in the chapter on developments in law firm marketing, law firms are discovering that they are subject to the same market forces as other parts of the business world, and viewing the firm as a marketable entity is central to future prosperity.

But what is good business development and what is marketing? This book seeks to examine a whole range of issues relating to business development, intertwined with some practical guidance as to how to get better at business development and what good business development looks like. We focus on both what individual lawyers and law firms need to think about. I am particularly pleased with the contributions that we were able to garner from general counsel all over the world as to how they view business development. If you read nothing in this book other than the chapter setting out the general counsel's comments, then you will have radically improved your understanding of what good business development is and how you should probably be rethinking, in some cases radically, the so-called 'business development' that you may presently be doing. You should make that chapter compulsory reading for all your lawyers!

It became clear to me whilst editing this book that building, managing and leveraging relationships based on trust and respect is fundamental to retaining and developing business. Engaging with your clients, understanding them and focusing on their needs should be your top priority. As Thorsten Zulauf says in the chapter on making the sale: "You need to ask yourself when was the last time a client complimented your firm on its exceptional understanding of its business and the excellent advice given, and if you cannot remember such an occasion, approach your client in order to find out what is needed to receive such feedback." This message of understanding the client comes through loud and clear from the general counsel, whose views we have deliberately kept in interview format so you can hear their opinions as they expressed them. Business development is effective only if it has an impact on the intended target.

After reflecting on these general counsel interviews, it is obvious that business development has to be seen in the context of developing a trusted relationship. Once you have it, you can do a lot of really effective business development, but without it, you will struggle. Winning new business from general counsel takes time and real thought. Clients want individual lawyers and law firms to demonstrate an understanding of their business and to be proactive and forward thinking in providing them with solutions to the challenges that they – not clients generally – may face. In other words, you have to do your homework before you start a conversation with a general counsel, whether you already have a relationship with that person or are trying to build one, and you have to tailor your approach and materials to have the greatest impact.

We also have to consider the rise of legal procurement in sourcing legal services and managing relationships with law firms, which Silvia Hodges Silverstein explains in more detail in her chapter. She suggests that the involvement of legal procurement is one of the side effects of a power shift to clients.

You need various foundations in place to implement good business development. Julia Randell-Khan describes the nuts and bolts of business development, which covers the practical infrastructure required to support the phases of the business development life cycle – the systems, tools and processes which enable a lawyer and a law firm to achieve their marketing and business development goals and wider strategic business objectives.

It is all very well having the foundation and tools in place, but do your lawyers know how to use them? Are they able to sell their firm? Technical expertise is critical but is also a given in a competitive and saturated market; it is not enough to retain business. Shelley Dunstone examines the lawyers' role in business development and questions whether lawyers can sell. Tom Bird takes this further in discussing how you can teach lawyers to sell and the importance of lawyers developing skills for developing business early to ensure future success. Following this chapter, André Andersson continues with the theme of starting early by suggesting that you should view your law students, applicants and associates as future clients and, therefore, market your firm to them to build a strategic long-term position for your firm in the local legal market.

All firms and lawyers are different and therefore need to develop varied approaches to business development. There is no magic formula or template that can be blindly followed. Good business development needs to be integral to a firm's strategy. Similarly, business development activities by an individual lawyer need to be appropriate to that individual. This book also discusses a variety of approaches to business development with three commentaries from law firms of different sizes in different countries: Tomasz Wardyński (and colleagues) from Wardyński in Poland, Daniela Christovão from TozziniFreire in Brazil and Paul Subramanian from ZICO Holdings Inc in Malaysia. As cited in the Malaysian section, the challenge to a law firm is to align its business development strategy with the professionalism expected of its lawyers.

Several contributors make very clear that effective business development can take place only when the law firm has answered some fundamental questions about what sort of firm is it. In his chapter on business development in firms of the future, Norman Clark states this very bluntly: "Each law firm must develop and agree internally a clear understanding of the fundamental nature of the services that are the core of its business and the clients that it wants in its client base." Law firms are discovering that they are subject to the same market forces as the rest of the business world. It is important for law firms to view their organisation holistically, as a marketable entity, as this is the key to future prosperity.

Business development has to take into account the ethical standards and the regulatory framework in which the firm operates. This premise is examined in the chapter titled "Advertising and marketing of legal services" by three officers of the Professional Ethics Committee of the International Bar Association (IBA), Martin E Kovnats, Rachel T McGuckian and Carlos Valls Martinez. This chapter provides a comprehensive comparison of how 13 countries from Asia, Europe, Oceania, North America and South America regulate the marketing and advertising of legal services, with roughly half of the countries basing their legal system on common law and the other half on civil law. A key concern in all jurisdictions is the behaviour of the legal profession in its promotion and publicity, which may affect the perception, and the confidence, of society in the legal sector. As the editors in that chapter mention, it would be a great topic for the IBA to investigate further and maybe promote a version of what good regulations for marketing and advertising might be. As the authors' analysis indicates, there is a huge variation across the world, and rules and regulations are not necessarily fully adhered to as they are out of kilter with modern reality.

As law firms continue to globalise and enter into a broader range of markets and legal disciplines, the demand for business development and communications professionals, with a better understanding of business development and communications methodology in the legal profession, has increased. The chapter by Christine Liæker Lindberg, a business development professional from Norway, considers a day in her life and the value that her expertise brings to her law firm. Chris Davis's chapter examines the case for communications professionals in law firms and the media tactics for getting recognition and attention.

It is also widely recognised that law firms are often slow adopters of technology – but with the rise of social media, there is no escape. As clients become increasingly sophisticated users of technology, Rainer Kasper observes the role of social media in business development and how we can utilise it in developing client relationships.

This book focuses on providing the reader with practical guidance on arguably one of the most strategically important areas of law firms' businesses today. I conclude with a practical guide listing 10 fundamental elements that all lawyers and law firms should consider to achieve good business development. However, as mentioned above there is no 'one size fits all' approach to business development. It has to be authentic and carefully considered as a central part of the firm's overall strategy.

I hope that you will find this book as insightful as I did; I am certain that you will benefit from the authors' knowledge and experience when developing and implementing your business development strategies in the future.

I would like to thank Sian O'Neill of Globe Law & Business for her patience and support in developing various chapters in this book which do not follow the normal pattern – we have interviews, we have surveys, but these were the best formats to convey the information. I would also like to thank Katie Cramond of Freshfields Bruckhaus Deringer for her help in putting this book together; without her, it would not have happened!

Developments in law firm marketing

Murray M Coffey
Emily Cunningham Rushing
Haynes and Boone LLP

Compared to other industries or professions, law firms are relative newcomers to the idea that the market or consumers drive the brand or persona of your company or firm. Law firms are finding that they are subject to the same market forces as any other sector or part of the business world. Which means that looking at your organisation holistically as a marketable entity is the key to future prosperity. Savvy law firms, whether global or regional, are learning this lesson as they evolve to compete in a changing market.

1.   Origins of law practice and marketing

A history rooted in medieval European colleges of legal educators gave rise to collectives of law practitioners and legal scribes who represented clients in courts of law. Governments and business grew in complexity as canonical and common law increased in sophistication, and the demand for lawyers increased. Lawyers evolved organisations to administer and govern various aspects of the various types of practice of law, like bar associations, law chambers and firms.

As law practice became more sophisticated and required more governance, rules and regulations developed to ensure ethical practices. In many jurisdictions these ethical rules restricted and strictly limited many forms of advertising to, or solicitation of, legal business from the public. These restrictions were designed to protect the public from fraudulent or avaricious law practice, but also to protect these early guilds of law practitioners, an essentially scholarly pursuit, from outside competition. Lawyers were allowed a monopoly on the practice of law as long as that practice was ethical and appropriate, subject to careful regulation by the lawyers themselves.

In most jurisdictions, lawyers were not permitted to publish advertisements and could publish only directories of lawyer contact information. In many jurisdictions, these restrictions on advertising also had a limiting effect on marketing activities generally, such as hosting client events or publishing articles and papers under the firm name and logo. Without the ability to 'go to market' as a business, law firms around the world lagged in developing sophisticated marketing strategies and disciplines.

Without marketing or sales tactics, as other industries and professions developed over time, law firms by the 19th and early 20th centuries relied on other means of developing relationships and securing valuable work as legal experts and counsellors to large clients. Social and community clubs and bar associations became critical sources of professional network development and a place to build relationships via peer-to-peer connections, professional referrals and corporate institutional relationships.

Social and community clubs included religious, civic, regional, alumni and special interest organisations. Bar associations included not only associations with the ability to regulate practice, but also bars for specialised areas of practice. The growth of these professional networks ensured that private practice lawyers had access to decision makers who retained counsel on behalf of their enterprises, and also referred legal counsel among their business associates. This system of professional relationships endured into the Industrial Age and the early Modern Era, until catalysing events, including a new regulatory environment, in the 20th century brought the practice of law forward from its traditional, protectionist early days.

2. Lawyer demographics and expanding market

Post-World War II, the number of lawyers worldwide saw a sharp increase, beginning a growth trend that would continue for the remainder of the century. By the latter half of the 20th century, the population of lawyers was changing and becoming more diverse. Also, lawyers began to shift from solo practices to new firm and corporate models.

Figure 1: Number of attorneys in the United States by year

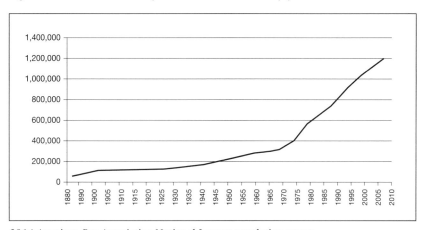

2014 American Bar Association National Lawyer population survey

For example, the rise in US attorney bar admissions following World War II was the result of returning soldiers picking up postponed plans and also a return to economic growth and prosperity following decades of global war and economic recession. Similar demographic trends were in evidence in other developed markets.

The 1970s saw a large increase in the number of lawyers in the United States, another trend driven by an ending global conflict with soldiers returning from Vietnam to begin careers. This increase in total lawyer population was also driven by new demographic trends, ushering in an era of change for many professions, in the United States and around the world.

Two of the global trends represented in the late 1960s were the coming-of-age of the post-war baby boom generation and also by the increase in the numbers of women entering the profession. With regard to the generational shift, the median age of US lawyers decreased from 46 in 1960 to 39 in 1980. Lawyers under the age of 36 made up 24% of the population in 1960 and 39% in 1980. With regard to the gender shift, by the late 1960s the rate of increase of the female lawyer population in the United States exceeded that of males, a trend that continued for several decades.

In addition to these changes in population, lawyers began to work and compete differently during this period. By the late 20th century, the distribution of the lawyer population by type of employment had undergone a dramatic shift from solo or private practice to law firm practice. An increasing number of lawyers joined corporations, signalling the rise of the in-house corporate legal department.

The mid-20th century saw the market for legal services experience rapid growth. The 1960s and 1970s saw new regulatory agencies forming in the United States, such as the Environmental Protection Agency and the Occupational Safety and Health Administration. Similar agencies and ministries were formed in other countries during this period, adding to the number of specialised areas of practice and increasing the demand by businesses for specialised advice in addressing new and changing laws.

By 1985, the year the first top law firm ranking was published by *American Legal Media*, there were 50 law firms in the United States with at least $44 million in revenues. The average revenues for these top 50 firms were $66 million and the largest US firm reported revenues of $129 million. This represented a $3.38 billion total market for just the United States. In June 1997 the *Wall Street Journal* reported in an article titled "Big Law Firms' 1997 Profits Evoke Boom Times of the 1980s" that "the revved-up economy gave major law firms another big lift in 1997, and attorneys say the good news has continued this year".

The first *Global 100* report was published in 1998, ranking firms by total revenues. In the first year there were only 50 firms ranked, with the smallest firm reporting more than $191 million in revenues. In 1998 these global firms represented a $14.9 billion market with an average firm size of $303 million. The largest firm, Skadden, headquartered in New York, reported revenues of $826 million. The largest English law firm, Clifford Chance, reported 1998 revenues of $629 million.

By 2015 the largest *Global 100*-ranked firm by total firm revenues was Latham & Watkins with $2.6 billion and the average revenues of the firms on this list was $927 million. To illustrate further the huge jump in firm revenues in this 17-year period, the top seven *2015 Global 100*-ranked firms with about $16.3 billion in combined revenue grossed more income than the entire *1998 Global 100* list with around $14.9 billion in combined revenues. Adjusted for inflation, this represents an increase of over 200% in the average revenues of these firms.

In addition, the value of the global legal market in 2015 is estimated at around $650 billion. Some $92.7 billion, or about 14.3%, of that global legal market value is accounted for among the *2015 Global 100*-ranked firms. This underscores the enormous gains in earning power of the largest law firms and the overall value and increased pressures of the market in which law firms currently compete.

Law firm growth was driven by expansion of the global economy and also an increasingly sophisticated legal environment. Law firms have enjoyed high profit margins, estimated by Clayton Christensen to be at least twice those of the United States' top-100 publicly traded companies.[1]

Hourly rates continued to increase and with advances in information technology, partners were better able to leverage low-cost junior attorneys for routine legal work. An increasingly complex and sophisticated global regulatory environment enabled an extended period of prosperity and high levels of attorney employment. Firms expanded during this period, opening offices around the world to take advantage of new opportunities in Asia, the Middle East and Latin America.

In addition to normal course-of-business legal issues, the late 1990s and 2000s saw growth in the number and size of company acquisitions. Government regulations and new corporate risk management models required law firms to expand their practices into new, specialised areas of law such as alternative dispute resolution, anti-corruption legislation and antitrust and competition law to meet the needs of their clients in this increasingly complex and globalised business environment. The formation of the European Union and the rise of new economies such as in Brazil, Russia, India and China, and in southeast Asia, opened more opportunities for law firms to provide specialised outside legal advice to companies around the world. As law firms grew in size and profitability, the requirements of managing those large, complex professional services organisations evolved.

3.   Law firms go to market

Throughout the history of modern legal practice, law firm marketing was restricted in many jurisdictions to in-person relationships and professional networks. In the United States, this changed with the landmark Supreme Court decision in *Bates v Arizona State Bar*, 433 US 350 (1977),[2] upholding the rights of lawyers to advertise their services. The State Bar of Arizona argued to maintain an air of professionalism among lawyers as justifying its ban on lawyer advertising, asserting that to allow advertising would "undermine the attorney's sense of dignity and self-worth", "erode the client's trust in the attorney" by exposing an economic motive for representation, and "tarnish the dignified public image of the profession". The court found against these arguments and held that allowing attorneys to advertise would not harm the legal profession or the administration of justice, and, in fact, would supply consumers with valuable information about the availability and cost of legal services.

This ruling opened up to lawyers in the United States normal business marketing practices, such as branding, advertising, mailings and other forms of promotion, and the engagement of marketing professionals brought new disciplines into the practice of law. Lawyers began to operate and manage their business more like their professional peers in banking, accountancy, engineering and other areas of professional practice.

---

1   www.drystonecapital.com/pdf/christensen_case_study.pdf.
2   https://www.oyez.org/cases/1976/76-316.

During the 2000s, law firms began to add professional staff to augment traditional support roles like secretaries, paralegals and office services. These professional roles include accounting and finance positions to help firms navigate increased data and reporting capabilities, advances in finance technologies, international finances, and client pricing and alternative fee requirements.

Firms also created dedicated executive functions overseeing conflicts, intake, records and risk responsibilities. Firms had long had librarians working as information professionals, but increasing numbers of information and knowledge technology staff were needed to develop, deploy and maintain productivity tools, rapidly evolving personal computing hardware, and increasingly sophisticated enterprise products required by finance, conflicts and other operational divisions.

Law firms also created marketing and business development positions. The Legal Marketing Association was formed in 1985 and by the 1990s enjoyed a robust membership among pioneers in this new field of professional services marketing. Many firms formed committees of lawyers to focus on marketing and business development, and oversee complex work in relationship management strategy and pursuit of client development opportunities.

Throughout the late 1990s and to the present time, company general counsel have become more involved in the strategies of their company. General counsel have gained access to the board and C-suite and are expected not only to control costs and risk, but also to advise proactively regarding the legal issues and possible threats to the business and its suppliers and customers. By the early 2000s, general counsel in these enhanced roles were beginning to hire and manage their service providers and vendors strategically, like outside counsel, using sophisticated data analytics tools to evaluate and manage costs and performance. Many clients developed 'legal operations' roles to help manage law firm service procurement processes, oversee complex engagements, negotiate vendor contracts, and scope and price high-risk, mission-critical legal work on behalf of their corporation. This has had a direct effect on the relationships between firms and their clients.

During the mid-20th century and into the early 21st century, experts characterised the law firm-client relationship as essentially monopolistic and based on intensive, long-term personal relationships. Companies selected outside firms and counsel for appropriate expertise and qualifications, but the ultimate hiring decision was primarily based on trusted adviser relationships, which were effectively exclusive and long-lived. General counsel leading in-house legal departments tended to enjoy longevity in their positions, and oversaw relationships with their peers and colleagues among law firm partners of the same generation. A relationship between one company and its firm counsel could extend into decades with little or no change. In the past five to 10 years the profession has seen a dramatic shift in the ways these relationships are created and managed.

4.   Market challenges

Even though the legal profession in the United States maintained its monopolistic practices, it was not immune to the kinds of market pressures experienced by every other sector of the business world. Law firms diversified their practices as a means of benefiting from whatever point of the business cycle it found itself in at a time of growth or economic retrenchment and dislocation. As described by one senior bankruptcy and reorganisation partner who was part of the great US railway liquidations of the late 1970s into the early 1980s, bankruptcy was a lagging economic indicator for the firm while the line of late-working hungry attorneys and staff lined up for the firm-proffered dinner buffet was a leading economic indicator for the firm. In other words, the firms made money on the way up and the way down of the economy. Firms enjoyed double-digit revenue growth year-over-year and a nearly unfettered ability to raise rates ever higher at the turn of each year – at least until the financial crisis of 2007 hit. Suddenly, the law firms faced unprecedented issues (at least for law firms) related to overcapacity and soft demand. Too many lawyers on the books with too little billable work and a pipeline of fresh recruits ready to start what they thought were promising and lucrative careers at firms that had, in some cases, promised them jobs two years earlier. Firm hiring models and revenue expectations built on what is now seen as a golden era of hyper growth were dashed. Partners with large and diverse portfolios of business were suddenly fighting for work that previously had been essentially bestowed upon them via long-term client relationships. And the clients, which were beginning to awake to the idea that they were the buyers, now exercised more control and pressure over their firms. Alternative fee arrangements, reverse auctions, panel counsel request for proposals and consolidation efforts laid waste to decades of comfortable relationships that benefited the firms.

Long-time pillars of the US business community, such as DuPont, began experimenting with new models and strategies related to the acquisition and management of outside legal services. In the case of DuPont, the company conducted an in-depth internal review of the company's legal services needs, legal capabilities and outside counsel relationships. With evidence and insight in hand, corporate leadership set about to redefine the company's procurement processes with an emphasis on alignment of value and service with specific company needs. Part of the value proposition sought by DuPont, and others, was a willingness and ability to share risks and develop a deep understanding of the company's business sector issues. This resulted in DuPont developing a stable of highly qualified firms, which in turn enjoyed a steady stream of work and revenue from the company while allowing DuPont to exercise much greater control over the relationship and deliver consistent cost and service levels to the company and its shareholders.

What is now well known throughout the legal industry as the DuPont Model[3] was viewed as a competitive advantage for DuPont by its competitors and the market. While not directly tied to the emergence of the DuPont Model, other large corporations such as Dow Chemical and General Electric, among many others, began to adapt a variety of models to rationalise their relationships with outside counsel. In some cases, these companies reviewed their outside counsel relationships and identified over 400 law firms with which the company might engage across the

---

3   www.nationallawjournal.com/id=900005407837/More-companies-now-follow-DuPonts-Legal-Model?slreturn=20160012220141.

spectrum of legal services. These reviews would then trigger a consolidation effort to whittle down the number of firms by as much as 90%, in some cases. This smaller set of firms may be referred to as 'panel counsel' and, for the first time, firms were finding that they had to answer highly structured requests for proposals that looked at an enormous number of metrics and characteristics upon which firms were never previously judged, including staffing ratios, geographic presence, 'most favoured nation' status, and diversity among its staff and attorneys in terms of gender, ethnicity and sexual orientation.

In addition to companies' own efforts at rationalisation, organisations like the Association of Corporate Counsel, Minority Corporate Counsel Association and general counsel round tables gave voice to the frustrations of the in-house counsel even going so far as to allow in-house counsel to rank their firms in an online forum. Attorneys started being asked to pass technology competency tests in order to work on client matters. In response to these pressures, many savvy firms ramped up their marketing departments' ability to produce proposals effectively, but also to adapt firm communications to changing client needs and expectations. The more long-term impact was to firm operations, which now needed to contemplate more accurate budget forecasting and billing transparency to provide clients with insights beyond just the actual cost of legal services such as attorney experience levels, diversity and overall leverage. In addition, firms found competition focusing on the more granular capabilities of individual attorneys, such as the technical degrees, advanced business education and industry experience. The rise of third-party tools for evaluating competing law firms such as Chambers, Association of Corporate Counsel, the BTI Consulting Group, Thomson PeerMonitor and ELM Solutions TyMetrix 360 also enabled the in-house community to put a finer point on their ability to compare and evaluate firms looking for their business.

Times had changed and the now tired trope of the 'new normal' settled in. Single-digit revenue growth, often fuelled by dramatic expense-cutting efforts, was applauded by the partners while the underlying business fundamentals of their firms remained essentially unchecked. Once the cost-cutting efforts ran their course, law firm mergers and consolidations – often defensive in nature – became increasingly common. Firms also began to buy market share in the form of lateral partner recruiting.

5.   Lateral movement

The US Census reports that the 2012 value of legal services in the United States was over $249.5 billion among about 173,000 law offices. This count of law offices indicates few new entrants and significant consolidation in the industry. Movement among these firms has increased as well. Partners and counsel begin their careers with one firm as an associate and then may go in house to a client department. That attorney may later return to outside firm practice, and continue to move firms every few years throughout his career.

Attorney moves affect knowledge transfer and culture and this mobility among law firm attorneys has reduced the former institutionalisation of firm-client relationships. Attorneys returning to law firm practice from in-house legal departments bring business discipline to their practice, along with the reasonable expectations that law firms should operate more like client business organisations in terms of efficiency, service and innovation.

Law firm attorneys moving among peer firms create challenging situations in terms of the portability of business relationships. The movement of client business from firm to firm can add to client perceptions that the service relationship is not with the firm institution, but rather with the individual attorney. This can also be complicated by panel counsel or approved vendor lists maintained by companies. After a review process resulting in some convergence and controls around outside service providers, a client company may find that the composition of that firm's specialist team may change dramatically in a short period of time, complicating the management of that service provider relationship from a business perspective.

Christensen's studies indicate that corporations have reacted to increasing outside legal costs by fragmenting their legal spend among service providers and bringing work inside the company – 'making' versus 'buying' the legal products and services.

The growth of in-house departments and the consolidation of firms have escalated the competition for talent. Law schools have seen a decrease in applicants and a reduction in the requirements for admissions. The retiring generations have lead to a 'greying' of the profession with attendant problems of knowledge attrition, succession planning and culture loss.

6.   New entrants

The competition for talent is complicated further by competition from non-attorneys. Carefully regulated by various bars, the practice of law is strictly limited to licensed attorneys. Large law firms sell many services that are not strictly related to the practice of law, but are rather a value-add product for the client or a necessary non-legal part of handling a deal or litigation matter, for instance. But what constitutes the practice of law is under scrutiny as new technologies and disaggregation of services threatens to disrupt the market of bundled services provided by firms.[4]

Some competitors working to unbundle services include legal service outsourcing companies. These companies may also be described as offshoring or direct contractors. Common outsourced services include document review and e-discovery work that a firm may not staff internally, but instead refer out to another service provider.[5]

Other competitors are large professional services firms like Big Four accounting firms looking to displace law firms. A March 2015 article in *The Economist*, "Attack of the bean-counters",[6] highlights the efforts of these firms to build up legal services divisions to focus on mid-tier process-oriented work, particularly in jurisdictions like Great Britain and Australia that allow accountants to own and operate law firms.

---

4   www.americanbar.org/content/dam/aba/administrative/litigation/materials/2014_aba_annual/written-materials/disruptive_innovation.authcheckdam.pdf.
5   ir.lawnet.fordham.edu/cgi/viewcontent.cgi?article=5006&context=flr.
6   www.economist.com/news/business/21646741-lawyers-beware-accountants-are-coming-after-your-business-attack-bean-counters.

Yet another sector of professional services is competing effectively with law firms, a rising sector of alternative legal service providers. Among the larger players are companies like Axiom, Pangea3 and Novus Law. In addition to document review and e-discovery services, these companies are also providing alternative staffing and pricing models, use technology in creative ways and leverage project management skills.

These new services have led to the rise of new professional roles to support the effective management of complex legal projects. These include knowledge professionals, pricing experts, technologists and consultants working hand-in-hand with lawyers to ensure, on one hand, the efficient and effective legal services for clients and, on the other hand, strong profit margins for law firms.

In addition to applying business and professional disciplines to the practice of law and execution of legal engagements, these professionals also work hand-in-hand with attorneys to develop and deploy new legal practice technologies. These new technologies fall broadly into categories including computerisation of law, machine learning or machine thinking, workflow or document automation and algorithms, decision engines and even artificial intelligence.

October 2015 saw an announcement from Thomson that it was engaged with IBM Watson, a leading cognitive platform supporting the development of artificial intelligence tools to support various industries that are driven by knowledge, data and decisions. Watson famously beat out two top champions on Jeopardy and IBM is working with its Watson platform and selected partners to develop thinking machines to solve healthcare and other fact-intensive industries' problems.

The potential for disruption from the application of cognitive computing technologies to the law is enormous. Legal technologies and business professionals are enthusiastic about the opportunity for these technologies to support the increase of law firm performance and profitability. Activists for public access to legal information are optimistic that machine-assisted technologies could make available to the average person those basic legal rights and services, but at a greatly reduced and thereby more accessible cost. For example, the average family could be advised and secure documentation to protect their family estate and wealth transfer, all using a machine-taught legal software, and at a much lower cost than the average trusts attorney. Understandably, this prompts concern about the unauthorised practice of law and the threat that lawyers will be replaced by machines. The argument against those concerns is that the use of technologies and cognitive computing will be prevalent throughout business and society and that no software could replace a lawyer. Instead, artificial intelligence-like applications will assist lawyers and ensure consistency and quality in the work produced, freeing the lawyer up to be more productive providing the thinking and judgement that only a human can do.

7.   Predictions

As the legal market reaches a new era of evolution, experts agree that high-end legal services needs will continue to increase, developing global economies and markets will mature and the regulatory environments in which large corporations do business will become increasingly complex. There is optimism among legal marketers that the amount of sophisticated, profitable legal work will remain consistent, if not grow, as the global economy continues to rebound.

Cost controls and efficiencies will continue to be areas of focus in clients hiring for those sophisticated matters, but large, complex matters are expected to continue to be a primary source of engagement for large law firms. A key question many law firm marketing professionals are actively considering is whether routine, repeatable legal work and tasks will continue to be served by large law firms at top rates, or whether those services will be automated or computerised, or subject to some other outcome.

In terms of automation, the business world is contemplating the success of BitCoin, built on blockchain technology and wondering whether future contracts will be written in blockchain code, and what that will mean for lawyers. It seems likely that artificial intelligence and decision algorithms will be programmed by attorneys as guided workflows to create standard agreements, draft pleadings and even quality control on legal work product. These technologies have the potential to augment and enhance legal practice to the extent that they create a competitive advantage for firms utilising these tools, but these new opportunities present huge challenges to the majority of law firms to adapt.

There is some concern that cognitive technologies are a threat to the billable-hour business model. Document assembly products, for instance, reduce the time that an attorney spends drafting a document. This has the advantage of freeing the attorney to spend that time instead on sophisticated issues, but some are concerned that this will reduce the number of hours that the lawyer can bill, making it hard to incentivise this work. This, in turn, brings into question the on-going relevance of the billable hour as a unit of value. Advocates cheer this potential disrupt to law firm pricing, but many lawyers and support professionals remain sceptical.[7]

Just as automation and the innovative uses of technology will disrupt the way firms do business, so the underlying fundamentals of the client relationships are changing. While the legal profession still is and will likely remain a relationship-based business, the clients are expecting these relationships to evolve as well. Use of metrics by in-house counsel to determine the relative value of the legal services that they are receiving, coupled with an increased precision in their ability to predict budget and scope, are having an impact on the overall relationship between attorney and client. Add to this the rise in the number of the legal procurement professionals and in-house legal operations managers, and today and tomorrow's law firm partner has a much higher bar to obtaining and retaining profitable legal work.

Bespoke legal services will continue to be required for legal issues that are extraordinarily novel, creative and of an existential nature to the client. And even then, firms will need to provide flexible solutions that can scale to client needs while protecting the integrity of the firm's operations and on-going business – a great example of which would be Jenner & Block's assignment as counsel to Anton R Valukas, the examiner in the Lehman Brothers Holdings Inc Chapter 11

---

7   www.kentlaw.edu/faculty/rstaudt/classes/justicetech_fall2011/darryl%20mountain%20document%20assembly170.pdf.

proceedings.[8] The assignment from the trustee was to determine the underlying causes of the collapse of Lehman Brothers, which many commentators cite as one of the primary antecedents to the global financial crisis. The complexities of this bankruptcy work were unprecedented in corporate history and to support the work of the examiner, the firm was required to bring together an extraordinary number of highly trained and qualified legal counsel and support staff to dedicate to this project, which needed to be completed within 18 months. The firm immediately brought in a significant number of contract attorneys and other staff to tackle this classic matter of first impression. Once the examiner's report was submitted to the bankruptcy trustee, the firm was able to quickly scale down and redeploy pre-existing resources to other firm business. In the end, the nine-volume examiner's report, which is over 2,000 pages long, became one of the best-regarded and most determinative statements on the collapse of Lehman Brothers.[9]

The past 15 years have created a sea change in client expectations and law firm ability to deliver on those expectations. As the market continues to become more sophisticated, these expectations will increase. It could be argued that the current rapid consolidation within the legal sector is symptomatic of this on-going disruption. To prosper, law firms will necessarily need simultaneously to reduce the number of equity shareholders or partners and increase the number of lawyers and paraprofessionals, to adjust leverage and enhance profitability. In turn, this will require firms to implement technology solutions including cognitive computing, blockchain and even artificial intelligence to handle routine, repeatable legal work and to automate production of legal services deliverables so that fewer lawyers spend more time on sophisticated issues. Fewer lawyers in the profession overall will result in fewer equity partners, a much more challenging path to equity ownership, and the increase in alternative attorney roles such as senior associate or contract counsel, along with the rise in non-attorney professionals, or legal paraprofessionals, practising in specialised non-advice legal roles like knowledge and practice management. These practices are well adopted and successful in global markets including the European Union, Australia, South Africa and the United Kingdom.

8.   Call to action

Marketing and business development have long been staples of corporate growth both in professional services and more traditional enterprises. As stated earlier in this chapter, the concept of structured marketing and business development is a relatively recent addition to the legal profession. Marketing and business development teams have grown substantially both in sophistication and numbers of professionals in the past 20 years. That said, the new realities that most firms are facing today pose a challenge and opportunity for the marketing and business development professionals in firms.

Just as the clients that pay the firm's fees expect the partners to provide proactive, business-centred advice and counselling, so too today's marketers need to be viewed

---

8   https://jenner.com/lehman.
9   https://jenner.com/system/assets/assets/81/original/AmLawLehmanArticle.pdf?1313766746.

as leaders – not simply order-takers. And, as the clients are expecting the partners to understand their business and industry so too must a marketer and business developer understand the competitive landscape and particular pressures and opportunities for the practices that they are serving. Senior leadership both in the firm and the marketing and business development team need to organise their resources so that the business development and marketing professionals are aligned with the practices, and not assigned to broad and non-descript geographies or practices that are not complementary or strategically aligned.

The firms that will succeed in business development and marketing in the future will take an integrated and multi-pronged approach to this mission-critical function. Traditional marketing and brand awareness through advertising and adroit profile raising needs to be done in the context of alignment with the strategic objectives of the firm, the practices and the partners. So too, the critical business and competitive intelligence needs of the firms should support and, in some cases, guide the strategy for growth in the firm. This means thinking critically about the pursuit of new business, client relationship management and application of appropriate resources. Business forecasting, agreement on success criteria, analysis for the always elusive return-on-investment and the professional development of the marketing and business development teams are the responsibility of the senior professionals in today's marketing and business development department. Some firms are also integrating true sales professionals into their ranks. While there has been some indication that these sales teams can help drive business, the firms often struggle with how best to compensate and reward top-tier sales teams in a partnership context. Empowered and deeply integrated sales teams could prove to be one of the more promising next steps in terms of accelerating revenue growth for firms ready to make this kind of commitment.

Today, happily, firms seem to be embracing a more mature and nuanced view of their marketing and business development teams and overall efforts. The business development team needs to be viewed as providing an integrated bundle of tools and capabilities to support the partners' business generation efforts. Increasingly, marketing and business development professionals have advanced business degrees and, in some cases, *juris doctor* degrees. The expectation of these professionals is to be part of a team focused on delivering exceptional results and not engaging in low-return efforts. All of the resources and tools that a modern business development and marketing department can provide should be used in furtherance of the firm's strategic objectives. The professionals within these departments need to reflect the client service mentality of the firm's highest unit partners. In sum, there is room at the table for business development and marketing professionals, but they need to prove their value before they can have a seat.

9. Conclusions

Law firms are businesses and their behaviour will continue to evolve to resemble corporations more closely, especially with regard to operations and service provision, to the extent possible for licensed lawyers bound by the rules of professional responsibility. One product of the application of business disciplines to legal services is the breakdown of a complex legal matter into its component pieces of services and tasks. This can make the practice of law seem like an assembly line and critics will argue that the most sophisticated legal work cannot be commoditised in this way. Most lawyers feel a sense of duty and obligation to represent the best interests of their clients that go beyond what some might characterise as 'widget production' highlighted in the preceding pages of this chapter. The challenge for the profession in this period of great change and opportunity will be determining when and how to apply enhanced productivity practices and technologies (making the best widget) while continuing to serve the client best, all while creating and maintaining a prosperous and rewarding environment for the best and brightest lawyers to succeed and engage in meaningful work and professional development as a firm. Today law firm leaders are faced with an unenviable number of choices and challenges that go to the very core of their firm's business model, firm culture, partnership structure and client relationships. Intellectual flexibility and a focus on the client's needs first have always been the hallmarks of successful lawyers with long-term client relationships. The application of these core principles may well provide the kind of insight and fortitude necessary for a firm to succeed in this era of change in the profession. To put it another way, what has made law firms successful in the past may well be the pathway to the future. The only constant is change and law firms can continue to expect plenty of change. Regardless of a firm's size, market, client base or demographics, continued focus on excellence in client services, and a deep and honest understanding of the client's needs, will continue to create success for the client, the firm and the individual lawyer.

Business development – the nuts and bolts

Julia Randell-Khan
Consultant

1. Introduction

This chapter covers the practical infrastructure required to support the phases of the business development life cycle – the activities, systems, tools and processes which enable a law firm[1] to achieve its marketing and business development goals and wider strategic business objectives. The life cycle has three core phases, all requiring distinct business development tools and activities.

Many of the activities can be led and handled by a firm's business development professionals if they are in place or by a combination of lawyers and business development staff depending on the firm's level of investment in business development and client relationship management (CRM) roles.

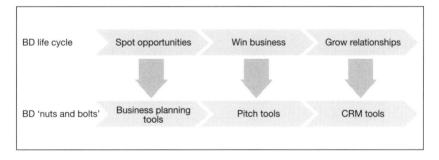

2. Spot opportunities

In today's competitive markets, businesses not only request greater value for less money from lawyers, they anticipate it. Competition is intensifying, the market is becoming more homogeneous and clients' demands are increasing. Clients' buying habits for legal services have shifted and they look to spread their legal work among their own in-house legal teams, alternative service providers (including legal process outsourcing and major accounting firms) and the full range of law firms – from low-cost providers for less complex work to a combination of generalist and specialist firms at both domestic and international levels. Faced with changing demand for legal services, law firms looking for new work opportunities can use systematic

---

1   The focus of this chapter is on the legal services provided by a traditional law firm. There is no 'one size fits all' approach. Every firm will opt for an approach which best suits its size, culture, structure and location.

business planning tools and processes to help identify priority and target clients, create awareness of the firm's expertise in specific legal services, products and markets, and build the profile of the firm and its brand.

The tools and processes include:

- priority and target client identification;
- client mapping;
- business opportunity plans;
- cross-selling activities;
- value-added services and tools;
- secondments;
- sponsorships and events;
- directory and awards submissions; and
- marketing campaigns.

2.1 Identifying the firm's priority clients and future prospects

Most firms will set out ambitious growth targets in their business plans, whether at firm/practice or region/office level. For example, a firm may aim to increase business in absolute volume by 25% over five years, grow the share of business in specific industry sectors or expand the number of relationships and practice group coverage in different geographical markets. The firm's business objectives and competitive position will inform the level of effort required to strengthen existing client relationships and target new clients.

The grid on the next page can be used to direct a more strategic and objective assessment of value potential versus effort to grow analysis. It is based on robust criteria and creates a balance between protecting an existing client base which generates steady revenue and investing more to support high-value potential clients where revenue margins may be much greater. A client's potential is a measure of how attractive the client is to a firm based on factors such as cross-selling potential, brand value to the firm (the value to the firm of having the company or individual as a client of the firm), potential to develop relationships and growth potential.

The client segmentation exercise will produce a list of clients that fit the agreed criteria and this list becomes the priority group for business development purposes and directing CRM efforts. The priority group may in fact be a small number of clients – this will encourage team work and cross-selling, generate economies of scale and offer opportunities to mentor junior lawyers on the team. Internal publicity of the agreed list and the criteria for client selection is critical to ensure transparency across the firm and to develop a common understanding of, and buy-in to, the firm's priority client base. This list can also be introduced in relevant internal training activities, on-boarding of new hires and other internal activities to ensure awareness and engagement across the firm.

2.2 Implementing a clear client targeting methodology

Firms will focus on different factors to inform their targeting approach. Factors to consider are:

- ease of potential to develop relationships;

Client targeting – segmentation of client base

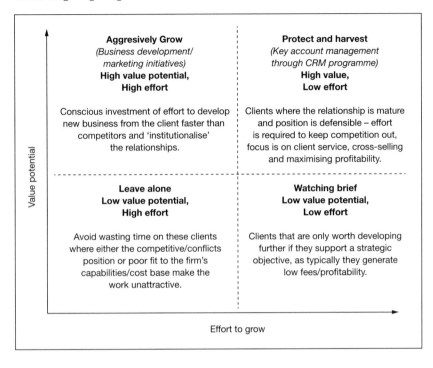

- size of billing prize – that is, the 'share of the wallet' if they become long-term clients (the focus being on profit, not revenue);
- level of activity in the sectors and practices which the firm intends to develop;
- brand enhancement;
- alignment with the skills and geographical reach of the firm; and
- ability to beat the competition.

Targeting clients with the most amount of continuing work allows a firm to sell more work to the clients with more compelling needs. This can translate into a long and reliable stream of business and the ability to deliver multiple services. Alternatively, firms may concentrate revenue in fewer practice areas than other law firms – that is, taking a narrower and deeper approach to targeting to ensure that they obtain the most lucrative opportunities in the priority practices.

2.3   Identifying the type of legal services or products to be provided
Firms need to be clear on the type of work that they want to compete for. For example, commodity services face pressure on fees and firms will require high volumes and efficient processes to run profitable commodity services. Clients increasingly use a mix of legal providers, including alternative service providers and specialist regulatory and compliance advisers, alongside their own in-house legal

teams. This demand for a variety of services at different price points will affect their buying decisions. The targeting exercise can help firms match their services and products with their clients' different business needs.

2.4   Mapping the client

A client map helps a firm really understand a client and which individuals to target for work. Building a map involves:

- finding out how the client organises itself – what the various parts of the organisation do and how their reporting lines operate; and
- identifying the key decision makers within the client, including the board and senior executive positions – especially the ones who have influence and budget for purchasing legal services.

The map is an iterative process and is a living tool which needs to be continually updated as the client organisation and business changes. Creating the map will involve gathering publicly available information, input from partners and lawyers with key individual relationships with the client and, ideally, validation with the client. The map can also be used to structure the law firm's own client 'attack' service team, assign key targets for relationship-building activities and identify cross-selling opportunities. At a practical level the map should be owned by the lead relationship partner. The firm can assign a face-off partner to each key decision maker at the client in order to understand the needs, business environment, products and issues of his counterpart and keeping regular contact with the individual. The map can also be used to facilitate efforts to build deeper connections with the client and track the progress of expanding existing relationships with the client's organisation. Lawyers of all levels of seniority can be involved in the mapping exercise. It is an ideal task for any lawyers on secondment at a client and is generally a practical way to engage lawyers in client relationship building.

2.5   Explaining the rationale for focusing resources on selected new opportunities

In addition to individual client business plans for the firm's priority clients and targets, business development activities benefit from detailed plans. They can define the type of activity required to create awareness of the firm's expertise in industry sectors, markets or practices, and to build the profile of the firm and its brand. Business plans require a clear view of who does what, together with the resources, budgeting dependencies and timings. A new business opportunity initiative needs to strike a balance between the size of the prize (eg, the estimated impact on profitability or the ability to open up new markets or areas of cross-sell, the ability to build a future successful pipeline of work rather than a one-off measure) and feasibility (eg, the spend required to undertake the initiative combined with the lawyer and business development time, whether the initiative plays to the firm's competitive strengths or leverages existing assets such as know-how, proven experience or campaigns).

An example of an outline plan is shown below.

Plan for new business opportunity Describe the opportunity. Include the size of prize. Identify the type of marketing and business development activity needed to realise the opportunity (eg, better targeting, building reputation, etc)			
Objectives and deliverables Include specific objectives. State what the opportunity requires (eg, thought leadership report, seminar programme, client workshop, marketing campaign or new publication)		**Measures of success** Measures should identify success (eg, acquire 50 new contacts, convert 10 prospects to new clients)	
Scope Be clear on what is covered and what is not. Who is the target audience?		**Dependencies** Assumptions on what all stakeholders will do	
Key Actions Include key actions needed for the initiative to succeed (eg, major building blocks)	**Owner** Assign one owner per action to ensure accountability. Confirm lead partner sponsor for the project	**Due date** Confirm delivery date with the owner	**Status** For example, not started, in progress, completed
Budget	**Forecast**	**Actual**	**Variance**
Progress report Include achievements and completed tasks. Include issues/risks which need escalation			
Review Establish a regular review process involving people outside those responsible for action			

2.6 Spotting opportunities through cross-selling the firm's expertise

Cross-selling is an excellent way to build client retention and develop relationships. It increases the 'touch points' with clients and can help them become advocates of the firm. The cost of selling a new service is lower when a contact is already warm. It can be a major source of new work given that many large, complex client organisations may currently do business with only one or a few practice groups or offices. Cross-selling outside of law firms is commonplace. Buyers are consistently offered other choices based on their buying and browsing history. Within law firms, there can be blockers to cross-selling such as lack of knowledge about what the firm can offer, an 'it's my client' or 'what's in it for me' attitude, limited recognition and reward for cross-selling or even a concern about being perceived as too much of a salesperson.

If cross-selling is to take place successfully and effectively, lawyers need to know:

- the full range of their firm's product offerings. When the opportunity arises, lawyers must be able to have a credible discussion about these services with the client and sell in a further meeting with a colleague. In-depth knowledge of the specialism of other practice areas is not needed – it is enough to recognise the client's need and make the personal introduction to the relevant expert. General knowledge of the firm – locations, sectors, major products/practices, recent awards and market recognition – is critical to cross-selling efforts. A client will not think about its needs through a law firm's practice group lines; rather, it will think, "we need a law firm which can help me do X, Y or Z". Lawyers who think holistically about their clients, their sectors and markets will be able to spot where to bring in colleagues from other practices. Never assume that the client has the full picture of what else your firm does;
- the firm's clients. If lawyers know what is happening in the clients' businesses, they will be able to spot opportunities beyond their own area of specialisation for colleagues in other teams or practice areas. But it is important to understand the clients' business issues and this may require putting together a bespoke service or solution drawn from a number of practices. Clients' needs do not follow strict practice group boundaries – it is not a random selling of other services that do not add value or address the clients' business needs. It is important to understand the clients' needs before cross-selling something that they do not need (and thus run the risk of looking ill-prepared);
- the firm's client strategy and who are the important clients. Familiarity with the firm's priority and target clients avoids wasted time and effort, especially with regard to conflicts. This requires knowledge of which partners act as the lead partners for a client relationship and being alert to opportunities to cross-refer to other colleagues while on the job. It also requires cross-sharing of internal expertise through presentations and awareness raising about what different teams can offer for the priority clients – that is, internal cross-selling. For priority clients, there are regular opportunities to review the depth of the relationship and use annual client reviews to promote expansion of the services offered. Access to internal reports which show a breakdown of practice and office coverage for a client can help inform cross-selling opportunities; and
- the process for fast and effective targeting. When an opportunity to cross-sell is spotted, the firm should ensure that its lawyers can act on it quickly in order to translate the opportunity into new business. This requires quick access to internal knowledge and information such as lists of partners who hold the client relationships, list of the target clients, guidance on how to reach the target clients quickly (eg, who should contact the client and how), materials to support cross-selling and a general understanding of how to identify the business opportunity and translate it into new business.

Cross-selling is also about encouraging and rewarding curiosity. People who are naturally curious about their clients' business, keen to network outside the firm, ask questions about the clients, think laterally about potential for wider relevance (eg, at a sector or regional level) and educate themselves about what the firm can offer are often natural cross-sellers. This behaviour can be encouraged and rewarded as 'cross-selling ambassadors'. For example, if new work is won from a cross-selling lead, this can be publicised and celebrated. Lawyers can be encouraged to reciprocate introductions to their respective clients in order to create a virtuous circle of success. Internal team meetings, news updates and internal communications channels can be used to promote awareness of materials and the success of cross-selling stories and anecdotes to encourage the mind-set change in support of cross-selling activity.

2.7 Investing in value-added services

Although the provision of value-added services can be viewed as part of on-going CRM activities, firms that invest in a range of value-added services which extend beyond the day-to-day fee-earning work can find that new opportunities arise. Value-added services include:

- training (bespoke training and seminars; legal hotlines to named experts; legal development briefings, hot topics and webcasts; training portals);
- knowledge management (access to information and know-how resources; advisory support from knowledge professionals; access to know-how tools and tracking of their usage and return on investment); and
- business operations (expertise sharing and secondments by human resources, community service teams, professional development, project management and IT professionals).

Clients expect non-chargeable value-added services and tools to be made available to them. Some clients will operate value accounts across their legal service providers to track what is being provided. Investment in innovative and client-focused tools to assist a client's business can be a practical way to open conversations about specific business challenges and ways in which the firm can offer new products and solutions. Clients will often be keen to work with their law firms to pilot, tailor and refine new tools which will benefit their business.

2.8 Spotting opportunities on secondments

Many secondments of lawyers to a client's in-house legal team arise from contractual obligations under the terms of engagement with the client. Internal processes can ensure that secondment choices are strategic and that secondees are used to the best advantage. For example, feedback and intelligence from a secondee need to be gathered systematically so that the wider firm can benefit from a secondee's knowledge of new business opportunities and competitor performance. A formal process of pre-secondment briefings and feedback sessions can capture client feedback and be used for cross-selling and relationship development opportunities.

2.9   Raising the firm's profile through sponsorships and events

Most law firms will have countless opportunities to participate in sponsorships of groups or events. Significant costs can be involved. For business development purposes, the opportunities can be helpful – for example:

- to demonstrate the firm's expertise to a clearly defined set of clients and prospects;
- to differentiate the firm from its competitors by what it does and what the brand is associated with; and
- to offer clients engaging opportunities to interact with the firm's people.

Before making a decision regarding any sponsorship, a number of key questions can be asked to assess the value of the sponsorship opportunity to the firm:

- What is the alignment with the firm's brand and strategy? Is there exclusivity without competitors in attendance?
- What marketing objectives are achieved in terms of audience reached?
- If the event is successful, what reputational benefits will be achieved?
- What contact and access does the firm have to the audience?
- What is the visibility of the firm's branding rights?
- Is the proposal cost effective and what is the true cost to activate the sponsorship opportunity?
- How will the benefits from the firm's participation be captured and measured?

2.10   Raising the firm's profile through directories and awards submissions

Annual directory submissions can raise the profile of not only the firm's expertise but also individual practices and lawyers. They are particularly important when a firm is in start-up mode or entering a new area of practice or market. Planning the target outcome of a submission and which clients to select as referees are important steps of the submission process and can support business development efforts. Winning awards which have a strong market reputation in terms of credibility and prestige can support a firm's positioning in chosen markets.

Given the regularity of the submission exercises, firms can streamline the process to ensure best practice is followed and submissions are managed effectively. The submissions and awards processes can easily be run by a firm's business development professionals. The following practical steps can be taken:

- Develop a toolkit and guidance to ensure consistent policy and approach (eg, with regard to client sensitive information);
- Create a research schedule log and timetable of dates and deadlines for submissions;
- Maintain an annual record of positions in directories;
- Conduct annual assessment of a firm's performance in directories; and
- Create templates for awards submissions.

At a practical level a central directory and awards submissions repository or database can be used to collate rankings, quotes, partner and firm profiles and submissions. This central repository provides the ability to capture and categorise the submission documents in a timely fashion, offers access to the materials for future submissions, and provides a source of experience for potential use in pitches. Wider business benefits from establishing a repository will be improved efficiency in collecting experience for pitches, the institutionalising of key information in relation to directory and award submissions (which minimises the risk of loss of knowledge as a result of staff turnover) and better levels of information exchange across the firm (which can be used for business planning, PR activities and in compiling internal know-how updates).

2.11 Running tailored marketing campaigns

The use of materials for multi-channel communications with clients supports business development activity. Campaigns can showcase the firm's services and expertise in specific sectors or markets, and prompt client conversations. Successful campaigns will have clear goals, a target audience (eg, the size and type of company and roles such as general counsel or chief risk officer), core messages and reporting measures. In general, marketing campaigns will be designed to:

- raise the profile and general awareness of the firm through activities such as:
  - PR strategy and press commentary;
  - social media – LinkedIn, Twitter, etc;
  - digital formats and animation for firm website and events;
  - conference and event sponsorship;
  - placed advertorials in industry publications;
- position the firm's lawyers as experts through activities such as:
  - thought leadership, client briefings and publications;
  - hosting client events;
  - co-sponsored features in industry publications;
  - speaking at conferences and external events;
  - issue-driven online and printed content;
  - social media alerts;
  - collateral, case studies for propositions;
  - inserts for pitches and experience summaries;
- develop and maintain relationships by means of:
  - client events, seminars or webinars;
  - promotion at networking and third-party events;
  - roadshows and workshops; and
  - value-added client tools.

Marketing campaigns – steps

Activity	Details
Sponsor	Agree on the partner sponsor or champion for the campaign and the wider stakeholders across the firm who will be critical for success (eg, dedicated business development resources).

continued on next page

Activity	Details
Aim	Confirm what the campaign will help the law firm to do (eg, position the firm to act as key legal adviser for a new practice or product; cross-sell different practices; grow a practice in a new market).
Target clients	Identify the target clients for the campaign including specific countries. Identify the specific contacts at the clients (eg, general counsel and legal teams, principals, board, chief executive officer, chief financial officer, chief operating officer, M&A teams, tax director, HR director, procurement teams).
Revenue opportunities	Estimate the revenue opportunities and expectation of fee income over a set period of time (eg, one or two years).
Messages and value proposition	Develop clear messages on why the campaign topic is important to the target clients and the value that the firm brings. Provide evidence and case studies of the firm's prior experience, including how the firm works with other advisers on the campaign topic.
Materials (internal and for clients)	Create a variety of materials to help lawyers understand and promote the campaign in different formats and through different channels (eg, talking points; template emails and letters; survival guides/road map on the product with full synopsis of the legal and business issues; presentation slides; key contacts and subject matter experts; training and know-how materials; frequently asked questions; hints and tips; precedents and templates for the new campaign product, pricing methodologies; inserts for pitches and credentials).
Tactics	Offer a range of ways (print, online, in person) to engage with the clients, such as presentations, one-to-one discussions, facilitated sessions with mix of a client's teams, know-how days, workshops and seminars, and client feedback.
Success measures	Identify specific success measures for client interactions such as set percentage of targets; agree to one-to-one meetings or to attend a know-how day; a set number of follow-up client meetings to which other practice areas are invited; a set number of new instructions; an increase share of business by a set percentage; winning a set number of awards, accolades, rankings.

3. Win business

The second phase of the business development life cycle is to win business. A firm needs to gain opportunities to pitch for the business that it wants and to convert opportunities into profitable mandates. During this stage the firm will want to complete the mandate successfully and profitably, leave a favourable impression, and create opportunities for repeat business.

The ability to deliver effective pitches which say why a firm is best placed to serve the client is critical to this stage of the business development cycle (see the section below on what makes a perfect pitch). Curated business development resources and toolkits are essential for effective pitching – such as capability statements, experience lists, lawyers' biographies and CVs. Internal processes to capture, update and provide easy access to this information are important nuts-and-bolts business development activities. Systems and tools can be categorised by the type of data that they support as follows:

- clients and matters – databases and online tools which enable searches to be made on client names and contact partners, client matters, client groups, client plans, policies for new business and pricing, priority and target clients, CRM programme information and client development resources;
- financial – template reports on clients and client groups, together with scorecards with key financial information including revenue, profit, debt, work in progress, value-added services and the firm's investment in the relationship;
- pitching – toolkits and templates for best practice to create pitch documents including resources to support each stage of pitch development (eg, pitch precedents, pitch briefing checklists, pitch project plans, experience, deals, referrals, pitch-ready biographies, CVs and photographs, review and follow-up materials, success/failure records and lessons-learned checklists); and
- marketing – databases and toolkits which contain practical guidance, checklists, templates and examples (eg, on effective LinkedIn profiles) and repositories for past directory and award submissions.

3.1 What makes a perfect pitch?

Selling something that you cannot see (advice) is notoriously difficult. It requires an ability to express, clearly and simply, what a firm does and how it does it. For law firms, the pitch document is an important part of the process to win new work or gain appointment to a client's panel of firms for pre-defined areas of work. Aiming for pitch perfection is every firm's goal. Law firms spend an ever-increasing amount of time working on bids, pitches or tenders. The downside of not getting it right can be costly, in terms of time, money and resources (of lawyers and business development professionals), and of the reputation of the firm and its brand. But the art of writing a persuasive pitch is also about thinking differently – thinking about seeing the world through the client's eyes – so that the firm shows an understanding of the client, its business and legal needs.

There are two main areas to focus on when looking to improve pitches and achieve higher success rates: first, the organisation and planning, which includes talking to the client, and second, writing the pitch document itself.

3.2   **Pitch organisation and planning**

Adhering to a consistent pitch process is critical to creating a successful pitch efficiently. Investment of time to standardise the front end of the pitching process and to follow a pitch project plan will ensure that the right questions are addressed upfront by the right people. The core elements are outlined below.

Conflicts: checking for potential conflict before anything is done is crucial to avoid wasting time and money, and potentially upsetting the prospective client.

Go/no-go approach: taking time to test in a formal way whether to pitch is an important decision. A go/no-go pitch protocol can set agreed criteria (eg, commercial viability, pricing, capability and client priority) to inform the go/no-go decision. A protocol can also state who should be involved in the decision (eg, the lead relationship partner, practice or industry leads, relevant business development professional). If a decision is made not to accept an invitation to pitch, the client should be informed without delay to avoid damage to the relationship and future prospects for new business.

Pitch team and project plan: assembling the pitch team and working through a project plan and pitch briefing checklist to deliver the pitch demands attention equal to fee-paying client work. The planning will decide who needs to be involved and who does what, breaks down tasks into discrete activities (eg, interrogation of the brief/tender; research on relevant expertise, market intelligence, prior relationship with the client, case studies and matter-specific examples, etc) and creates a timetable. Business development professionals can lead the organisation of this work. Post-pitch follow-up with the team and a client debrief should also be included in the timetable, ideally combined with lessons learned for the team (eg, what worked or things to do differently), which should be done even in a win situation. An independent de-brief of the client is almost always more candid and open, providing valuable information about what went right and wrong, and how the competitors performed. Win or lose, the pitch exercise is an opportunity to develop the relationship.

Discussion with client: taking time to speak to the client before submitting the pitch gives a firm the opportunity to understand better both what the client is looking for and the client's priorities. It also helps understand what the client does not want. The conversation also starts to build the relationship, particularly if the pitch is to a new client. Taking a proactive step to engage with the client about the brief/tender before submitting the pitch document will give a positive impression of the law firm's interest and commitment to tailor the proposition to the client's specific issues and needs. For example, compatibility of technology solutions to support cost-effective delivery of the legal services may need to be discussed and understood by not just the lawyers, but also the IT and other technical support teams. The client can also be asked for feedback on the pitch document before any face-to-face presentation.

Rehearsal of the pitch presentation: an impressive pitch document can often be let down by a poor pitch presentation. A minimum of two rehearsals in real time with relevant technology and software being tested as well (eg, web conference, video link ups) is advisable with pre-agreed roles, key messages, written presentations and pre-agreed questions. The team should look and sound like they enjoy working together. A rehearsal in front of a group able to challenge and test the proposition also gives an opportunity to refine and change the pitch to create the winning proposition.

3.3 Access to experience records

Successful pitching requires evidence of a firm's experience. Maintaining a parallel process to capture and record examples of experience is vital to support the pitch process. The process wheel below is a visual explanation of key aspects of the pitching and experience capture cycle, as well as of the steps to be taken. It is assumed that a conflicts check and clearance has been carried out before the pitching steps listed below take place.

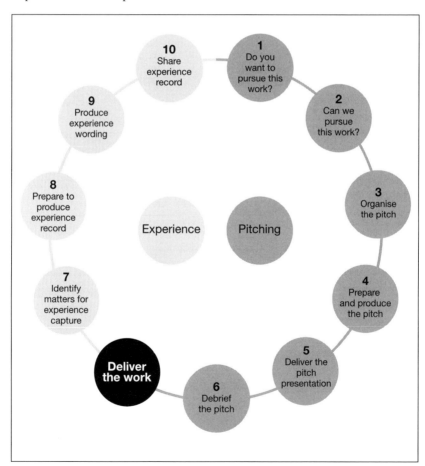

3.4 Writing the pitch document

The content of a pitch document, whether it is a short, informal email or a formal panel pitch, needs to be clear, consistent and persuasive. The structure of the document must make sense from a client's perspective. The format needs to be easy to read, using features such as headlines and graphics to help reflect how people read online and using different devices. Increasingly, clients will preset the structure of the pitch document, particularly if the pitch process is run by procurement teams (perhaps using a scorecard). If this is the case, the firm must work within the client's parameters and may be constrained by limited word counts and other formatting limitations. Careful reading of the client's instructions at the outset is critical given that law firms can easily make inaccurate assumptions about what a client has requested.

Below is some guidance for writing a winning pitch.

Think like a client: it is likely that different audiences at the client will read the pitch document – general counsel and the legal team, the board, financial and operational managers, procurement teams, etc. The pitch document needs to answer the questions that these people will ask. An effective pitch document will be written with the client reader in mind and will not focus on the firm. The reader wants to know how a firm will support the transaction or fix the dilemma, and does not want unnecessary information about the firm and its history. Clients will often say:

- "I want to know the legal difficulties they anticipate, the business issues and how they have handled these things previously";
- "I want lots of ideas as to how to tackle the problems";
- "The savvy firms prepare questions and make sure they understand the business; the conservative ones don't do anything";
- "The best service comes from empathetic lawyers who identify with the business"; and
- "I want consistent service whatever the geographic location".

Anticipate a client's questions: the pitch document needs to pick up on what will be going through the client's mind when he reads the document. For example, he may wonder:

- "How much thought have they put into this?"
- "Are these lawyers who think strategically?"
- "Will I enjoy working with them? Will they work well with my team?"
- "Have they worked out the strengths and weaknesses of our position?"
- "Do they understand the issues or are they just airing their knowledge?"
- "What's the cost? Have they done what they can to reduce/provide certainty over the fees?"
- "What is the firm doing to demonstrate cost effectiveness and efficiency?"
- "Will I get the A-team on the project? Will we be a priority?"
- "Will they be familiar with our culture and procedures?"
- "How will they collaborate cost effectively with my other legal services providers on the very complex matters such as compliance and regulatory areas?"

Use an executive summary with three clear 'reasons why': a client may not have time to read the pitch document fully. The summary, which may be a paragraph or up to three pages, is therefore the most powerful section in the pitch document. The summary will state clear reasons why the client should select the law firm for the new work. With a true executive summary, a reader should not have to read the whole document to form an opinion on whether to select the firm for the work.

Spell out the facts and benefits: a client will want to see the facts that demonstrate the benefits of using the service of a particular law firm. The client needs to see substantiated statements with facts that back up the claims, ideally combined with a concrete example. This answers the 'so what?' test. For example:

Claim
"Our team has extensive experience and excellent reach"

Substantiated statement
"Our team has six partners and 25 lawyers in the team – a total of 75 years of tax experience"

Statement with benefits
"Whatever situation you face we have the skill and the manpower to work out the best course of action. By way of example we helped X do Y".

Spelling out the benefits gives a client a clear view on why a particular firm should be instructed, for example, avoiding duplication, saving time and money, knowledge of the legal team and how it works, and having the right people.

Tell the client about the team: the client is buying a parity service and a law firm is trying to prove that its service is better than a competitor's. If the client knows who will be on the team and who will do what, including this information in the pitch document will address the anxiety about who will do the actual day-to-day work. People buy from people whom they like and trust. The client will want to know who is the lead contact, who are the experts on niche topics, how the team will be managed, etc. A clear pitch document will give a precise explanation of how the team will work with the personal attributes of the lawyers involved rather than simply a large set of CVs in the appendices. Additional evidence about how the team has worked together before is also important, in addition to a firm's history of working with other parties such as regulators or law firms in other countries.

Highlight relevant experience: a persuasive pitch document will explain how a firm's experience is relevant to the client's needs. Using case studies is a powerful way to illustrate the relevance, rather than providing long lists of transactions or cases which require the client to trust that the firm has the expertise. A small number of good examples of relevant projects count far more than pages of bullet points with two line descriptions where the reader has to guess the relevance. Use of third-party quotes is also a way to demonstrate experience.

Keep language simple, use short sentences: lawyers have a tendency to use language which comes across as long-winded and formal. Using everyday language instead (eg, 'so' rather than 'accordingly', 'use' for 'utilise' or 'before' rather than 'prior to') will make for a faster read and improve readability, while shorter sentences will avoid the trap of making simple points sound overly complicated. Writing in a conversational style will also help bring out the firm's personality.

4. Grow relationships

This is the third phase of the business development life cycle. The focus of activity is to maintain, develop and grow the relationships with clients. At the most straightforward level, this can be achieved through doing the work well and efficiently, thereby generating repeat business. But it is also about regularly talking to clients and cross-selling the wider expertise of the firm to deepen the relationship. A range of practical CRM tools can be used to support this activity. The approach to successful CRM would ideally apply to all clients of the law firm, but given the varying sizes of clients and resources available firms may opt to focus the full range of CRM activity on a core group of valued, long-term and developing clients.

4.1 Why is CRM so important?

Clients expect firms to deliver value and active relationship management. A good CRM programme drives favourability and will help a firm build deep, long-term, loyal and profitable relationships with clients. Firms which stay close to their clients and have the most relevant business judgement delivered through broad business relationships are normally the winning firms.

The goal of good CRM is to institutionalise CRM practice across the entire law firm so that:

- the approach to CRM is focused and an integral part of what the firm does;
- all lawyers and business services staff understand the importance of the firm's highest priority clients, know how these clients are selected and are confident in teaming up with colleagues around these key clients;
- the firm's client base is actively managed by identifying key clients and future prospects so that strong client relationships are built to secure a firm's future; and
- the firm becomes skilled at engaging with key clients and becomes a more relationship driven law firm and a trusted adviser rather than a firm which is used only for one-off advice. The trust is built when lawyers take time to educate themselves and understand the client's business, and show interest and commitment in the client at a personal as well as a corporate level.

Over the past 10 to 15 years, many law firms have adopted basic CRM programmes. Some firms have well-established programmes and are on their second or third iterations. The key to success is to build solid CRM process and procedures which are well supported by senior leadership to foster buy-in from the partnership for time spent on CRM activities. Firms will need to take a bespoke approach to reflect the culture of their firm and its clients. Clients will normally take it for granted that their lawyers have the technical legal skills to advise them on the law – so good CRM can be a real differentiator.

4.2 Clients need to feel valued

Proactive relationship management is an issue that clients regard as amongst the most important for professional services firms to get right. When a firm gets CRM right, the client feels supported by a motivated team of lawyers working in partnership on their priority issues. Here are examples of what clients feel:

- "The relationship delivers the whole firm – that is, the right expertise at the right time to help them achieve their objectives."
- "There are regular opportunities to provide feedback which is taken seriously and acted on to improve the relationship."
- "Pitch promises are kept and the quality of service delivery is actively monitored."
- "Perks don't matter – what matters is that when I go to sleep I know my lawyer is still awake and thinking about our problems. The fewer matters I have to think about, the better my life."
- "Real value is added by making know-how available via training and seminars."
- "The price of services is predictable, transparent and fair, and there are no surprises at the point of billing."
- "The lawyers visited our manufacturing facilities – this shows they are interested in our business and the relationship."

4.3 Focus on the core group of highest revenue-generating clients

Law firms find that a significant proportion, often over 80%, of their revenue, comes from about 20% of their clients. A targeted approach to CRM to protect the established 'superclients' representing the largest proportion of revenues will lead to best return on invested time and effort – it is easier and less costly to develop an existing client relationship than to establish a new one. But a CRM programme will also need to focus on developing clients which offer the best growth prospects for the firm as a whole and cross-selling over time.

4.4 Building blocks of good CRM activities

The activities are a mix of direct interactions with the client and time spent on internal management of the client relationship in order to get the most out of client-facing activity. This balance keeps client relationships well coordinated and aligned with the client's strategy. Client service should also improve through the CRM efforts and generally be guided and measured by regular feedback at both the client and market level. Depending on the size and scale of the client's business, the CRM activities can be the responsibility of a client team led by a client partner or an individual responsibility. Where the culture of the firm allows, introducing dedicated roles in the marketing and business development teams to run CRM activities for valued clients alongside the lawyer teams is worth considering.

The core building blocks are outlined below.

(a) Senior management engagement in the CRM programme

The success of a CRM programme is highly dependent on the engagement of senior leadership. They can take a visible role in the initiative, regularly communicate to the wider firm about the importance of the CRM programme, and help drive accountability of partners with a lead role for specific client relationships. If CRM is seen as a purely business development-led exercise, it may gain less buy-in and active support. Senior management can also help manage potential tension between a central versus local approach to developing the client relationships. Centrally run programmes may have the benefit of additional resources and the ability to coordinate the administrative matters, but the regional and local offices need to engage and have a voice on the central programme to reflect cultural differences in business practices.

(b)   **Setting the strategy in a client plan**
An understanding of the client's strategic and business objectives is critical. The account plan for the client needs to answer questions such as:
- What are the client's business priorities and legal needs?
- What is the growth strategy for the client?
- Do the firm's short, medium and long-term client development objectives align with the client's pipeline of new work?
- What are the current strengths and weaknesses, and what are the steps in place – for instance, SWOT (strengths, weaknesses, opportunities, threats) analysis – to address them?
- Have the objectives been discussed with key contacts at the client?
- How can the firm help support the pipeline of work?

(c)   **Managing the relationship on a national, regional or global basis**
There should be a big picture view of how the relationship is managed at a geographic and people level, as well as through on-going work, pitches, hospitality and pro bono activities. As a risk management issue, clients expect firms to deliver a uniform client service across practices, offices and regions. Questions to consider include:
- Who are the key client contacts and what are their preferences and influence?
- What is the client's organisational structure?
- Who is maintaining regular contact with the key individuals even when there are no active mandates?
- Is there a regular people tracking process to record contacts (including job titles and leavers/joiners) and activities done with the individuals?
- How is succession planning handled for key individuals at the client organisation?
- What is the firm doing for the client across different practice areas/offices/countries? Does the client receive a uniform client experience?
- Is there alignment between practices and offices to effect introductions, maximise cross-selling and organise multi-disciplinary and multi-jurisdictional projects?
- Will a secondment enhance the client relationship?

- Is the selection of secondees made with a tactical view of the longer-term client development objectives – for instance, to extend the relationship into a new practice area?
- Are all the pitches to the client on message?
- Are the hospitality arrangements joined up, focused and tailored to the client?
- Have pro bono activities been discussed with the client?

(d) **Seeking feedback and dialogue with the client**

A regular programme of relationship and satisfaction reviews, matter and pitch debriefs and post-transaction reviews should be set. These activities provide an opportunity for clients to see that a firm values their opinions and they are being listened to. Clients tend to react positively when approached for feedback, especially when there is active follow-up on issues raised. Regular client dialogue also offers opportunities to introduce a wider number of partners to the client to allow people to know each other, trust each other and openly share. Cross-selling becomes a natural part of the client relationship. A firm needs to address practical questions such as:

- Is there an established timetable of reviews with the client?
- Who is involved in the client review – senior management, lead partners, CRM managers?
- What topics are covered in a review – fees, staffing, matters, external data on deal activity, broker reports to identify strategic issues?
- Is the agenda structured to achieve valuable, qualitative feedback?
- Would the relationship benefit from an independent third-party review?
- Following reviews, is there a follow-up action plan to address client issues or concerns within a 24/48-hour timeframe?

(e) **Researching and reporting on the client's market activity**

This is key to developing an understanding of the competitive position and market activity. The following questions should be considered:

- What is the client's relationship with the firm's competitors?
- If the firm loses work to a competitor, why does this happen and what could have been done differently to win the mandate?
- What work do competitors do for the client?
- How can the firm differentiate itself in order to win the work?
- What is the firm's share of the wallet in comparison to competitors?
- How is the client team kept up to date with news stories about the client and its market?

(f) **Managing and communicating internally**

A range of internal communication activities should be put in place. The following team management actions can be considered:

- Who will lead the client relationship and who is in the client team?
- What are the individual roles and responsibilities of client team members?

- Is there a regular team meeting of the core client team and any wider members?
- Is action from the team meetings documented and tracked?
- Are there internal distribution lists to facilitate communication with team members?
- What internal tools (eg, intranet pages/shared files) exist to share client information easily?
- How are key successes and best practice shared with the wider client team?
- How is the client team performance reviewed internally in order to stretch the ambition and action?
- How is success measured and communicated?

(g)   *Skills training to create a consistent and coherent approach to CRM*
Firms should invest in training courses and workshops to develop lawyers' CRM skills and to improve confidence and competence in CRM and business development activities. CRM competencies and behaviours can be included in career development programmes in order to raise the standard of skills across the firm.

(h)   *Sharing knowledge*
This is an assessment of value-added services for the client. Topics to address include:
- Is a tailored know-how programme required for the client to include know-how consultancy and bespoke products?
- What publications and know-how should be circulated to the client and in what format?
- What training needs does the client have and how can the firm assist?
- Is a tailored training programme required for the client with bespoke training and access to client seminars and workshops?
- How does the firm proactively identify ideas for training based on an understanding of the client's business and industry sector issues?

(i)   *Setting fees and billing protocols and reporting*
This consists of a set of routine activities to monitor and track financial and other metrics of the client relationship. The factors to address include:
- whether there is a process to review fees, to track progress against budget, to prompt the issue of bills and to monitor work in progress;
- how a pricing strategy is reinforced across the firm – for instance, in pitches or new mandates; and
- how non-chargeable CRM time is captured consistently and reported on to communicate the amount of 'value-add' time to the client.

(j)   *Setting service standards*
This is to gain a clear understanding of the client engagement and internal processes for running the client relationship. A variety of topics will cover whether:
- the client team is aware of the terms of engagement and the terms and conditions;

- there is a set of operating principles for new instructions, billing processes and fees reporting;
- internal processes are in place for matter management, including team selection, briefing team members on client protocols and fees arrangements;
- there is a set of golden rules for working with the client.

(k) *Measuring success*

Any CRM activity should have clear, measurable goals which can be reviewed and reported on at regular intervals. Scorecards (see below) are practical ways to measure progress over a 12-month period. Third-party market feedback and client feedback can complete the picture for measuring the success of initiatives and the return on investment.

Standard resources can support the CRM activities and offer a more consistent and systematic approach and ability to track and measure progress. Easy-to-use tools and resources can help client teams, individual lawyers and business development professionals deliver successful CRM activities. There will be a range of resources to reflect best practice and help people to stay in touch with their clients, provide ideas for broader business discussions, and provide access to key information about clients. Examples of CRM tools include scorecards, calendars, reviews, client themes for cross-selling and template reports.

Scorecards: they measure what 'good' looks like. A scorecard can help a client team assess how effective it is in building and maintaining the relationship for the firm. It also helps firms benchmark the client relationship. A scorecard can include financial metrics and other successes for the overall relationship.

Example of CRM scorecards

1. Financials

Total/average for client	Last financial year	Current financial year	Target next financial year
Time/costs ratio			
Average billing rate			
Profit per partner			
Gearing on matters			
Gross margin			
Practice Revenues			
[Practice areas]			
TOTAL			

2. Client relationships

Example activities	Scores	4	3	2	1	0
When was last key account meeting with the client?		In last 3 months	In last 6 months	In last 9 months	In last 12 months	More than 12 months ago
When was the relationship map for client last updated?		In last 3 months	In last 6 months	In last 9 months	In last 12 months	More than 12 months ago
Do we know the key decision makers?		90%		50%		No
Number of practice areas which have generated >US$50,000 in last 12 months		5+	4	3	2	1
What percentage of time spent on the client is non-chargeable?		10–15%	8–10%	5–8%	3–5%	0–3%
TOTAL						

3. Understanding the client's business

Example activities	Scores	4	3	2	1	0
Is there a SWOT analysis for client's business?		In last 3 months	In last 6 months	In last 9 months	In last 12 months	No
Has client been asked for update on its business?		In last 3 months	In last 6 months	In last 9 months	In last 12 months	No
Is there a coherent client plan?		In last 3 months	In last 6 months	In last 9 months	In last 12 months	No
Has client's value chain been mapped?		In last 3 months	In last 6 months	In last 9 months	In last 12 months	No
TOTAL						

4.   Client team

Example activities	Scores	4	3	2	1	0
Do any alumni work at client?		In contact		Know	Don't know	
Are there succession plans for team members?		Updated in last 12 months		Yes		No
Is business development involved in client team?		Active		Inactive		No
TOTAL						

Calendars: they offer a forward three-month view, updated quarterly, of the key events and important updates that client teams should be passing on to their clients. The client team will assess what is relevant for their clients.

Post-transaction reviews: a review with the client at the end of the transaction is an excellent opportunity to strengthen the relationship. A range of topics can be covered such as overall performance of the firm and the team including support services; responsiveness; meeting the client's objectives; delivery against deadlines; levels of creativity, proactivity, anticipation and flexibility; teamwork; handling of costs and managing client's expectations on billing and fee levels; and communications generally.

Client themes guide: they support cross-selling, developing a guide which summarises topics and questions designed to help client teams raise relevant issues with their clients. For example, a discussion with a client on growth strategies can cover:
- Which markets are you focusing on (eg, South Africa, Turkey, South Korea)?
- How are you monitoring your investments in high-growth and new jurisdictions?
- How do you get the right legal support?

The guide can include references to relevant lawyers at the firm who have expertise in the area and observations on the topic.

Client plan templates: a client plan provides a comprehensive view on the strengths and weaknesses of a client relationship and the objectives and action plan to progress the relationship.

The big picture of the relationship would be an annual exercise covering topics such as:

- client's business strategy – main macro and future business issues for the client and its market, competitive operating environment, legislative and regulatory position, sector and industry issues;
- financial summary – total fees, work in progress, profitability figures, time/costs ratios, gearing, average billing rates, debt levels on unpaid bills;
- relationship summary – SWOT analysis, spread and scope of work across the firm, pricing pressure, ability to sell in other parts of the firm, client feedback;
- competitive position – legal spend, key competitors, key differentiators from competitors, work pipeline, significant mandates missed; and
- value-added services – training, secondments, online tools and know-how support.

The practical activities to track activities on client contacts mapping and man-marking, objectives and action plan and meetings can be updated more regularly (eg quarterly).

Client reviews: an in-depth review by senior firm management can be beneficial to support the client team and drive more disciplined follow-through on CRM activities and progress on the client plan. Detailed upfront research and data is required to support this type of client review such as analysis of fee deals, top matters, deal activity, staffing levels, external research to identify strategic issues and what is likely to be on the mind of management teams. The outcome of this type of review can stretch ambitions and action plans for the relationships. Any performance issues in the client teams can also be addressed during these reviews. Learnings from successful client relationships can also be shared across the firm.

4.5 What is needed to support CRM activities systematically?

The desire to acquire a 'silver bullet' CRM technology system can often get in the way of what is needed to support and implement good CRM practices. Systems are only as good as the data that they include. Firms will have vastly different budgets available to support the purchase and licensing of the different systems and software available on the market. Taking a bottom-up approach by working out what is needed to support the efficiency of practical day-to-day CRM tasks is the starting point to inform what type of system may be needed to support CRM activities. Cultural change led by senior management is also vital to encourage consistent and open sharing of client information and buy-in to the use of consistent CRM practices.

An integrated CRM system will bring together all aspects of client information in one place. It will support contact management for communications with clients and potential clients – that is, having the ability to run mass mailing lists for events and publications and distribute, track and report on the activities in a systematic manner. Broader CRM-related information such as Outlook integration and wider contact management (client meeting information, who knows whom and relationship mapping), account management (client plans, action plans, client teams, financials, client organisational structures and activity tracking), external client content (newsfeeds, links to social networking sites – LinkedIn, Twitter etc, research and profiles), internal client documents and data (pitches, research, databases for client information – matters, experience, training , personal data) and reports and analytics can all be accommodated in more sophisticated CRM systems which integrate to relevant information sources.

The variety of structures and approaches to business development in a law firm

Stephen Revell
Freshfields Bruckhaus Deringer

As discussed in the introduction to this book, to be successful in today's market lawyers and law firms need to treat the firm as a holistic business and ensure that they have a business development strategy that is aligned with the firm's overall strategy. Unfortunately, there is no single formula to implement such a strategy successfully. Different firms and individuals have different strategies and priorities. A successful business development plan also depends on jurisdiction, culture and client relationships – to name but a few variables.

For this chapter, I invited three individual law firms from Asia, the Americas and Europe to write about their approach to business development – Daniela Christovão from TozziniFreire Advogados in Brazil; Tomasz Wardyński, Darius Wasylkowski and Szymon Kubiak from Wardyński & Partners in Poland; and Paul Subramaniam from ZICO Holdings Inc in Malaysia.

What is clear from their commentaries is that a firm's strategy needs to reflect its values and project itself to its existing and target clients as a trustworthy and ethical business. There are many ways to do this and the authors discuss the approaches that their firms take. They all agree that a clear business development strategy is a way to differentiate your firm in the market. In developing a business development strategy that suits your firm and differentiates it with your clients, you can look at what your competitors are doing, you can look at what law firms are doing in other countries and you can talk to a wide variety of consultants. Many of the latter can provide helpful input on the development of a business development plan, but remember that they are only consultants and you must make the decisions. Thus, you must take the inputs, whether by looking at others or taking advice, and then determine your own strategy. Many consultants will advise that a 'unless you measure it, it will not happen' approach is essential to business development; certainly, ensuring that you have a results-driven plan is crucial.

Mr Subramaniam highlights that lawyers need to have business understanding as well as legal expertise to be successful at business development. Yet in reality lawyers are rarely equipped with the business skills which enable them to implement successful business development. As a result of business development's increasing significance to a lawyer's career, one obvious question is whether it should be taught at law school or early on in a lawyer's training. As part of any firm's business development strategy there needs to be a clear training component to ensure that all the firm's lawyers understand the overall strategy of the firm and, more importantly, their role in the business development activities of the firm. Although there is much learning on the job to be done, the relevant skillsets are essential to the success of the individual and the firm emphasis must be placed on appropriate training.

Ms Christovão highlights in her section that the key to success in business development in the Brazilian legal market is primarily about relationships and reputation, which therefore influences the approach that her firm focuses on in that market. Importance is placed on personal experience and direct empathy, which reflects the social, people-focused culture of Latin America. Culture is an important factor when considering your business development strategy and its impact on your approach should not be underestimated. Similarly, you must reflect on the needs of your existing and target clients. As is clear from other chapters in this book, it is essential that in developing your business development strategy you talk to your existing and target clients about what they want and how they want it delivered. Poor business development activities can harm a law firm and an individual lawyer. Getting it wrong is not just a waste of time and money, it may also damage client relationships and turn off target clients.

Wardyński & Partners have seen success from their three-pronged approach – namely, strengthening relationships with existing key clients, accurately identifying the new needs of existing and potential clients, and creating and effectively executing external communications. For these three areas, they have launched a series of internal programmes and tailored them to the realities of their firm and available resources. This commentary takes you through the journey that the firm has been on to implement a successful strategy and emphasises that when you put a model in place, you cannot expect immediate results, particularly for new initiatives like customer-relationship management programmes. However, if you invest time and effort into your approach to business development, either firm wide or as an individual, the benefits will become clear.

The case of Wardyński & Partners in Poland
Szymon Kubiak
Tomasz Wardyński
Dariusz Wasylkowski
Wardyński & Partners

1.　Introduction
The term 'business development' stems from commerce and is associated with producing and selling goods. It may thus appear inappropriate at first in relation to law firms, which provide professional services. In the context of this chapter, however, it may be helpful to consider business development as referring not to marketing, selling or cross-selling, but rather to the client's trust in the law firm – a trust based on integrity and experience.

About three years ago our firm decided to change the way that it approaches business development, which had previously been pursued rather independently by individual partners, with few initiatives coordinated on a firm-wide basis and with only limited involvement from associates. The financial crisis and increasing competition in the Polish legal market resulted in a continuing excess of supply over demand for legal services. (This imbalance seems to have become a permanent feature.) This made it necessary for the firm to consolidate its business development initiatives and to overhaul the way that it approaches business development in general, particularly in terms of streamlining efforts and focusing firm-wide priorities. While doing this, we tried to strike a fair balance between individual initiatives of partners and associates, and the implementation of new firm-wide programmes.

We would like to stress that while we consciously decided to increase our business development activites, we also agreed never to compromise the core values underlying the firm's overall strategy. Clients feel and believe that law firms that behave like salespersons are untrustworthy. They perceive such firms as business counterparties with whom they have a conflict of interest. Such an impression among clients makes it impossible for a law firm to gain any credibility and consequently the trust of such clients.

Lawyers are there to help. This can be proven only by the willingness and ability of a firm to invest in the client's matter by devoting a sufficient amount of time to the assessment of the facts and strength of the client's case. Such appraisal makes it possible to form a competent judgement as to the client's expectations and will help to formulate a financial proposal, which must always remain within the limits of professional ethics. Potential clients should never feel treated as cash cows.

Ethics and the core values of the legal profession must always underpin any kind of business development. Lawyers must not forget that their role in society is to provide social value, and that they are representing not only legitimate client matters, but also the interests of justice and the rule of law. Only such philosophy will translate into a credible image of the law firm serving as a basis for future trust.

2.   Model adopted

The model for business development that our firm adopted comprises three areas:

- Strengthening relationships with existing key clients, other professional service firms and the foreign law firms that we cooperate with in other countries;
- Accurately identifying the new needs of existing and potential clients, developing necessary expertise, and effectively communicating the firm's capacity in these areas to the interested parties; and
- Creating and properly using external communications materials containing practical knowledge and timely information that we want to share with existing and potential clients to show them our expertise.

In these areas, we launched a series of internal programmes based on the best market practices in Poland and abroad, tailoring them to the realities of our firm and the available resources.

These initiatives have already brought significant improvements, although we will continue to monitor our programmes and tools, abandoning those that do not work and, as the need arises, considering new approaches and adjusting those already in place.

Below are five examples of firm-wide programmes that we introduced.

2.1 Key client programme

This programme is designed for our most important clients. The main goal is to strengthen our status of trusted adviser. To achieve that, we established a three-tier supervision over each key client, involving a client partner, a senior client partner and a main coordinator.

The client partner is the first port of call for the client and is responsible for both maintaining day-to-day contact with the client and coordinating the work of all lawyers working for the client. The senior client partner ensures the proper composition of the teams for major projects, monitors the quality of the work performed for the client, its efficiency and consistency, and maintains strategic relations with the client. Both the client partner and the senior client partner should have a deep knowledge of the client's business, industry, strategy and challenges, as well as of existing and potential legal risks. Both are involved in setting up a client service plan and a strategy for key projects, including any crisis situations that may arise. The main coordinator is responsible for implementing the key client programme and in case of a crisis signs off on the strategy to be followed. He supervises the work of the client partner and senior client partner.

We have also established a similar programme for key foreign law firms that we cooperate with.

2.2 Identifying niches and seizing opportunities

In today's rapidly changing environment, responding quickly to changing circumstances and taking action by being at the right place at the right time is an absolute necessity. So is investing in relationships, making new contacts and the willingness to devote a great deal of time to building these relationships genuinely and not be limited by a narrow understanding of networking. This includes relationships with cooperating foreign law firms and professional service firms, particularly sharing with them market intelligence on existing opportunities.

On the basis of an in-depth analysis including a number of internal discussions and meetings with outside experts, we identify areas of strategic focus. We concentrate on one such area for a given period. The successful creation of our multidisciplinary new technologies practice two years ago shows that this approach works. If the practice area complements our existing business and adds value, we will involve non-lawyers (eg, IT experts and forensic and cybersecurity professionals) to work hand-in-hand with our lawyers to create this new practice.

2.3 Sharing our knowledge

We feel that as lawyers our role in civil society implies widely sharing knowledge both to provide social value and to strengthen the rule of law. Consequently, sharing our knowledge is an inherent element of our strategy and firm culture (also allowing us to deliver information to clients and potential clients very effectively – knowledge that is useful and timely). We pursue this most notably through the publication of:

- the *Yearbook* – a collection of articles by the firm's lawyers, written in accessible business language, inspired by matters handled for our clients, published in print and electronic versions in Polish and English. The *Yearbook* is popular among clients, and we published the fifth edition in 2015;

- the LexisNexis "Law in Practice" casebook series (eg, civil and commercial disputes, competition law, real estate transactions, public procurement law and legal risks and environmental law in mergers and acquisitions) – high-profile publications in book form intended to serve clients and advisers as guides to particular areas of law and practice, and also an important knowledge-sharing mechanism via traditional commercial channels (as the casebooks are also sold in bookstores). They are often prepared by our multidisciplinary working groups; and

- specialist reports – for example, reports on virtual currencies and crowdfunding, prepared in areas (often innovative and pioneering) where an opinion-shaping, highly specialised presence based on expertise is crucial for the firm, but reports on internal investigations, subcontracting in public procurement, reprivatisation, outsourcing in Poland, protecting creditors against dishonest actions by debtors and IP protection.

2.4   Building a presence in the virtual world

It is trivial but true to say that today the first source of information is the Internet. In addition to our traditional website, we are present online through:

- *In Principle* – our own knowledge portal for the business community. We write about key rulings by Polish and EU courts, proposed and adopted changes in regulations, and nuances of the law that may have a special impact on business. The site receives over 65,000 visits each month;

- Wardyński+ – the first Polish-language mobile application on legal topics for iOS and Android, offering users current and archival editions of *In Principle*, the *Yearbook* and other firm publications. The app is available free on the App Store and Google Play. New texts appear every week; and

- social media – the firm maintains a profile on LinkedIn. Several times a week posts are added about key publications, firm seminars and conferences, as well as issues of *In Principle*. Individual lawyers are encouraged to create individual profiles and receive assistance to maintain them.

2.5   Joint activities with non-lawyers

We emphasise joint activities with providers of other professional services, where complementary areas of legal and non-legal expertise and services may be presented as integral parts of one common solution for clients and prospects. This can take a variety of forms, including joint publications, seminars, workshops and so on.

3.   Our experience

3.1   Increasing activity, aligning priorities, monitoring and rewarding successes

One of the hardest goals to realise is increasing the level of business development activity among the firm's lawyers. Identifying priorities, elaborating model solutions and reaching a broad consensus on the correctness of the assumptions does not mean that everyone in the firm will be equally eager to get involved and committed to performing concrete tasks.

For the past three years we have taken a number of measures aimed at aligning lawyers' individual priorities with defined firm-wide priorities and introducing business development habits into our daily working style. Our experience shows that action is required on several different fronts at the same time. First, the people engaged in programmes and pilot initiatives must be correctly identified. These are the people who can encourage others to step up their activity by setting an example. Second, individual business development goals should be defined which are consistent with firm-wide goals, as well as following the SMART (specific, measurable, achievable, realistic and time-related) concept for setting goals. Third, activity must be persistently monitored, with reminders and encouragement. Fourth, successes should be recognised and rewarded – particularly in the areas of bringing in new clients and adopting a proactive approach to initiatives undertaken by our colleagues.

3.2 Adaptive strategy of small moves, flexibility

We strongly believe that it is important to take a flexible approach to the solutions that are adopted, eliminating those that do not work and launching new ones. A periodic review of the existing programmes and instruments can help. Last year we conducted our first internal 360° survey covering all business development initiatives, to verify what had been done so far, test partners' and associates' recognition of the available tools, and brainstorm for new ideas.

Our business development strategy is based on the belief that an adaptive strategy of small moves and small wins works better than a big long-term strategy. It is crucial to understand the possible risk of rejection of any grand theories and magic plans by individual lawyers who might feel paralysed by the high expectations. That could foster frustration and result in less involvement or no involvement at all.

3.3 No immediate results

Our experience shows that one should not be discouraged by a lack of immediate results. In our case this can be illustrated by the launch of a new customer relationship management (CRM) module. The initial launch was only moderately successful despite an adequate amount of training. It was only when we re-launched the scheme with a very precise assignment of responsibility for feeding the database with the appropriate data and current monitoring that it began to generate the desired results.

4. Our priorities for the immediate future

4.1 Better use of business intelligence

Although most business development decisions are based on intuition, a great help in making these decisions and a factor limiting the risk associated with them is using analytical business intelligence. Obtaining information from the marketplace is fairly straightforward. It is much harder to gather and exploit your own internal information.

The natural tendency is to rely primarily on internal financial information, which is easily accessible and used as the basis for making all kinds of evaluations affecting the functioning of the firm, specific practices and individual lawyers.

In our opinion, the most useful information is integrated internal information containing financial data and other easily measurable data, together with information that by its nature is hard to quantify.

Our immediate priority, which we are working on now, is to develop a model based on technology solutions available on the market that will enable us to generate the necessary internal financial and non-financial information. Such information could be very helpful in making any kind of evaluation of activities and the effectiveness of initiatives that have been taken. A subsequent priority will be to combine relevant internal and external information that can be used to take the right decisions on allocation of the firm's resources in business development.

4.2   Ethical pricing

Any business opportunity resulting from business development activities eventually requires an appropriate pricing proposal. Without this, even the best-planned and implemented business development effort cannot succeed. In today's practice, this is rarely if ever a result of simple multiplication of hours by a certain hourly rate.

Although we have been using alternative pricing arrangements for some time, we feel that further changes are needed. Our pricing model will continue to be founded on relevant rules of professional ethics and fairness. It will reflect the intellectual value of the services and their practical applicability, be competitive, and never attempt to translate the weight of the client's problem or the value of the matter into our financial advantage.

When pricing our services, we will also never attempt to make up for our own potential deficiencies – for instance poor management of the firm's resources or ineffective handling of the project. In this context, it is important to underline that we strongly believe that efficiency in handling all phases and elements of the process of providing services to our clients is our absolute obligation. In our understanding, this follows from the duty of loyalty to our clients and partners, as well as the whole legal profession.

4.3   Best practices, peer-to-peer learning

We have always tried to follow the latest trends in business development best practices. We have done so by inviting leading foreign and domestic experts to lecture or conduct workshops in-house, and by sending our lawyers to conferences and workshops. We will continue to do this, but plan to concentrate more on internal peer-to-peer initiatives.

The main reason for this change is that we have noticed that initiatives that allow for open sharing of ideas, knowledge and experience have a positive impact on the level of participation in business development activities. We plan to extend peer-to-peer learning to all areas, from gathering business intelligence, feeding the CRM database and organising successful seminars, to better functioning of the key client programme and winning the trust of new clients.

The case of TozziniFreire in Brazil
Daniela Christovão
TozziniFreire

Many of this book's readers will already know that different firms will take different approaches to business development. However, it may be helpful to demonstrate this variety of structures and approaches by reflecting on the peculiarities of the Brazilian legal market, which present exciting challenges.

The term 'business development' was first used by UK and US law firms to describe and conceptualise the systematisation of sales and marketing processes that they used in order to build longer-lasting and more fruitful relationships with clients. But while the advertisement of legal services is not prohibited *per se* in either the United Kingdom or United States, Brazil imposes a variety of restrictions on these activities. Accordingly, ensuring that the relationship-building tools that they use comply with the Code of Ethics of the Brazilian Bar Association is a matter of high priority for top Brazilian firms.

For example, the Code of Ethics restricts the use of dissemination tools for legal activity, such as direct email, advertising on television, radio and outdoors. In Brazil, the understanding that generally prevails is that publications about a lawyer or law firm should be informative and such dissemination should be moderate, without constituting client solicitation or commercialisation of the profession. This situation pushes business development professionals to be creative and to seek more efficient tools to sell to clients. Above all, the legal profession is recognised in the Brazilian Constitution as essential to justice, and not simply as another form of business.

As a result of privatisation and the economic stability achieved in the late 1990s, a 'magic circle' of Brazilian law firms gained access to the global market; not only did these firms experience a period of rapid growth, tripling in size in just a few years, but they did so without relaxing their standards of excellence while simultaneously undertaking important structural reforms to be in line with their international counterparts. The big firms developed corporate structures and relationship programmes with the press, introduced international cooperation, hired professional managers and started providing career development opportunities for lawyers and administrative employees.

Along with these structural and economic changes came a cultural shift in the professional activity of the lawyer, whose work was now undertaken as part of a service profession increasingly focused on serving businesses. A Brazilian lawyer no longer had the luxury of waiting for the customer to come to him, he now had to be more proactive; this included both being more attuned to the business world and understanding the market better, in particular in order to assess how the needs of his clients are affected. Many of these lawyers obtained LLMs in the United States or United Kingdom before working in international law firms. As a result, they were fully aware of the deep changes that the revolution in corporate customer service practices would bring to the Brazilian legal services profession.

In this combination of international best practices and Brazilian reality, the key to success in business development in the Brazilian legal market boils down primarily to relationships and reputation.

1.   Marketing tools

In the light of the dissimilarities mentioned above between the rules governing lawyers and their activities in Brazil, on the one hand, and their US and UK counterparts on the other (especially as egards the use of advertising), it comes as no surprise that Brazilian law firms find it nearly impossible to follow international marketing recipes when it comes to selling their services and products. Of course, even Brazilian law firm marketers, such as myself, follow the lessons of the great Philip Kotler, especially his concepts of holistic marketing,[1] but we must adapt them to the reality of the provision of professional legal services in Brazil. Thanks to my relationship with marketing colleagues from the United States, United Kingdom and other Latin American countries, and my experience of over 10 years in business, I know that this holistic approach is the most appropriate.

Holistic marketing of the service industry translates, in the legal profession, into directing the law firm's efforts towards focusing on customer aspirations and exceeding their expectations. Since client/service provider relationships are complex and affected by a number of variables, such an undertaking is as much art as science. Ultimately, the aim should be to maintain loyalty. Susan Keaveney's approach was to group under eight categories over 800 critical behaviours that led customers to switch service providers.[2] If one takes the overall picture generated by Keaveney and transposes it to the reality of law firms, the result is striking:

- pricing – high price, price increase, unfair price, misleading price;
- inconvenience – waiting for a visit, waiting for a service (the infamous unavailability of partners);
- core service failures – error, billing error, sloppy service;
- service encounter failures – inattentiveness, rudeness, indifference, lack of preparedness;
- response to failed service – negative response, no response, reluctant response;
- competition – customer finds elsewhere a service that better meets its expectations of quality or price;
- ethical problems – cheating, aggressive sales practice, insecurity, conflict of interest; and
- involuntary switching – customer moved or provider closed down.

To avoid the defection of clients as a result of any of the above, business development in law firms requires external, internal and interactive marketing.

It is generally understood that 'external marketing' refers to the normal processes of preparation, pricing, distribution and promotion of services to a customer; 'internal marketing' refers to the processes of training and motivating employees to provide excellent customer service; and 'interactive marketing' refers to the ability of employees to serve customers in a real culture of service.

---

1   Philip Kotler and Kevin Lane Keller, *Marketing Management*, Pearson Prentice Hall, 2007.
2   Susan M Keaveney, "Customer switching behavior in service industries: an exploratory study, *Journal of Marketing*, April 1995.

2. Relationships

According to David Maister,[3] large full service law firms that adopt the 'one firm' concept distinguish themselves from the competition not through technical excellence but through the ability to generate an experience of receiving personalised service from their firm. After all, when it comes to top law firms, technical ability and pricing are largely comparable. If this is the case, then the specific difference between firms and, thus, the crucial factor in a client's decision to choose one firm over its competitors is the client's experience of being served according to a certain standard and in a certain manner – of knowing that the chosen firm will deliver services with a level of transparency, openness and trust that it would not find elsewhere. In this sense, to talk about holistic marketing is also to talk about creating an internal culture focused on the client, one that permeates all areas of the firm and communicates this to all its stakeholders: clients, employees and community.

I maintain that the key ingredient to the cultivation of successful corporation-client relationships in a law firm is empathy, where real human interaction is cultivated in all the firm's daily activities, from meeting clients across the table, to interaction on the telephone, and even in and through the billing process. A successful marketing department is one that can spread this culture throughout the law firm.

Thanks to new marketing techniques and tools, we can now collect data that gives better insight into a client's needs. These tools allow a deeper understanding of any particular client and thus go some way toward offering that personalised service that has become so important in the service-oriented business environment. Carrying out customer surveys on a regular basis, for example, is essential for continuous improvement in service delivery. It is an established form of dialogue, but not the only one. Conversation itself is essential and should be embraced by each partner, each lawyer and each administrative employee who interacts with the client. According to Maister,[4] the characteristics of this business development tool are nothing but the characteristics of a real, open-hearted conversation, including:

- It is person to person, not role to role. People use ordinary language, not corporate speak;
- Both sides talk and, more importantly, both sides listen; the meeting between corporation and client is a real conversation, a collaboration;
- Both parties are engaged in joint problem solving – neither is trying to win or prevail; and
- It is designed to allow people with different views to learn from one another.

Marketing (and selling) begins to work when a conversation moves away from being a role-to-role exchange of capabilities, contracts and costs, and becomes a person-to-person interactive dialogue about ideas, beliefs and perspectives. Only then can the chemistry, confidence and commitment that lead to new revenues begin to grow.

The goals of initiating and deepening relationships are vastly more important

---

3   David H Maister, *Managing the Professional Service Firm*, Free Press Paperbacks, 2009.
4   David H Maister, *The Trusted Advisor*, Touchstone Books, 2000.

than conventional marketing's emphasis on the goals of building awareness and generating leads. And nothing builds relationships better than regular, meaningful conversations.

To have these interesting, meaningful conversations, you must have something new to say. Developing fresh points of view means reframing issues, and creating new metaphors and language to talk about them.

As Maister says, the message itself is only the beginning of marketing. Its value exists only if it leads to a dialogue with clients: "That was interesting, tell me more!"

3. Reputation

In any business, reputation should be treated as a chief asset. It is a matter of the long-term nature and personality of the corporate entity, and is based on the ongoing maintenance of efficient corporate communication – the kind of communication where a person or organisation speaks of itself, outside of the narrow confines of the administrative or seller discourse – something always consistent and aligned to the mission, vision and values of the organisation. When a company follows ethical practices, communicates openly, listens to its audience and serves its interests, it strengthens its reputation and raises the confidence of stakeholders regarding its future. There is little doubt that a firm's careful and consistent cultivation of a reputation for integrity correlates favourably with its position in the market. If we take reputation to refer to what an institution has built up to the present, then it is useful to view confidence as referring to the generally accepted expectations for an institution to thrive into the future. Though reputation and trust are fundamental to the sustainability of business, they are notoriously difficult to measure. However, studies conducted at Aston Business School demonstrate a strong correlation between reputation and profit in the top 50 UK law firms.[5] After all, reputation is a signalling device to clients and other stakeholders about the firm's products, strategies and professional quality compared to its competitors – a sorting mechanism to stratify firms into status-based groups. Those with high status obtain benefits, which in turn tends to reinforce their reputations.

Reinforcing the importance of attentiveness to holistic marketing, reputation is important not only for attracting clients, but is equally important in both attracting staff of the right quality to work for the firm and in retaining them by offering work assignments of the appropriate challenge and variety.

Because corporate legal advice is a complex phenomenon, a customised, client-centred product, including a number of variables not susceptible to quantification and unyielding to any type of 'one type fits all' calculus, a firm's reputation is of paramount importance. In the absence of clear indicators of the difference in quality of professional services, or the technical competence of firms to provide these services, reputation is perhaps the chief criterion by which clients sort firms. Data indicates that reputation is more strongly correlated with profits than with revenue.[6]

---

5   Michael Smets, *Reputation and Performance in Large Law Firms*, Aston Business School, 2008.
6   Zhaohui Chen, Alan D Morrison and William J Wilhelm, "Individual and Institutional Reputation" – paper submitted at Saïd Business School, University of Oxford, 2012.

This suggests an interesting conclusion about the importance of reputation as a proxy of service quality for different types of service: it is particularly important for attracting premium high-margin/low-volume work. In practice, high reputation combined with high performance generates a cycle that is self-sustaining: reputation allows hiring top talent who, in turn, deliver cutting-edge, high-margin/low-volume services. These services, both highly profitable and highly visible, help recruit high-quality staff and further attract high-status clients, which further enhances a firm's reputation.

The next step in the evolution of the law firm's reputation is how it is transferred to its professionals and practice areas, facilitating cross-selling. Once again, this raises to prominence the importance of dialogue and conversation, but with the focus now on how such conversations and dialogue can be facilitated in-house, between lawyers from different practices of the firm and from the different areas of specialisation. Though the focus here is on the internal structuring of the firm so as to facilitate open communication, this is all undertaken ultimately as a means to provide the client with the most appropriate integrated legal solution for its business or problem.

The case of ZICO Holdings Inc in Malaysia
Paul P Subramanian
ZICO Holdings Inc

With apologies to George Lucas and fans of *Star Wars* throughout the universe...

1.   A long time ago in a galaxy far, far way...
Judge Panganiban of the Philippines said:

> *In this day and age, members of the bar often forget that the practice of law is a profession and not a business. Lawyering is not primarily meant to be a money-making venture, and law advocacy is not a capital that necessarily yields profits. The gaining of a livelihood is not a professional but a secondary consideration.*

Except it was not that long ago. It was in 2002 in *Burbe v Magulta*. With the greatest respect to the learned judge, his characterisation of the practice of law today is somewhat simplistic, and, some may say, idealistic.

There is a disconnect between the ideals of the law and the realities of practice. To most of today's practitioners, the practice of law is the primary, if not the sole, source of their livelihood. The reality is that legal practice today is a business, facing the same challenges that business enterprises throughout the world face. For lawyers and law firms to survive, the need to develop sound business practice runs parallel with the need to observe sound legal principles.

The challenge to a law firm is to align its business development strategy with the professionalism expected of its lawyers. The strategy has to take into account the ethical standards of the practice and the regulatory framework in which the firm operates. A critical examination of the comments of Panganiban J quoted above will show that the judge was not objecting to treating practice as a business *per se*, but to a business development strategy that promotes profits to the exclusion of the professional responsibilities inherent in the practice of law.

So what then should be the objectives of a business development strategy of a legal practice? In my view, it must strive to reach four outcomes:

- It must articulate the values that drive the law firm in addition to its service offerings.
- It must aim to strengthen the relationship of the law firm with its existing client base.
- It must reach potential clients which would benefit from the service offerings of the law firm.
- It must build public trust in the law firm.

This is easier said than done. The reality is that the education of lawyers before they come into practice rarely equips them with a sense of the business aspects of practice. Also, increasingly, the ability of the profession to control entrants is being rapidly diluted by quasi-governmental agencies dictating entry requirements and the opening of areas of practice traditionally exclusive to the profession to non-lawyers. Young lawyers are often overwhelmed by the competition that they face, not only from their fellow practitioners but also from non-professional consultants equipped with effective business tools and techniques. Knowing the law is no longer the primary challenge for the young lawyer. Getting his skills recognised and earning a livelihood with those skills is the real challenge. It is the young Luke Skywalker coming to grips with the discovery of the Force.

2.   The phantom menace

A quick Internet check on law societies globally will show that most are acutely aware of the need for their members to be equipped with business tools to run their operations. However, this realisation appears not to have permeated to the law schools which provide the basic training for lawyers that come into practice. In many jurisdictions there is no barrier to a fresh law school graduate opening his own firm immediately upon completing his pupillage. Pupillage itself does not touch upon the tools required to run or grow a legal business.

Herein lays the phantom menace. The reputation of the profession hinges on public perception of the capabilities of its members to handle not just their legal problems, but also the financial affairs attached to those problems. Lawyers who lack a sound understanding of business practices are more likely to run into financial difficulties and mix trust funds with revenue, thus leading to the perception that lawyers as a whole are untrustworthy, or that they are primarily in it for the money.

Ironically, sound business development practices in law firms – far from diminishing the focus on professionalism – will enhance their ability to uphold the professional aspects of practice.

Of necessity, the objectives of these business development strategies will take into account the necessity for the law firm to portray itself as trustworthy, committed to the required standards of practice and ethical in the discharge of its engagements. For such strategies to work, the firm itself will need to develop programmes that promote those values. The ubiquity of social media today will give the lie to any enterprise which says one thing and does another. For business development strategies to work, they need to be backed up with professional practices that are aligned with them.

So how should law firms achieve this? At my firm we have the following in place:

- an induction programme for all who enter into the firm outlining its vision and values;
- a succinct statement of the vision and values of the firm in its publications and website; and
- development of specific policies to promote the vision and values of the firm.

3.   Attack of the clones

The question then arises whether all legal businesses should have generic business development strategies. Is it a case of developing a 'one size fits all' programme for law firms either at university level or at the professional law society level? Will the public be assaulted by an attack of cloned business development strategies?

The development of business strategies begins with objectives. The function of the strategy is to make known the strengths of the legal firm and its areas of focus. While professionalism should be a necessary element of all business development strategies of law firms, it cannot be the sole element. The development of the strategy should seek to highlight the differentiating factors of the law firm in question with the other law firms operating in the same business space. While advertising and publicity rules generally restrict the amount of information that can be put in the public space, the business development strategy of the law firm should ensure that the required information that distinguishes it from other law practices in general, and those in the same practice space in particular, is able to be articulated and put in the public space.

In short, a successful business development strategy needs a communications team that is able to connect with the public and potential clients. Any business strategy that does not reach the ears of the market that it is operating in is, by definition, a failed strategy.

In our firm, we articulate how we differ from other firms. This covers the following areas:

- our working culture;
- our areas of practice; and
- the way that we engage with clients.

When one is assaulted by clones, the distinctive article stands out.

4.   The revenge of the Sith

It should not be forgotten that law firms today compete not only with other law firms, but also with an increasing number of consultancies, multi-disciplinary practices and private enterprises providing the same or similar services offerings. Except for litigation and some elements of conveyancing, law firms have lost, and continue to lose, the exclusive right to offer professional legal services across the board. Many of these competitors have long mastered the art of sound business development programmes. The revenge of these 'Sith' awaits law firms positioning themselves as businesses under a business development programme.

To compete with these other players, a sound business development programme needs to have two components. The first is a mechanism or team to make the law firm itself aware of these competitors and their strengths and weaknesses. The second is the adoption and implementation of business tools within the legal practice. Project management, Gantt diagrams, fishbone analysis, SWOT (strengths, weaknesses, opportunities and threats) diagrams – none of these are taught at law schools or in law societies, to my knowledge. Yet they are standard tools in the business world to plan strategies and communicate them to clients. A sound business development strategy would empower those framing proposals or facing clients to be familiar with and speak the language in which business is done in that space.

Traditional knowledge management and training functions in law firms tend to focus on legal developments, precedent building and internal practice skills. A sound business development programme would incorporate industry knowledge and business tools as necessary modules to be offered by the knowledge management and training team within the firm.

We achieve this by including business practices and industry knowledge in our training programmes. We stress the need for a holistic approach to legal problem solving and to focus on the client's needs and responses in the process. We exchange training sessions with other disciplines to encourage collaboration and knowledge sharing.

5. A new hope

In the previous paragraphs, I have spoken of the need to have a sound communications team and a knowledge management team as part of the business development strategy of a law firm. Both, however, will be heavily dependent on technology to function efficiently and effectively. The coming of the personal computer has enabled lawyers to become more productive and has raised management standards to new levels. Coupled with the ubiquity of the Internet, new technology brings new hope to law firms to extend the reach of the services that they provide to a global audience.

However, keeping up with modern technology and its ever-increasing rate of change requires both capital and focus. In developing a sound business strategy, law firms will need to factor in the cost of staying abreast with the changes in software and the need to upgrade hardware regularly.

Server downtime is a luxury that few lawyers can afford these days. Clients expect to have instant and ready access to their lawyers. Any significant break in the line of communication will lead to a loss of business. Frequent breaks in the line of communication will lead to the loss of clients. The business development strategy should factor in the possibility of back-up systems or, at the very least, reliable customer service response from the firm's IT provider.

Ultimately, a long-term view needs to be taken of the IT enablement of the law firm together with the possibility of maintaining an in-house IT team aware of the needs and direction of the firm. All business development strategies will necessarily ride on the back of the IT infrastructure and capabilities of the firm. An IT strategy should be part and parcel of the business development strategy of a modern law firm.

As part of the firm's engagement with our clients and the new generation of lawyers, we maintain an active online presence. We train our lawyers in online etiquette and encourage our IT unit to keep abreast of new disruptive technologies that could enhance the way that we serve our clients.

6.   The empire strikes back

The empire that is the Internet is a two-edged sword. An online presence allows a business to position itself on a global level and offer its services to all and sundry. However, the Internet also allows for misinformation, bad experiences and rumours to spread literally at the speed of light, or the time taken to click a button. While a communications team is tasked with the job of making the presence and abilities of the law office known, a brand-building team is necessary to make sure that their efforts are supported and not undermined by negative publicity or news.

The growth of social media has led to peer reviews rapidly becoming the resource that most consumers and clients depend on to seek out new service providers. This includes law firms. While there are many authoritative industry-wide publications which rate law firms and are a source of information to the more discerning consumer of legal services, the vast majority of clients will not rely on those sources, assuming that they are even aware of them, to determine who they will choose to be their legal service provider. Social platforms such as Facebook, Twitter, LinkedIn and specific-interest blogs are likely to be the first places where a potential client comes across a law firm. In a quick survey of such sites shortly before writing this chapter, I came across the following comments about specific law firms:

- "Were we wrong about this law firm? Probably, yeah."
- "As a legal firm, they are pretty bad."
- "Bad to the bone."

With mystery still surrounding the marketing executives' dream scenario of being able to control what goes viral and what does not, should any of the above articles go viral, the law firms in question would be facing serious problems if not survival issues. A brand development team within a business development strategy must have the ability to respond quickly to situations such as those behind the comments above, and to put the law firm's position across briefly and succinctly.

Time is of the essence. While publicity rules may limit the ability of law firms to engage in social media, addressing issues on a firm's website is just as effective as it can be the trigger for those who have had positive experiences with that firm to come to its defence in the social media arena to give some balance and perspective before the issue gets out of hand. Firms today ignore the power of social media at their peril.

We have a team which keeps an eye on social media so that a quick response can be sent out if there are rumblings of discontent with our services or our approach. We encourage our clients to engage with us through social media channels to contain and deal with dissatisfaction.

7. The return of the Jedi

A law firm's sound business development strategy should take into account its position in the community in which it operates. It is a challenge to stay relevant in an ever-changing business environment. Commercial law firms are rarely seen in a positive light. There are no positive jokes about lawyers. Engagement with the community through corporate social responsibility programmes is a great way to keep public awareness of the brand. At one time lawyers were seen as knights in shining armour battling for social justice in an otherwise unjust world. Today the tendency is to align corporate and commercial lawyers with predatory lenders and greedy corporations.

Active corporate social responsibility programmes will not only aid the business development strategy but will also position the firm as being opposed to the dark side. In our firm we focus our efforts on children. We champion healthy fund raising activities such as distance running teams and other sporting events, and collaborate with our clients in reaching out to orphanages, shelters and child patients in palliative care. This not only increases the profile of the firm and its brand but, more importantly, strengthens the tie between the firm and its clients.

8. The force awakens

Today's law firms need to go the extra mile in their business development strategies. Merely issuing regular publications and updates to clients and organising social gatherings are no longer enough. When I started practice some 30 years ago, there were barely 1,000 lawyers in my jurisdiction. Work flowed to the law firms and lawyers were generally seen as noble, reputable and trustworthy. Certainly, the lawyer was subject to the odd joke, but it tended to be more about his verbosity and pomposity than being characterised as predatory or self-serving. Little needed to be done by way of business development – the public needed lawyers and no one else would do.

Today the tables have turned. Lawyers sit on the dark side, as far as the public goes. Business development strategies are required not just to stay competitive, but also to combat such negative perception. Lawyers were seen as a force for good. The force needs to awaken.

Interviews with general counsel

Stephen Revell
Freshfields Bruckhaus Deringer

1. Introduction

As editor of this book I concluded that it was essential to talk to the recipients of a law firm or lawyers' business development message – namely, the client. How do the clients think about business development from the receiving end? What do they like or dislike? What is a waste of time? What is the most effective form of business development?

I think that all law firms and lawyers should talk regularly to their clients to determine whether their business development activities are effective. If they do not, they could well be not only wasting their time but also damaging the relationship that they have by poor business development or unthought-through and unnecessary contact.

Accordingly, the key message of this chapter is: talk to your own clients – existing and targets – about how they are receiving and reacting to your own business development activities; it is as simple as that.

I interviewed nine general counsel from a wide range of companies and jurisdictions. To keep some order to their various comments, I used the same set of questions with each general counsel. As you will see, some chose to provide succinct answers in writing, but others generously gave their time for an extended telephone interview which I then transcribed. I have kept the interviews in broadly the spoken form so as to allow the character and the comments of each general counsel to come through – this is deliberate. I hope that you will find reading the thoughts of these general counsel as illuminating as I did. I would like to thank them all for the trouble that they each went to in contributing to this chapter.

Based on these interviews, it is clear that business development has to be seen in the context of developing a trusted relationship. Once you have that trusted relationship, you can do lots of really effective business development, but without it, it is really hard. The chance meeting or the cold call is not going to cut it with a general counsel, and you have to find ways of 'triangulating' a relationship – find out who they know and whether there is somebody who knows you. See if one general counsel will introduce you to another. To win new business, you have to work at a relationship because general counsel are not just going to read your brochure, they are not going to read your marketing materials, they are probably not going to read your alerts and, therefore, will not suddenly instruct you. Unless you have a knock-out piece of information for them because you have really closely studied them and their company, you are not going to get their attention; and even if you have that piece of information, you might still not get their attention because they do not know you. Finding a way to be introduced rather than any variety of cold marketing is probably the single biggest takeaway of these interview sessions.

A close second is the need for good business development to be based on a real understanding of the business of the company from which you want to develop business. By understanding the company, you can not only understand better their needs, but also ensure that any business development is clearly targeted at those needs and, through that, demonstrate an understanding of the business – that is clearly appreciated by general counsel. Many companies, especially those with a listing, regularly publish detailed information (including financial information through their audited accounts). In many instances lawyers will approach a company without doing even the most rudimentary of research, such as reading the latest annual report, let alone doing press searches etc, on what issues the company may be facing. There is some basic homework that all of us should do before we start a conversation with a company, whether it is an existing client or, more particularly, when it is a new relationship that we are trying to build.

Additional takeaways include:

- Clients clearly like training and there is a general view that training and seminars are among the business development activities that clients appreciate most. Again, though, the message is clear – it has to be targeted and well presented.
- Secondments are a very good example of longer-term thinking from a law firm. They signal a financial and relationship investment which often results in more work from the client.
- Joint *pro bono* activities are a great way to build the relationship and provide a platform for client and law firm to work together as one team. It is also a commitment from the law firm for a long-term investment rather than a short-term gesture. By finding opportunities to do more together, you consequently work more together.
- Post-transaction reviews are a very useful exercise to learn lessons and also an opportunity to introduce areas where you can add value to the client. Clients also appreciate regular relationship meetings.

2. The interviews

2.1 Alex Dimitrief, General Counsel, GE

1. Thinking about the best relationship that you have with your lawyers, what business development do they do that you value most?

Firstly, writing exceptionally well is important – routinely, as well as for the 'big stuff'. Ascertaining and then sharing our objectives is also crucial. Good firms deliver excellent services with integrity and cost-effectively. Also important is improving our profession by developing young lawyers through training and promoting diversity, as well as collaborating with us to give back to our shared communities. This helps develop and build relationships between us, as well as being a good *pro bono* opportunity.

2. What does good business development by a lawyer look like to you?

Selflessly promoting others within a law firm (or at a different firm) who are more suited for a particular assignment. Continuing Legal Education (CLE) and other 'early warning' tutorials that are provided ahead of the pack. Insightful articles that stand out from the pack (harder than people think) – by lawyers or about lawyers (but requires modesty and humility). Earning referrals or testimonials from other in-house colleagues. Creating optimal opportunities to build relationships (ie, *pro bono*, CLE, charitable activities).

3. What does bad business development by a lawyer look like to you?

Bad business development is the production of slick brochures that brag and puff with no substance. Being sent poorly-written and superficial articles that have no relevance to me or my business and with no substantive content. Being taken out for an extravagant meal or outing which is out of proportion to the business relationship. Lastly, presentations and/or meetings that do not include younger lawyers. It is really important to me to develop and nurture young talent.

4. What materials (if any) do you like receiving from law firms? What materials (if any) are likely to lead to you giving law firms work?

I like insightful articles and newsletters. There is a handful that I tend to read every time. Annual reports are also interesting, particularly to see what firms emphasise and how. I am also very interested in reports regarding diversity programmes, *pro bono* and charitable activities.

5. Do you get newsletters/alerts from law firms that you actually read?

Yes. There are three in particular from three different firms about financial services regulation, litigation (with an emphasis on lessons learned from trials and evidentiary hearings) and diversity. The content of these three newsletters is always timely and insightful.

6. Tell us the things you like/dislike in a law firm pitch?

I like humility, writing samples and credible references from other clients. What I dislike is bragging, exaggeration and disparagement of other law firms.

7. With regard to the law firms that you regularly work with, how do you like them to seek to develop more work from you?

They need to have proven they can provide great and cost-effective results. Also demonstrated knowledge of our businesses and innovative approaches to new engagements. They should also be introducing GE to rising talent within the law firm so we can continue to develop our relationships across experience levels. CLE and other mutually beneficial professional development activities. Another very useful exercise is post-matter reviews for lessons learned, for both GE and the firm.

8. Think back to a time when you met a lawyer that you had not worked with before, what did he do or say to pique your interest in working with him?

They have told me stories about developing younger talent at their firms and also intriguing stories about successful engagements for others and why they like being lawyers. Another characteristic I like is people that are compelling and charitable, especially efforts by lawyers outside of the United States to promote *pro bono* initiatives in their countries.

9. Do you have any other comments on business development?

It is important for a lawyer to acknowledge any past mistakes and explain how lessons were learned and will be implemented in future engagements. What they do to make work at their law firms less of a grind for their teams. Also discussions about shifting away from hourly rates to value billing (and how to measure that value). I also value learning experiences in emerging markets as this is a whole new world to me and one I am extremely interested in.

2.2   Felix Ehrat, General Counsel, Novartis

1. Thinking about the best relationship that you have with your lawyers, what business development do they do that you value most?

Lawyers need to have a deep understanding of our business and of our organisation. This is the first, second and third priority for me. They need to know how we work, what our challenges are and, of course, provide us with top-notch quality and creative advice. Responsiveness and pragmatic commercial advice are equally important, but I really appreciate lawyers adding real value and, if circumstances allow, providing us with options (and the different risk profiles associated with these options) and unexpected ideas and thoughts, rather than just one way of approaching the matter.

2. What does good business development by a lawyer look like to you?

A lawyer needs to show familiarity with our business and come to us having identified specific issues relevant to our business. The traditional pitch – "we are the best and we have so many partners and so many offices" – is of little value. A good first approach is if the lawyers have already familiarised themselves with our business and really thought about how they can add value. For example, for new business pitches in the United States, rather than to ask lawyers to provide us with the traditional capability statement, we invite them to present on a specific topic where they believe that they have deep subject-matter expertise and where they could add value to us. This also allows us to get to know the lead experts who would actually work on the matter.

3. What does bad business development by a lawyer look like to you?

An example of bad business development would be if after the pitch I didn't have any understanding of why I should use this lawyer or the firm. Information is so readily available to us that I would not want to spend time on information which I can have at my fingertips anyway. In other words, telling me information I already know and introducing me to lawyers who would not be involved in the actual work is not helpful.

4. What materials (if any) do you like receiving from law firms? What materials (if any) are likely to lead to you giving law firms work?

There is sometimes interesting content in the materials I receive from law firms, but I think the answer – in order to avoid a feeling of being inundated and being randomly sent materials from all over the globe – is to talk with the client to find out what their targeted needs and objectives for this kind of information are. I am not negative *per se*, but it has to be targeted, it has to add value and it has to be something that the client needs.

5. Do you get newsletters/alerts from law firms that you actually read?

If it is relevant to me, then I will read it, but as I mentioned before it must add value. It should have depth and quality – not something I could have read in the paper that morning. It has to be good or otherwise I would prefer not to receive anything.

6. Tell us the things you like/dislike in a law firm pitch?

It really depends on the type of pitch – whether it is a general pitch or for a specific project – but what is really important is providing me with the credentials and experience of the key individuals that will actually be working on the deal, not just a senior or billing partner I will never see again. If the project is going to be led by a senior associate, then we should get a feel for that person, too. I cannot understand the rationale behind law firms having specialised pitch teams that I never see again.

I think it is absolutely natural for a law firm to seek more business, as we are talking about a business relationship and partnership. Obviously, there are limits dictated by common sense and appropriate manners. I also think that law firms should pitch for work only where they have real experts and where they can add value; otherwise, they may put their credibility at risk. I personally believe that it is a strong indication for a good partnership if a firm tells us that they do not have particular expertise in a given area and guides us to somebody else. I would never see this as a weakness – quite the contrary.

7. With regard to the law firms that you regularly work with, how do you like them to seek to develop more work from you?

The way in which a law firm seeks new business enables me to understand whether it actually understands my business. I am not interested in hearing about their excellent data privacy lawyer from their Sydney office if it is reasonably clear that I have no need for data privacy support in Australia. It is all common sense, even though it does not always seem to be obvious to everybody. For example, an appropriate occasion to raise new business opportunities would be in a debrief of a project, with the lead partner highlighting areas they discovered during the course of the project that we might appreciate support on. Following this, they would introduce me to their specialist contacts in the areas highlighted and send me their credentials. To me, that is a normal relationship, but again I think a sophisticated client has a good understanding of its own needs and if this is being matched by more information from the law firm, that is perfect – but if it is being pushed randomly by a 'marketing machine', then it is sometimes unpleasant.

8. Think back to a time when you met a lawyer that you had not worked with before, what did he do or say to pique your interest in working with him?

To be honest I am not sure how bumping into someone would add value. This is sometimes an issue at congresses and other lawyers' events because a general counsel might be seen by many as a potential client. It is about creating an impression that the lawyer is interested in our business and challenges, not only in his business; about creating an impression that he might be able to help me and is interested in learning more about my challenges and where I might need support.

Something that is important to mention is that we are definitely not looking at outside counsel as mere vendors and suppliers of some services. We are looking to them as partners and we try to establish a long-term partnership. This is a two-way street, with obligations on both sides. I think with clients such as my company, it is really about identifying the areas where outside counsel can create value, especially as we have a large in-house department; this requires a bit of an investment on the part of outside counsel.

2.3   **Julian Gooding, Managing Director, General Counsel Division Asia, Credit Suisse**

1. Thinking about the best relationship that you have with your lawyers, what do they do that you value most?

We highly appreciate law firms that can act as our eyes and ears – our 'antennae' that feel what is coming on the legal and regulatory front – and can identify the key issues we should be thinking about. These 'crystal ball' updates (or thought leadership if you prefer) are usually more tailored than a general bulletin, and so can be more effective. I particularly value a quarterly email from litigation teams which provides a summary of what we have seen from the regulators over the previous quarter and identify key enforcement themes. Good insights from our relationship firms inform our strategic planning: at the start of the year, I ask all our internal legal teams that service businesses to formulate a coverage plan, identifying the business strategy, key legal and regulatory risks, new business and product initiatives, and any potential issues or concerns.

2. What does good business development by a lawyer look like to you?

For me, it is about regular dialogue with the law firm. We like to meet our key firms quarterly, where we receive in advance information about the overall relationship, identifying where it is working well and where it is spotty, where we have received secondments, training and other value-add services. The quarterly meetings allow us to keep up with new arrivals and leavers on both sides, and to make new introductions where it builds the relationship. As part of our quarterly agenda we discuss other ways to work together – jointly supporting charitable initiatives, sharing insights regarding people development, or how to build engagement within our teams. We are happy to ask our people to deliver training to our key legal providers, and we will also send our people on secondment where this makes sense. In essence, we would like our relationships with law firms to be truly reciprocal in the long term and prefer to work with law firms that think the same way. A relationship partner who understands the importance of this will be able to deliver the entire firm.

3. What does bad business development by a lawyer look like to you?

Bad business development is the lack of a regular dialogue – relationships can only thrive with good communication. At introductory meetings, it goes down well if lawyers are prepared to give a thematic overview of their area of business which is tailored to our bank. The quality and relevance of the insights will mark the lawyers out. Also, the courtesy visit by the global partner who is visiting the region can be a source of frustration if the meeting simply goes through the motions.

4/5. What materials (if any) do you like receiving from law firms? What materials (if any) are likely to lead to you giving law firms work? Do you get newsletters/alerts from law firms that you actually read?

In the context of the quarterly relationship meetings, an informative and well-prepared deck for the relationship meeting makes a difference. For example, we find it helpful when a law firm has prepared a year-on-year comparison of the amount of work done for us, identified by business line and location areas. Sending the pack well in advance of the meeting means we can digest it and make the meeting more meaningful.

Law firm bulletins on key topics can be useful in giving a check on the topics we need to factor into our thinking. Although there may be a number of law firm bulletins produced by various law firms on the same topic, it is difficult to get a sense of who the real expert is from a bulletin. It is often helpful to supplement the bulletin with an offer of training, which is still the best way to launch or strengthen a relationship.

6. Tell us the things you like/dislike in a law firm pitch?

The content is key – it must reflect proper due diligence by the law firm. Written materials must look professional. A sloppy pitch document is hard to come back from.

7. With regard to the law firms that you regularly work with, how do you like them to seek to develop more work from you?

There is nothing wrong with a law firm approaching me and having a frank conversation about why they are not getting business in a particular area. I am very happy to give honest and transparent feedback. It helps the law firm with its hiring plans, and may ultimately lead to better capability in the areas where the relationship is spotty. As long as those conversations are handled sensitively and in confidence, they are usually mutually beneficial. Ideally, these conversations would flow from the quarterly relationship meeting.

8. Think back to a time you met a lawyer you hadn't worked with before, what did he do or say to pique your interest in working with him?

It would be foolish of us not to take up an initial invitation of a conversation or a meeting. If we decide not to use a firm, it is better to have good grounds not to do so. Lawyers who are engaging, smart people who have done good work and are able to communicate this in a clear way will be well received. Ideally, a successful introductory meeting should lead to an offer of training. A lawyer who presents to a group of 20 or 30 lawyers or compliance professionals, shows his expertise, uses case studies and is personable stands an excellent chance of winning the instruction. The onus is on the law firm to ensure that lawyers who give training create that positive impression.

9. Do you have any other comments on business development?
What will usually pique my interest are intelligent thematic insights that make our complex markets easier to comprehend, and reflect an understanding of what it means to be a general counsel. A good sense of humour also helps, of course!

2.4   Lisa Luo, Head of Legal, COFCO (Hong Kong) Limited

1. Thinking about the best relationship that you have with your lawyers, what business development do they do that you value most?
We value external lawyers who demonstrate not just technical legal skills, but also good communication skills and creative thinking qualities. We appreciate lawyers who demonstrate a deep understanding of the industry and of our business, and are able to offer commercial insights, and proactively provide counsel on business risks, reputational risks, governance practices and best practices rather than simply follow specific client instructions.

2. What does good business development by a lawyer look like to you?
Lawyers need to demonstrate that they are knowledgeable about our business and industry in their business development approaches. Willingness to offer in-depth topical training programmes to in-house and business people is much appreciated.

3. What does bad business development by a lawyer look like to you?
Bad business development is when you have no focus on the clients' interests and business. The materials are general and broad, with no tailoring or thought.

4. What materials (if any) do you like receiving from law firms? What materials (if any) are likely to lead to you giving law firms work?
I like receiving topical materials with in-depth analysis or practical tips.

5. Do you get newsletters/alerts from law firms that you actually read?
Yes, I do read them. I find newsletters and alerts particularly useful. They are wonderful resources to help me keep updated with legal, regulatory and practice developments and trends.

6. Tell us the things you like/dislike in a law firm pitch?
We like to see that law firms are open and honest about the areas they are best at and

acknowledge the areas where there are challenges. We like law firms/lawyers to be accountable for their pitches. We also expect those who pitch to us to be the ones that will actually do the work.

7. With regard to the law firms that you regularly work with, how do you like them to seek to develop more work from you?
We expect our external lawyers to be flexible on billing and take a long-term view about fees – don't try to charge on small matters or phone calls. We appreciate when they are willing to spend time to have reviews and evaluation of cases/matters with us after the work is done.

8. Think back to a time when you met a lawyer that you had not worked with before, what did he do or say to pique your interest in working with him?
A lawyer who is open and displays humility and sensitivity to cultural issues and shares a genuine interest in the client's business is likely to catch my attention.

2.5   Nina Macpherson, Chief Legal Officer, Ericsson

1. Thinking about the best relationship that you have with your lawyers, what business development do they do that you value most?
Being proactive is what I value the most in lawyers. I like them to have thought about what I should be worrying about and proactively say, "Have you set up this process?", "How are you preparing for this piece of regulation?", etc. Being a good adviser, a proactive adviser, is what I really appreciate.

2. What does good business development by a lawyer look like to you?
Being a proactive lawyer and sharing content. Bringing to my attention the latest legislation or things to be aware of that are helpful in my daily business.

3. What does bad business development by a lawyer look like to you?
I won't start to use a law firm because they come and say they are the best in the world. I start to use lawyers because they are experts in their field. If I really like a lawyer, then I might try someone else in the same firm because they gave me a good impression and I like their ethics, professionalism or the relationship we have. If my usual contact is efficient, sympathetic and nice, it is likely he has a nice colleague in some other field that I need advice on.

It is very difficult to say how you should go about developing a relationship from a cold start – you need to have proven yourself in a particular field. For example, the firm we would usually use might have a conflict, so our next step would be to look for the best, say, litigation firm in the market. We then might start to use that firm for our litigation matters going forward.

4. What materials (if any) do you like receiving from law firms? What materials (if any) are likely to lead to you giving law firms work?
At the moment the *Safe Harbour* ruling by the European Court of Justice is very

topical so I get a lot of memos from various law firms about it. I will send that over to my expert in data privacy and she uses this as she forms her opinion on what we should do. This is a very topical issue which I am interested in so materials on that topic are relevant and useful. As a chief legal officer, I am interested in a wide variety of subjects. Often, if it is not useful for me personally, I will send it over to the person in my team I think should read it. I would not throw away everything, but I do throw away quite a lot. If one firm produces a good publication which is not just facts but is more their opinions on particular topics and their view of developments, I usually save that for long trips to read.

5. Do you get newsletters/alerts from law firms that you actually read?

Newsletters and alerts go much further down in priority because I have to skim-read them to see if there is anything of interest. Sometimes I quickly scan through the headings to see if there is anything that catches my attention, otherwise they might just 'disappear'. The shorter alerts which are topical are more useful to me.

6. Tell us the things you like/dislike in a law firm pitch?

The ones I like contain a preliminary view of the case because I like to see how the law firm is reasoning and it actually can be a differentiating factor if that is done well. My other requirement would be a good specification of the fees so I understand how the firm intends to charge and, of course, the best possible rebate or fee structure that they can propose. I also like to get an idea of how the law firm will work with me and the team, so I can get a good understanding of how they would take on the case and who would be working on it. A bad pitch is when it is not structured, especially when I have been clear about what I want.

7. With regard to the law firms that you regularly work with, how do you like them to seek to develop more work from you?

Yes; for example, if I work with a particular law firm on antitrust and they say, "We have a really good litigation lawyer I would like you to meet", I am very happy to meet that person. I am fine with this approach, as long as it is not all the time – I don't want to be sold to all the time, but if it is something particular that they think would suit my needs, I'm absolutely fine with that. If I really like the firm and the lawyer I work with, I will probably be proactive and ask, "Do you have someone that could help me with X?"

8. Think back to a time when you met a lawyer that you had not worked with before, what did he do or say to pique your interest in working with him?

I am a relationship person and I feel that I need to be able to approach my lawyer even at 3am if I have a crisis on my hands.

9. Do you have any other comments on business development?

To impress corporate clients, you need to demonstrate that you are trying to make your own business more efficient and that you transfer some of the efficiency gains to me as a client. Many law firms work with efficiencies, but it is not until you ask them that they show you. Law firms need to find a way of sharing more on the technological side enabling us, for example, to work together on the same document.

Another thing that I think is beneficial for law firms is when you send really good lawyers on secondment at a reasonable price as this really creates a close relationship. If you send me someone that is really good, then I will be impressed by that person and naturally by the firm. That is a very good way for the lawyer to get to know our company and for me to get to know your firm.

You could also think about making sure that both the law firm and the in-house lawyer benefit from the lessons learned after any large project. You don't necessarily have to do a debrief, but you can have a conversation on:

- what worked well;
- what could have worked better;
- what could have been prepared better;
- whether there were any issues between the teams in a particular stream working together (eg, confidence issue);
- why a particular negotiation didn't go very well; and
- most importantly, how can we improve that next time.

This builds a bond between the in-house lawyer and the external counsel that I think is really beneficial for both. This does happen, but most of the time on our initiative. You could probably find a way to institutionalise that and I think that is probably a good way for the law firm to cross-sell without doing it overtly – it is a lost opportunity if you don't do it.

2.6   Abhijit Mukhopadhyay, President (Legal), Hinduja Group

1. Thinking about the best relationship that you have with your lawyers, what business development do they do that you value most?

Every day I meet with lawyers from around the world. I already know many of them personally and whenever they are in London they drop in and have a chat. Some who I do not know also seek an appointment and they will come and meet me and introduce themselves. In the past couple of years law firms have become quite aggressive in their approach – I like this very much because, honestly speaking, my belief is that law firms need us and we also need them. This should be a win-win situation. I want to understand law firms, how they work, what kind of expertise they have, what kind of fee structure they propose, what kind of flexibility they have, etc. At the same time, they should also understand us as a business, what we do and what kind of requirements we have. I have also been requesting law firms to think of us when they come across business opportunities relevant to the businesses that we are in. Most have no problem with this and they keep referring business opportunities to me. My approach is very clear – if there is a business proposition which ultimately comes to fruition and we sign any kind of joint venture agreement or supplier agreement, or any definitive legal agreement, there will be an element of legal work involved and that legal work will go to the referring law firm. Law firms are becoming not only more aggressive, but also more innovative in terms of the services they offer to clients.

I really value lawyers who have expert commercial and legal knowledge in our kind of businesses, that is the most important thing. They need to help us in our transactional legal matters. For this, we are ready to provide them with business/commercial inputs to help them understand our requirements better.

2. What does good business development by a lawyer look like to you?

There are two things I value above all others. One is personal contact because, ultimately, it is all relationship based. If I know you well, if I have worked with you, and vice versa, and I'm happy with your expertise, then whichever firm you will be joining I will first come to you, no matter whether you are in a global law firm or a magic circle or a mid-level law firm because I know you. So for me personal contact, personal relationship, wavelength and chemistry matching are the most important thing.

The second thing is that I am very disappointed when I receive an impersonal kind of email, either without the name of an individual sender or my name on it, which has very clearly been sent to a large number of people; there is no personal touch in that. Having said that, I also recognise that it is not possible for everyone to send me a tailored personal email. However, I do value targeted information. If the subject matter is interesting, if it is relevant to me, if it's important legal information or an important case that interests me, then I will read it. Whatever is concise, clear and relevant attracts me most.

3. What does bad business development by a lawyer look like to you?

If a law firm does not have the capability to undertake a specific task and yet somebody is trying to project that they do have that capability, that disturbs me. This does not generally happen with established/reputable firms. If they do not have the expertise, most of the time they will say, "I am sorry, we do not deal with that, but if you want us to give you some references, we will be very happy to do so". At the end of the day, if somebody says I know how to do this job, they are taking a great risk if I engage them and they cannot perform. Therefore, most people are very clear about what they can and cannot do. I also dislike too much pushing; every other day an email comes for a personal meeting as law firms try to be 'in the mind' of the client or potential client, but how to do it cleverly is something of a challenge. I think the best way is to maintain personal contact and I find that most people who contact me do it on a personal basis. I welcome a telephone call or an email saying, for example, that they are coming to London and would like to catch up. That is the best kind of relationships because it is two way – we learn from them, they learn from us.

4. What materials (if any) do you like receiving from law firms? What materials (if any) are likely to lead to you giving law firms work?

Honestly speaking, it depends upon the content. However, I can give you a 100% guarantee that all materials we receive by email, we read. If I find something really interesting or very relevant to our business, then I will definitely read it and often distribute to our global operations; we operate in 40 countries around the world and many of our CEOs and legal personnel are interested in this type of material.

5. Do you get newsletters/alerts from law firms that you actually read?

It depends on the content, but most law firms are not naïve: if they spend their time and energy producing something, it is usually worthwhile reading. It does not deter me if the newsletter is big or small. There is one US law firm which prepares and circulates once every three months a huge arbitration journal and it is really informative. It runs into around 50-60 pages, but I make a point of reading it and then get in touch with them if I have any further comments or questions. So, it does not really depend on the number of pages, but rather on the content.

6. Tell us the things you like/dislike in a law firm pitch?

The problem we are facing is lawyers not understanding the commercial issues and business issues relevant to our particular business groups. I do not like to receive a generalised pitch – full stop. So, if I ask somebody to pitch for a particular transaction relating to a particular business (and we have 10 business verticals), then I would expect them to come back not with a generalised view, but specifically about that particular business because that demonstrates their own knowledge and understanding of commercial issues. I am impressed when someone highlights the problem, the issues and the cost. This makes me feel special, having a tailored and thoughtful response. Sometimes, I have limited time to discuss a problem I am having with a lawyer. In this case, when they can give me some answers based on just one 30-minute phone call, that shows they really understand our business and what I am asking for.

7. With regard to the law firms that you regularly work with, how do you like them to seek to develop more work from you?

Trust and confidence are central – I do not change my lawyers frequently. Having said that I also do not have a panel. How do I select a lawyer? When work comes in, I review our law firm database and approach the most appropriate firm for the work and ask them if they can assist on the matter in a particular country. If they have expertise, presence and we are happy with the fees, then we move forward straightaway. If firms are unable to assist, then I will expect some suggestions, which are always gratefully received. Timing is often key as well, sometimes a matter finishes and then another matter comes up and since I have worked with that law firm recently I might contact the same lawyer because I like working with them. That is the approach I take because I do not believe that you can use one law firm, for one job, only once.

8. Think back to a time when you met a lawyer that you had not worked with before, what did he do or say to pique your interest in working with him?

After the recently concluded IBA [International Bar Association annual conference] in Vienna a lot of law firms contacted me. However, I do not get irritated by it, I welcome it and I will always meet them. No matter whether they are small, big, global or non-global, I enjoy meeting new people and you never know what you will learn. It is important for me to build my network of firms that cover all areas of law, including the slightly niche ones as we have got 10 business verticals. My advantage is I do not have a panel so I do not have any restrictions – it primarily comes down to three considerations:

- Do you have the expertise?
- Do I have a personal relationship with you? (Even if I don't know you, we can start a business relationship if you can demonstrate your capability); and
- How flexible are your fees?

9. Do you have any other comments on business development?

Lawyers need to understand our group and our businesses (we have 90,000 people operating in 10 business verticals in 40-odd countries with $15 billion in revenues). I do not want a generalised approach. People should come after doing their homework, so that even if I ask them a very specific commercial question they are able to answer. I am always looking for more than a very general pitch.

2.7 Shella Ng, Chief Legal Officer, Yum! Brands Inc (China Division at Yum! Brands Inc)

1. Thinking about the best relationship that you have with your lawyers, what business development do they do that you value most?

Firstly, they have a good knowledge of the business of the client and the decision-making process. Secondly, good commercial sense is also important. I also appreciate lawyers who have good soft people skills and are good at relationship building.

2. What does good business development by a lawyer look like to you?

They have to have an ability to understand the business needs of the client and a willingness to share their other clients' experiences – in other words, to act as a window to see the industry's best practice. These kinds of insight are invaluable and provide me with a sense of the firm's experience and also what is going on in the industry. Lastly, cost: they need to have a reasonable fee range.

3. What does bad business development by a lawyer look like to you?

The worst business development is when lawyers promote a service or an area of service that I do not need as it is neither relevant nor suitable for my business or just something I can't relate to. Another bad example is contacting my colleagues at the same time as me, which is embarrassing to me and makes me feel that my relationship is not valued.

4. What materials (if any) do you like receiving from law firms? What materials (if any) are likely to lead to you giving law firms work?

I like receiving case studies and 'war stories' – how other people make mistakes or achieve success so that we can learn from real experience. I don't think any materials will directly lead to an engagement opportunity, unless there is a need. However, showcasing the capability and the know-how will be an added advantage when the need comes and they will be front of mind.

5. Do you get newsletters/alerts from law firms that you actually read?
I probably read about 50% of what I receive. As previously mentioned, it has to pique my interest by being relevant.

6. Tell us the things you like/dislike in a law firm pitch?
I like to see a genuine desire to work together despite the size of the engagement or fee. I also like open-mindedness and a demonstration of a good understanding of the engagement. Most of the pitches I receive are thoughtful and well structured, so I have little to complain about.

7. With regard to the law firms that you regularly work with, how do you like them to seek to develop more work from you?
I welcome all options which add value and might develop into a formal engagement. Very often, law firms also provide good training seminars (that must be tailor-made) for my team as they identify an interest or need, even without the promise of substantial legal work. This is something I really appreciate.

8. Think back to a time when you met a lawyer that you had not worked with before, what did he do or say to pique your interest in working with him?
Attitude is very important. Lawyers from big or top law firms should be cautious and sensitive to the feelings of smaller clients. If they sound too arrogant to a potential client, it is detrimental. After all, the law business is a service industry!

9. Do you have any other comments on business development?
For a lawyer to pique my interest, they need to be helpful and give me a good sense of trust and confidence. The reputation of the lawyer also counts a great deal because accreditation of lawyers is primarily done by word of mouth or hearsay of clients.

2.8   Howard Trust, General Counsel, Schroders

1. Thinking about the best relationship that you have with your lawyers, what business development do they do that you value most?
I value lawyers that use their imagination when working with me. Of course, experience and technical excellence are very important, but they are not really a differentiator, particularly among the top-level law firms. What really sets someone apart is their approach. I also need 'cultural empathy' – the lawyers I work with have to have an understanding of our business and our business culture.

2. What does good business development by a lawyer look like to you?
To be honest, we really appreciate training and in effect, free advice. Seminars, 'lunch and learns' and other forms of training are a good way for us to discover more about the law firms' areas of expertise and get to know the lawyers.

3. What does bad business development by a lawyer look like to you?
Bad business development is when lawyers clearly have no understanding or interest

in the revenue and profit drivers of our business. At the end of the day, we are a business and our revenue and profit are high priorities for me and the company.

4. What materials (if any) do you like receiving from law firms? What materials (if any) are likely to lead to you giving law firms work?

The best materials are those that deliver quality know-how from a global perspective. They should be comprehensive and targeted at my sector. I prefer longer pieces that go into detail on a particular topic rather than the short and snappy alerts. The material has to educate me, otherwise I won't read it.

5. Do you get newsletters/alerts from law firms that you actually read?

I receive newsletters and alerts from a lot of firms and I do make a conscious effort to look at all that cross my desk – but see 4 above.

6. Tell us the things you like/dislike in a law firm pitch?

The worst things a law firm could do in a pitch is to portray 'cockiness' or to have absolutely no sense or understanding of cost and value. I want the fees to be presented upfront in a clear and understandable way – not as a side thought. I can't stand lawyers who are arrogant because they work for a prestigious firm. I want to know what experience the team has, not how wonderful your firm is.

7. With regard to the law firms that you regularly work with, how do you like them to seek to develop more work from you?

The best way to develop more work from me is to provide training and to develop the relationship through invitations to seminars and events. These types of event are a platform for the firm to showcase their expertise to me, so I might think about using them on a future matter.

8. Think back to a time when you met a lawyer that you had not worked with before, what did he do or say to pique your interest in working with him?

Any lawyers that approach me should have a good knowledge and understanding of Schroders and the services we offer. They need to focus on areas of law that are relevant to my business and comment intelligently on what areas we should think about more closely, hot topics in the market, etc.

2.9 Solms U Wittig, General Counsel, The Linde Group

1. Thinking about the best relationship that you have with your lawyers, what business development do they do that you value most?

Business development is a significant part of the lawyer–client relationship. First of all, of course, they must do excellent work because if they do not, I will not work with them again. Second, a long-term relationship is supported by information provided by the law firm thinking ahead in a specific industry maybe with legal topics, legal problems, statutory developments that are being communicated and developed including offering seminars. One example – several law firms that we work with have approached me with the following questions: do you need anything about shareholder activism, can we help you, can we give you some information? Being proactive is extremely helpful.

2. What does good business development by a lawyer look like to you?

I do not like approaches from a lawyer for 'business development' if I separate this as a function. If lawyers approach me, they should approach me directly and establish a base of trust and confidence, not by trying to sell me something that I do not need at that point in time, but trying to draw me into discussions on particular matters and show their relevant expertise and know-how by leading the discussion with me. It must be based on a substantive matter or topic.

3. What does bad business development by a lawyer look like to you?

Getting overwhelmed by law firm brochures which are in no way connected with my business or which I did not ask for is unhelpful and rather irritating. I do not wish to be sent materials that do not help me and only provide me with information that is out of context and unrelated.

4. What materials (if any) do you like receiving from law firms? What materials (if any) are likely to lead to you giving law firms work?

I prefer materials which show or tell me that this particular lawyer or law firm has carefully considered my company or my department and thought about what we could need. For instance, I have certainly received a few on the recent energy law developments in Germany, but only very few are customised. It is the customisation of information that attracts me.

5. Do you get newsletters/alerts from law firms that you actually read?

I rarely read material which comes unsolicited. In my opinion, the best approach is when law firms ask you to select which areas you are interested in. This allows me to choose the content that I want to receive. For newsletters in particular, I have no interest if they come unsolicited. To the extent that I have asked for them, then, of course I flip through them as it was my choice to receive them. If I get several sets of information – triple or quadruple times – that is my problem, not the law firm's problem.

A differentiating factor for me, if I get three or four newsletters I have elected to receive which are essentially all addressing the same issues, would be the language: I personally would prefer German over English.

6. Tell us the things you like/dislike in a law firm pitch?

Customisation is the key word, understanding what you are pitching for and customising your approach to the client's needs. If the presentation is general with little or no thought about how to apply their expertise to my business, I will not be interested. If I get a standard brochure on their expertise with x many deals for x number of companies which is basically name-dropping, I rather dislike that.

7. With regard to the law firms that you regularly work with, how do you like them to seek to develop more work from you?

Generally, yes, it depends on the method of presentation. I meet regularly with partners of law firms who obviously try to get more business and when I get the impression that they have put some thought into my needs and tell me why they think they could do more and why they would be strong in this or that field, then we can start a discussion and then maybe next time something comes up I will consider them.

8. Think back to a time when you met a lawyer that you had not worked with before, what did he do or say to pique your interest in working with him?

An important point is: do not start with a general pitch, how great your firm is, having just met me. I prefer to develop and build on a personal level first. You can talk about general non-legal topics, for instance, politics, and try to feel the chemistry. Then if the chemistry is right you can go to the next step of a meeting. If when first meeting me someone tells me how clever they are and how superior they are, then it's a turn off – I prefer to go through the small talk at first to get the measure of the person.

9. Do you have any other comments on business development?

It is all about customisation of the offering and gaining the trust of the client through the right approach and not just through general marketing. I would probably not meet somebody from the business development function who cold calls me and says, "I would like to come in and talk to you about a law firms' services"; I'd rather talk to my normal relationship partner whom I have a trusted relationship with.

The lawyer's role in business development – can lawyers sell?

Shelley Dunstone
Legal Circles

1.   Salesperson or ambassador?

There is a common misconception among lawyers that the best marketing is simply to do good work. While doing good work is essential, in this very competitive world it is no longer enough. This is partly because of the difference between being an expert and being perceived as one. A lawyer who keeps a low profile risks being overlooked in favour of another lawyer who is better at self-promotion.

Another aspect of the 'good work only' marketing approach is to believe that all work can come from referrals, which is what successful lawyers often say is their case. However, such a gold standard can not only create unrealistic expectations, but also become an excuse for not undertaking any form of marketing. Simply waiting for referrals is a slow way to build your practice.

Lawyers need to be involved in business development. They cannot simply delegate it to the marketing department. Marketers can build the firm brand, but it is usually the lawyers who need to make the sale.

Some lawyers have negative thoughts and feelings about marketing and business development. They can feel uncomfortable about being a 'salesperson'. Instead, though, lawyers should think about business development as an ambassador role. Being an ambassador is prestigious and carries a glamorous image. An ambassador takes initiatives, networks to meet new people and forges new connections. An ambassador represents the values that the firm embodies. An ambassador is both receptive to different cultures and well informed about the surrounding world, expresses interest in every new acquaintance and follows up each meeting with personalised communication. The skills of an ambassador can be learned and developed.

The first step is thus to start thinking of yourself as an ambassador.

Conferences and networking events are all opportunities to be an ambassador where you create conversations and build relationships that can lead to business for your firm. When you act in a business development role, you are representing your firm and your profession. Why not think of this as an honour, and aim to be the best ambassador that you can be?

This chapter discusses the seven steps that will help lawyers to succeed in business development:

- understand the strategy;
- know your strengths;
- build your network;

- understand your market;
- demonstrate your value;
- help contacts to buy your services; and
- set goals.

2.   Understand the strategy

Start by getting a clear idea of what sort of business you are trying to build. What type of work and clients are a good fit for your firm?

Make an effort to understand the firm's strategic plan. It is best if you can align your own career aspirations and profile-building with the firm's strategy. Can you build your ideal practice within this firm? Will your goals serve the firm, as well as yourself?

Competitive strategy is the choice of how and where to compete. It consists of three main elements:

- your choice of target market;
- your differentiation – that is, how you intend to serve that market in a way that differs from your competitors; and
- the strategic assets that will support the first two decisions.

A firm achieves competitive advantage through a combination of what it has (its strategic assets) and how it chooses to use these assets to create value for its market. It is a matter of using what you have to get what you want.

Strategic assets are usually intangible and are:

- unique to your firm;
- costly or difficult for your competitors to acquire;
- difficult for competitors to copy;
- path-dependent (ie, you have developed these assets as a result of the unique path that your firm has followed);
- contributing to something that customers want, at a price that they are prepared to pay;
- durable; and
- superior to those of your competitors.

Examples of strategic assets include knowledge, know-how, systems, networks, relationships, reputation, brand image and awareness, culture and capacity to innovate.

An effective strategy builds on the firm's strategic assets and also aims to enhance them in order to create further competitive advantage for the firm.

All marketing, including business development activities undertaken by the lawyers, should be consistent with the firm's competitive strategy. That strategy should be shared with the lawyers, so they understand exactly what the firm is seeking to achieve.

If you are a lawyer seeking to build your profile, a good starting point is to answer the question, "What do I want to be known for?" Be clear about the sort of clients that you want to attract and the area in which you intend to position yourself, in a manner that is consistent with the firm's marketing.

3. **Know yourself**

What would make a client choose you instead of some other lawyer? Your professional expertise is just one factor. Who you are, and the way that you connect with your clients, are fundamental to the value of the service that you offer.

Your aim is to stand out from the crowd. Aspire to be of unique value. Strive not to be 'fungible' (a commodity). You do not want to be interchangeable with others in your category.

Law exerts a strong influence of conformity. It is natural to imitate what you see as a model of the successful lawyer. It is good to learn from those who are more experienced, but do not lose what is distinctive and individual about you. If you imitate others' behaviours, you risk appearing inauthentic. Clients can easily sense when a lawyer is presenting a façade, when that person's true self is being concealed, and this can cause discomfort.

Be yourself. Your personality is a unique asset. Law is a personal service, and to a large extent, you are the product that clients are buying.

There are many ways to engage in business development. Find an approach that suits your personal style. Consider what you can best contribute. Do you like socialising or are you an introvert who prefers to write?

However, your natural strengths and preferences should be a starting point, not an excuse to avoid learning new skills. Over time, we can all stretch ourselves and develop our abilities.

4. **Build your network**

The more people you know, and who know what you do, the faster your practice will grow.

This means meeting more people, letting them know what you can offer and keeping in contact with them.

It is worth taking deliberate steps to widen your circle of acquaintances.

There are many ways to meet people, for example:
- through mutual friends;
- going to networking events such as breakfasts, lunches, cocktail parties or dinners;
- joining clubs or associations in accordance with your interests;
- joining a service club; or
- joining a group in which the members refer business to each other.

Some people dislike networking events, but these provide excellent opportunities to meet new people, in a setting where everyone is there for the same reason – to build business.

Do something to make yourself memorable – for the right reasons. You could wear something colourful or flamboyant. Have an unusual business card. Be a great conversation partner. Be a good listener. Ask thought-provoking questions. Be witty.

Meeting people is just the first step. Very rarely will you get work simply by meeting someone at an event and giving them your business card. You will more likely need to initiate an acquaintance upon which you can build a relationship. The person whom you meet might one day buy your legal services, or refer you to someone else who becomes a client.

Most people do nothing with the business cards that they bring back from events; some people file them in a business card box; others throw them away. Instead, you should follow up after the event by making contact with the people that you met. If you are a member of an online networking site such as LinkedIn, invite your new contacts to connect with you. At its simplest this is like an online business-card box. But it also stores much more information than a business card box. You will find out what you have in common and the interests of your contacts. Reading their online profile will give you a lot to talk about next time you meet. Another benefit is that if they move to another company, they will update their own contact details, so you will not lose touch with them. And by posting updates, you can easily keep your business contacts informed about what you are doing.

Relationships are built in layers. Each time that you make contact, you add a layer. A layer could be:

- sending a 'great to meet you' email after the networking event. In your message, refer to some aspect of the conversation that you had. This shows that you were listening and interested in what the person had to say;
- sending a relevant article that you have written;
- sending a relevant article that you have read;
- offering to introduce them to someone whom they might be interested to meet;
- referring them to someone who might be able to use their services;
- referring them to someone who can provide a service that they need;
- inviting them for coffee; or
- inviting them to accompany you to another event.

Find out what your new contact will regard as valuable. Ask questions to get them talking about their business activities or leisure interests. When you go to a networking event thinking about the follow up, you are more likely to obtain relevant information.

Make a particular effort to have regular contact with people who refer work to you. Referrals are valuable. Never take them for granted. Professional referrers such as accountants, financial advisers, doctors and even other lawyers are constantly targeted by lawyers seeking referral work. If you do not maintain contact, they might send the work elsewhere. Do not wait until you need some work; it can look as if you contact them only when you want something.

It is also becoming increasingly acceptable to meet new people online, through networking sites such as LinkedIn. People search using keywords, so if someone invites you to connect, they could be seriously interested in what you have to offer. By ignoring their request to connect, you could be rebuffing a potential client.

There are two ways to meet people online: responding to approaches from people whom you do not know and making your own approach to people whom you want to meet.

If someone that you do not know invites you to connect, do not immediately reject the request. Look at that person's profile to see if there is any potential synergy. If you decide to accept the invitation, treat it as the beginning of a relationship, just as if you met at a networking event. If they live in your city, invite them to meet you in person. Arrange a meeting at a public place such as a café.

Conversely, you could invite someone whom you would like to meet to connect. Make sure that you do this in a manner consistent with the rules of the social media platform that you are using (so that your message is not reported as spam). The safest way is to ask someone in your network to introduce you. It is easy to find out who is connected to whom.

Aim to meet everyone in your contacts list. If you are travelling, search through your connections list to see who lives in your destination city. See if you can set up a meeting with them.

Sometimes, relationship-building activities feel unproductive – as if you are not working. Naturally, you need to control the amount of time spent on non-billable work. But building your network is an essential aspect of your legal practice.

5. Understand your market

Positioning yourself as a lawyer who is familiar with the challenges that your clients are facing makes you more valuable to them and helps you to achieve 'trusted adviser' status. To do this, it is necessary to invest in your client relationships. Initiate contact with your clients outside of the formal legal work that you do for them. Clients may be wary of engaging in general conversation with you while you are doing paid work for them and the timer clock is on.

Examining trends in the world around you can help you to gain a deeper understanding of an industry, practice area or a client's business. You can do this by:

- asking your clients what the most important issues are for them;
- paying attention to common issues that are affecting clients in your practice;
- reading industry journals to gain insight into trends that are causing concern;
- subscribing to blogs and podcasts published by opinion leaders in an industry;
- attending conferences and seminars that your clients attend; and
- reading business magazines – they often run features on the broader trends that may affect business and surveys in which executives report on their concerns about the future.

Your thinking and research will give rise to questions which can serve as conversation starters. You will thus express curiosity and interest in your clients. They will appreciate your investment of time and effort in learning about their challenges. You will learn about what your clients are trying to achieve and what may be standing in their way.

Demonstrating an understanding of trends that may have an impact on your clients is a way to differentiate yourself from other lawyers. You may even discover new types of legal need which you can meet.

6. Demonstrate your value

You may have excellent technical abilities and client service skills. But people can receive a complete experience of these qualities only after they have started working with you.

There are two main ways to promote your services: asserting your expertise and demonstrating your expertise.

Advertising asserts your expertise. Advertising is regarded as the weakest form of promotion, because it is self-serving. Everyone knows that you are the one making the claim of greatness in your advertisement.

What can you do to demonstrate your expertise? Think about the concept of samples. Samples enable people to try before they buy. You can use the same idea to give potential clients an experience of your approach and what you are like to work with.

Engaging in thought leadership is a powerful way to position yourself as an expert in your field.

A thought leader is someone who is recognised as an authority in a specialist area and whose expertise is highly regarded and sought after.

There are many ways of engaging in thought leadership. The two main ones are writing articles and giving presentations. These are effective ways for lawyers to build profile and attract clients.

Central to thought leadership is the importance of original thinking. Not every informational article or presentation counts as thought leadership.

Most lawyers tend to write and speak about new developments in the law. They wait for something to happen, to give them a reason for writing or presenting.

While it is important to inform your clients about important changes, whenever such changes occur there is a race to be the first to report on it. This puts you in a highly competitive situation and makes it hard for you to stand out from the crowd.

In addition, your clients might not be as fascinated by new legislation and court decisions as you are. Even if you make it relevant to them by predicting the effects of the changes, new developments in the law rarely address clients' most pressing problems. The issues that interest lawyers are not necessarily the same as the ones that interest clients.

How can you find topics that are more interesting for your clients? Instead of using the law as a starting point, start with an issue that you know is a common problem for your clients. Ask your clients what is happening in their world. Find out what is keeping them awake at night, and write or speak about that. Draw on your own unique experience of the kinds of problems that arise. Go to seminars that your clients attend. Pay particular attention to the questions attendees ask – it gives a clue as to what they are thinking about. Talk to people during the networking breaks. Ask questions and listen to their responses. Join online groups frequented by your clients and target market, and examine the questions and comments posted there.

Here are some ways to focus your article or speech on something other than recent developments:

- Present a case study (and of course you would either keep the client information confidential, or obtain the client's permission to make it public).
- Discuss an interesting trend that you have observed.

- Examine common problems and how to fix them.
- Consider common mistakes and how to avoid them.
- Share pieces of wisdom and tips for success.
- Comment on survey results – people love to know what other people do and think.

Focus on what the clients want to achieve. People are looking for ways to improve what they are doing, make more money, feel less stressed, reduce risk, and have better relationships and a happier life. There is always plenty to write about.

Maintain two lists: one of potential topics and one of topics that you have previously addressed. From time to time you can update and republish these pieces.

Constantly build your lists. Every time you have an idea for a topic, write it down. That way, when you are ready to write an article or speech, you will have plenty of ideas to draw from. When you have that elusive spare half an hour, you will have something to work on, instead of spending that time wondering what to write about.

Speaking at conferences and seminars is a very powerful way to position yourself as an expert in your chosen field of practice. It gives decision makers the opportunity to evaluate your level of expertise and to get a feel for what you might be like to work with.

However, lawyers are not renowned for being interesting speakers. Delivering a speech that grabs more people's attention will put you in good stead.

Start by thinking about the needs of your audience. If you are presenting to an audience of lawyers, by all means begin by outlining the legislative framework, describing the law prior to the introduction of the current regulatory regime and defining key legal terms. But if your audience consists of non-lawyers, it will quickly tire of watching PowerPoint slides crammed with statutory provisions or long quotes from cases.

Begin your preparation by identifying some of the valuable messages that you could impart. What problems might these people be experiencing that you can help them to solve? Instead of simply summarising the law, relate it to some typical issues.

Reviewing court decisions is not necessarily the best way. The particular situation faced by the parties in a case might be uncommon and therefore essentially irrelevant to your audience. It is just a situation that ended up in court because the parties were unable to resolve it between themselves. It is thus possible that no one in your audience will relate to that particular story. What other situations do your clients frequently face? What misconceptions do you regularly encounter? What mistakes do people make? Draw on your experience. Demonstrating your understanding of the audience's needs instantly differentiates you from a lawyer who simply outlines the law.

Organise your presentation around several key points that will have value for your audience. A 'point' is not the same as a 'topic' or 'heading'. To make a point, you must write a sentence which offers some sort of advice. For example, "evidentiary issues" could be a topic heading, but it makes no point. Conversely, "keep accurate and comprehensive notes of all telephone conversations" is a point which provides advice that all clients can adopt to improve their business practices and reduce risk. Emphasising points that are relevant to your audience instantly gives your presentation more impact.

It may feel risky to provide anything that resembles advice outside of a lawyer/client relationship. But if you do not provide any value to take away, your audience (readers or listeners) will feel cheated. They spent their valuable time reading or listening to you, and may feel that it was not worth it.

You can offer plenty of guidance without risking liability. Your article or presentation should include some practical steps that people can apply, even if they do not hire you. Here are some examples:

- Establish a regular review process.
- Have that difficult conversation with your partner!
- Ask yourself these five questions…
- Make a list of all your assets.
- Use this seven-step process…
- Fill out this template and maintain these records regularly.
- Next time you are about to have an argument, take a deep breath and count to 10.
- Write a note summarising every telephone discussion.
- Prepare a list of selection criteria.

Simply telling people what the law says is neither hard nor particularly helpful. Providing real help takes more effort and a switch in mindset, but doing so will position you as a valuable resource and a potential paid adviser.

Thought leadership is a great way to build your profile and attract clients by positioning yourself as an expert in your field. It showcases your knowledge, demonstrating your expertise instead of simply asserting it.

When people are referred to you, they are likely to search for you on the Internet. If you have been engaging in thought leadership activities, these potential clients will find a body of work created by you, such as informative articles and references to presentations that you have made. It provides proof of your expertise. It gives people the confidence to act on the recommendation and make contact with you. It also keeps your name in front of your clients, potential clients and referrers. Sometimes it will give you a reason to make contact with particular clients and arrange to meet with them, either individually over coffee or in a group for a seminar or discussion, further deepening your business relationship.

7. Help contacts to buy your services

No one enjoys being on the receiving end of a hard sell. People like to buy products or services that they have chosen freely. But sometimes they need some help to make a decision to buy.

It is never a good idea to try to sell your services to someone whom you have only just met. You would not propose to someone on the first date. And why would a person buy services from someone they have only just met? Why would they switch from their existing provider?

However, there is no point in having countless coffees and lunches and just talking about family and hobbies. There comes a time when you need to ask for the business. If you have built a professional relationship, provided some value through informational articles and presentations, and listened to what they have told you about their work, their aspirations and their concerns, you have earned the right to offer your services.

This is the 'selling' part of the process, and it should feel like a natural progression. If you have done the groundwork and you know that what you are offering is a good fit for their needs, you can feel confident to offer it. Explain the connection between what you do and a problem or issue that they have expressed. You cannot assume that they will automatically make that connection and book the appointment. This does not have to feel uncomfortable. What you have developed is a business relationship, after all.

Here are some ways to ask for the business:

- Can I help you with this?
- If we take action on this now, we have a good chance of sorting it out.
- Our firm has an expert on this issue. Would you like to meet that person?
- This is exactly the sort of work I do. Would you like me to come to your office to discuss it with you and your colleagues?
- Would you like to do that?
- When would you like to do that?
- Here is what I would recommend for you...
- This is very exciting. I would love to help you make it a big success.

When you ask for the business, do so in a helpful, not pushy, way. If the answer is "no", or "not yet", accept it with good grace. You cannot force someone to buy. At least you have planted a seed that might grow.

Do not put all your hopes on one particular person or company. The higher the stakes, the more anxious you will feel, and the more disappointed you will be if you do not get the business. If you are having discussions with lots of people, you will feel less upset about a "no, thanks".

People are looking for leadership. Teach them how to use you. Help them to take action.

8. Set goals

Many lawyers feel uncomfortable about promoting themselves. They tell themselves that they are not good at building business. By labelling themselves in this way, they dramatically limit their career potential and their income.

In private legal practice, your ability to attract clients is an important part of your value-proposition to a law firm.

First, consider how you will benefit from building your practice. If you have a strong reason for wanting to do it, you are more likely to make the effort than if you are doing it because someone has told you to. Will you earn more money? What will that enable you to do or buy? Will it mean you have more of the work you enjoy? Will you be working with your favourite kinds of client? Will you enjoy a greater level of job security?

Set yourself some business development goals. These should be goals over which you have control. For example, a goal to win a certain number of clients by a given date might sound entirely reasonable, but you cannot compel clients to sign up with you. Conversely, you might challenge yourself to write a certain number of articles in the next six months, create a presentation or have lunch with one client per week. You have complete power over this.

Achieving your goals requires determination and good time management. The practice of law tends to be reactive. Clients come in with problems and we do our best to solve them. But if you spend all your time reacting to things that happen, and never exert any control over how you spend your time, you are leaving your practice development to chance. Do not simply wait until you have some spare time.

Here are six ways to find the time for your business development activities:

- Always use a 'to do' list. Include on it the business development activities that you intend to do, such as write that article, reconnect with potential clients or contact conference organisers to be featured on their programme. If it is not on your list, it will not get done.

- Break the work into its component parts. If the job is too big, you will never find the time to do it. On your daily list, write specifically which part of the task you intend to undertake. Complete this part of the task, then set yourself the next one.

- Impose a time limit. Some tasks tend to drag on. Other tasks are ones you prefer to avoid. In either case, set yourself a defined amount of time, say 30 minutes or an hour. Set a timer to sound when the time is up. Working to a time limit makes you work more efficiently. And it is a good way to get started on a task that you have been avoiding.

- Take breaks. No one can concentrate indefinitely. Divide your day into blocks of one or two hours, and take a break before commencing the next one. Go outside and get some fresh air. Stretch and move around the office.

- Batch your work. If you have several phone calls to make, doing them all in quick succession can be more efficient than doing them in isolation. Once you are warmed up and ready to pick up the telephone, it feels easy to keep doing it.

- Make a start. To get better results in business, you have to try different things. Success comes not from a single activity but from consistent activity. Do not wait for the right opportunity; just make a start. Your profile will build gradually.

Business development requires different skills from legal work. It also requires a shift in mindset. It is easy to become set in our ways and think that we know best. Do not reject business development opportunities too quickly. You never know whom you will meet at that networking function, or who might be in the audience at that presentation.

Be receptive to new ideas. Your marketing staff or external experts have reasons for the ideas that they propose. Resist the natural temptation to challenge or resist their suggestions.

When opportunities arise, take them up, and learn from each experience. You will build your skills, and over time you will win work. Some activities such as being interviewed on radio or television, or making an informational video may seem daunting at first, but all your experience will accumulate. Focus on what you will learn, rather than how good you will look. To achieve your chosen future, you must make a start and work towards it.

Everyone can learn the skills of business development.

How do you teach lawyers to do business development?

Tom Bird
Møller Professional Services Firms Group

1.   The reality for lawyers

It is reasonable to assume that rare are the lawyers who chose a career in the law, involving years of study and accumulation of knowledge, in order to become sales people. And yet, as a legal career progresses, the need to develop business, from both existing clients and new ones, grows. Within most firms, however, relatively few partners (often known internally as 'the rainmakers') seem naturally adept at developing business; they remain, to a large extent, an enigma to the rank and file of the partner and associate population.

The reality, though, is that the legal market is populated with a number of firms achieving profit margins that other businesses would die for. This implies a dilemma: despite what some would see as impressive success, will what has always worked in the past be enough in the future to win business in the face of increased global competition and strategic market changes? This is the reality within which we are seeking to improve business development skills.

For any investment in building business development capability to succeed, we need to recognise the reality that lawyers work within and the mindset and priorities that drive their activities. This will enable us to address the real barriers and interferences that exist to building their business development skills.

Life as a lawyer tends to attract a certain profile of individuals that is sometimes at odds with the concept of business development.

Lawyers are academically bright – their passion is for the law, the application of their expert knowledge in service of a client's needs. Business development can appear as a dark art in the face of this intellectually rigorous and logical discipline. Lawyers also focus on their utilisation – most of a lawyer's long working day is spent on the urgent and important task of delivering a solution to a client's need. Value, in the mind of a lawyer, is often linked with hard deliverables, whereas the return on business development effort seems less tangible. However, lawyers are less confident in areas where they lack competence – confidence is situational and business development is an area where lawyers perceive their own skill deficiency. In these situations, it is easy to let perfect be the enemy of good; lawyers can over analyse and be slow to action. Lastly, lawyers are self-directed in how to use their time: business development becomes an increasingly important part of lawyers' careers as they progress towards and into partnership. However, no one is giving them clear direction as to how much of their discretionary time should be spent pushing their business development ability. Contrast this with life in a corporate organisation where clear development, training and direction are often given.

Figure 1: The development of professional skill

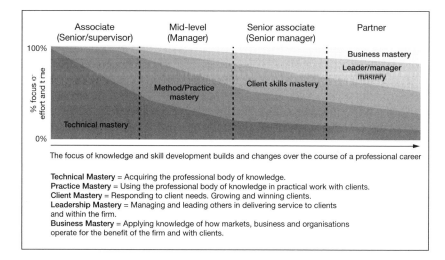

The focus of knowledge and skill development builds and changes over the course of a professional career

Technical Mastery = Acquiring the professional body of knowledge.
Practice Mastery = Using the professional body of knowledge in practical work with clients.
Client Mastery = Responding to client needs. Growing and winning clients.
Leadership Mastery = Managing and leading others in delivering service to clients and within the firm.
Business Mastery = Applying knowledge of how markets, business and organisations operate for the benefit of the firm and with clients.

The chapter on the nuts and bolts of business development summarises the three core phases of the business development life cycle. If we are to teach lawyers how to engage with, and deliver on, these phases of spotting opportunities, winning business and growing relationships, we need to consider first the obstacles that they need to overcome.

2.   What gets in the way of business development?

At the heart of the challenge of developing business development skills in lawyers is the reality that the time spent on it is discretionary. This requires the lawyer to want to take action. But even that is insufficient. If five frogs are sitting on a log and one decides to jump off, how many frogs are left? The answer is: five – there is a big difference between deciding to jump and jumping.

Tim Gallwey, in his "Inner Game" series of books, states the simple equation:

Performance = Potential – Interferences

Gallwey suggests that one way of increasing performance in any area is to start by identifying what gets in the way and then working to reduce these interferences, thereby releasing more of your natural potential and increasing your performance. This is a useful way to think about developing business development skills: what stops or hinders professionals from doing more business development and being more effective in their efforts now?

So, what gets in the way of business development activity for a lawyer? At a high level, there are three main causes for failing to achieve desired performance in most situations. Individuals either:

- do not know what is expected of them, or indeed what business development involves;
- lack the skills; or
- lack the motivation or supporting mindset.

These main obstacles are considered below in the context of business development in law firms.

Expectations: business development is rarely formally recognised or rewarded. When there is a choice between utilisation and business development, utilisation often wins.

In addition, individuals often lack clear and specific business development goals and the metrics for related activities that enable performance to be monitored and, therefore, managed and developed.

Lastly, business development is considered 'important but not urgent', and therefore often takes second place to the 'important and urgent' client deliverables.

Skills: lawyers are used to having answers, to providing solutions based on their legal expertise. Business development is more about relationship building and the skills of asking questions. It is often about not knowing an answer and encouraging the client to talk. It is easy for lawyers to see their value in business development as still being their legal expertise and this can lead to driving to a solution too quickly.

Further, people buy emotionally but justify logically. Lawyers frequently deal with logical argument, but this will not be enough when seeking to differentiate the firm and themselves as individuals, or in developing an existing relationship to deeper levels of trust.

Motivation and mindset: the motivation to engage in business development is hindered by a misconception of what business development is in a professional firm. Most lawyers equate business development with selling, which often has negative connotations for them. But in a law firm the professional is the product and so business development is about helping people to buy, rather than selling to them. This is the only approach that will support developing long-term and trusting client relationships. These limiting beliefs, combined with a focus on utilisation and a perceived lack of competence (and, therefore, confidence) in business development hold people back from taking action.

Some other interferences combine both internal (firm-specific) issues and individual challenges. These include:

- the lack of a clear, cohesive and fully aligned strategy for business development. Too often, business development is seen as a thing to do when you have time rather than a core aspect of the lawyer's role and so the business does not build a formal strategy around it. This leads to an *ad hoc* approach with some lawyers taking action, others doing nothing and everything in between. This lack of strategy and clear goals for which individuals are both supported and held accountable does not build personal accountability;
- the absence of suitable internal systems to support business development. If lawyers are to engage in business development, they need it to be as easy as possible from an internal customer relationship management and process perspective;

- the fact that people will cross-sell only people whom they know and trust. While most firms articulate an expectation that lawyers should proactively cross-sell, this is unlikely to happen unless lawyers know each other well enough to trust each other with their clients; and
- poor support. Business development support within firms varies in its scope, availability and quality. Lawyers will assess the credibility of those delivering internal business development support and work only with people whom they see as adding definite value to them by providing the right level of expertise, support and challenge.

Of all of the interferences, mindset often has the most significant impact and is, therefore, the barrier that must be addressed first if business development skills are to be developed and, more importantly, implemented systematically.

3.   One size does not fit all

As mentioned above, most law firms have a small percentage of partners who are outstanding at winning work and developing profitable long-term client relationships. These individuals seem to naturally 'get' business development and are often held up as exemplars. The trouble is that while these 'rainmakers' might be naturals at winning business, they may not be role models. Often, they have the reputation of being mavericks or difficult to manage. If they are held up as examples and used to define success, it can have a negative effect on a population of fee earners who, quite understandably, will resist anything that implies the need to change their personality in order to be effective or be more like these rainmakers.

Business development needs to feel authentic if partners and associates are to engage with it. It is critical, therefore, to recognise that there is no one 'right' personality for business development.

Toby Hoskins (a partner at our firm) has worked with a large number of international law firms and has found from his research a simple way of analysing a complex population of partners. It is a model that senior and managing partners often recognise in the partnership that they lead. Hoskins articulates four categories of partner behaviour where the differences are based on whether a partner sees business development as driven by either relationships or legal knowledge and skills.

What does this categorisation mean to developing business development skills in a law firm?

The smallest number of partners fit into the first category. These category 1 partners simply 'get' business development and relationship selling. They are the naturals, the rainmakers within a firm, and are really good at their 'speed to intimacy' – to have an understanding of the client and the client's business.

The category 2 partners are larger in number than category 1. They are not the business development naturals that defines category 1, but they understand the need for business development and they want to improve – they see the need and have the desire.

Category 3 is often the largest grouping in a law firm. These people focus on credibility and reliability rather than on the relationship side of developing business

Figure 2: Leadership of the firm

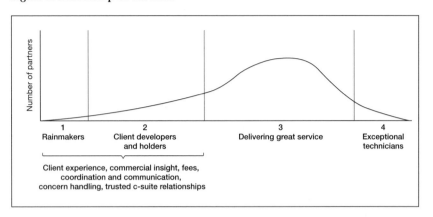

(despite what the firms website might say). They value legal service delivery over really understanding their client's needs.

Lastly, there are the category 4 people. These individuals do very well in the 'rocket science' aspects of law as these projects are often won on the basis of technical reputation rather than relationship. This category can win significant projects, but not necessarily through creating great client relationships.

What the graph shows is that category 1 and 4 are rare, but the more you have the better. (Anecdotally, a partner who used to work for one of the Big 4 accounting firms felt that his firm never had more than five category 1 partners at any one time.)

From a business development training perspective, a firm should focus on having more category 2 individuals than its competitors as these lawyers represent the best investment in any training. This implies that a sheep-dip approach to a total partner and/or associate population is likely to be less effective than selecting groups who understand the need and want to develop their business development skills. While this will vary from firm to firm, we often see this hunger within new partners and more senior associates (who see business development as a way of improving their chances of partnership). Investing in the category 3 lawyers may well produce less of a result – they do not want to get business development and, as mindset is so critical to business development success, it might make sense to let this category of individuals focus on just doing the work. This holds true for work that is not standardised or commoditised, as decisions around those matters are often more price driven.

A managing partner at a large accountancy firm (and his thinking is transferable to all substantial partnerships) said, "a disproportionately small number of partners make a disproportionately large difference to all partnerships".

One thing that we have seen as being particularly helpful when building business development capability within a law firm is an approach called modelling, which, when applied to the category 1 partners, can help elicit and define the firm-specific DNA of success. Modelling is a process that uses structured questions and, ideally, observation, to identify subtle nuances in how effective business development exemplars achieve their results. This includes surfacing their mindsets, particular approaches or techniques that they use and questions that they ask. If we model the successful category 1 partners, it brings firm-specific credibility to any business development training and paces the practical needs of participants.

1.   What works?

A wide spectrum of approaches is available to develop the desired skills. At one end is a fully integrated business development skills programme for a large number of participants and at the other end is the individual business development coaching of partners.

If you decide that a programme involving training is the most effective solution to your needs, then you must also recognise that training, in isolation, is unlikely to work. This is especially true with business development where the issues relate to mindset as well as skills. It is not enough simply to learn the approaches and techniques; lawyers must believe that they can apply them to good effect, and they need the motivation to make the time to do this in an already busy schedule.

While each firm might create a programme that is specific to its own needs, culture and participant profile, we believe that the seven-step approach summarised below is relevant to all.

4.1   Identify your goal and why it is so important

It is surprising how many firms still make a decision to train their fee earner population, or a sub-set of it, without spending due time considering the tangible objectives of such training and the return on investment.

There may be one or more high-level drivers which, once identified, will help you clarify the scope and nature of any programme. You might be looking for a growth in revenue or an increase in profit, or even more effective targeting of the work that you want to win, for example, but it is critical to know what you want to achieve before you start planning. One law firm with which we have worked aligned some of the business development metrics with specific firm-wide metrics concerning the number of clients bringing over £1 million in revenue, the revenues derived from FTSE 100 clients and an upward trend in billable hours.

Thus, you should define the success criteria and be specific. Wherever possible, focus on a combination of metrics. Some of these might be revenue based or might identify a certain target of key clients or account penetration, but other metrics relating to the relationship and the individuals' activities are no less important.

There is a difference between having an aspirational target (which can contribute to drive and motivation) and setting specific objectives that are in the control of the individuals and can, therefore, be measured and managed. These latter, activity-based goals become important proof of activity and enable conversations to develop improved performance, whereas achievement of revenue and account penetration targets are sometimes longer term and not in the full control of the individual. Business development is an area where activity is critical and focusing on the right activities will lead to longer-term results.

If any programme is to succeed, then senior buy-in is critical. For a business development programme to work, it is likely to involve a number of different components and stakeholders. This implies a cost in terms of both hard investment and people's time and effort. Being clear on the goal and the benefits will help secure this. If you can engage people using the potential positive impact to the firm and put revenue or profit numbers on it, you are far more likely to engage the hearts and minds (and purse strings) needed to guarantee success.

Involve the firm's management in this step to build both an understanding of, and agreement to, what you are seeking to achieve and create a dialogue about relevant metrics.

Identifying why the programme is relevant and important to the firm as part of this objective setting phase will also contribute to gaining the necessary support from senior management to see the programme through. It is likely that senior stakeholders will have an important part to play in the success of the programme. This might be through being visible during the learning elements, supporting the desired activities through role modelling or changing processes and rewards to support the desired behaviours. If the senior stakeholders do not take ownership, then any programme is unlikely to succeed and helping them connect with the benefits is one way of increasing ownership.

4.2   Define who you are going to develop

Once you have clarified the objectives of the programme, it is easier to define the population that you want to work with to achieve these objectives. A couple of questions to consider are particularly important in this phase. First, what level of the fee-earning population are you going to target? Partners are often the obvious community as they have the most direct and regular client contact and, therefore, the greatest opportunity to conduct business development conversations. But often it is the associate population (especially those aspiring to partnership) who demonstrates the greatest hunger in this area. When developing associates, however, you need to define the focus of any programme to take account of the degree of client contact that they have and the nature of that contact. For some firms, our focus with associates is on building the right relationships with their counterparts within the client (who will become the buyers and decision makers of the future) and on building their internal and industry sector profiles.

Second, if it is partners, how will you target the right people to develop? As the author Robert Heinlein said: "Never try and teach a pig to sing. It wastes your time and annoys the pig." Not all partners feel the same about business development. Think about how we see the spread of partners across the four categories defined in section 3 above. This suggests that not all partners will benefit equally from development in this area. Those partners who get the need, but may lack the knowledge and experience, might yield the most significant positive result from a business development initiative. Conversely, those partners who have either no interest, or even an active dis-interest, in engaging in business development are unlikely to change their behaviour. In some instances, perhaps where the law is 'rocket science' (ie, highly specialised), that is acceptable as clients are likely to take the initiative to contact the firm anyway.

4.3 Build an approach and structure that recognise the real barriers to success

Once you have clear outcomes and senior buy-in, and have identified the community to be developed, you can define the right approach and structure for the programme. Remember that training in isolation is unlikely to work; the programme needs to recognise and address the wider needs of participants and the challenges that they face in applying what they learn in the work environment.

In one study carried out several months after a training programme had been completed, participants in the programme were asked: "What are the significant barriers that limited your effective application of these skills/behaviours in your job?" The top three barriers were:

- My immediate manager does not reinforce/support my use of the skills/behaviour;
- It is difficult to break away from the way I have done it before (old habits); and
- I do not have enough time to apply the skills/behaviour.

In the complex and pressured environment of the professional service firm, there may well be other inhibiting factors.

Some likely components of the programme, their rationale and content are summarised below.

Component	Rationale	Content/considerations
Needs analysis	• To identify the real need • To challenge assumptions • To create a programme that addresses what is needed in order to apply any learning in the work environment • To maximise the chance of success	• Look at the whole system – internal systems, firm mindsets and behaviour norms, skills needs/gaps and competing priorities • Engage in a meaningful dialogue with key stakeholders to elicit expectations and build awareness about their roles and responsibilities • Build programme credibility through surveying participants views
Engagement	• To build personal and firm-wide motivation for success • To ensure stakeholders engage with their roles • To raise awareness about expectations • To ensure that participants arrive at any learning event motivated to engage	• Communicate the compelling reason for the desired change in behaviours and personalise this for participants (build the 'why?') • Ensure that people understand the scope and expectations of the programme • Communicate a clear vision for the future (provide direction and build motivation) • Show the importance of the programme through key stakeholder support and involvement (eg, through launch events, video, etc)

continued on next page

Component	Rationale	Content/considerations
Pre-work	• To maximise the value of the workshop touch-points and personalise learning • To raise awareness of the needs, opportunities and issues in participants minds • To build personal accountability for learning and application	• Focus participants on their own specific needs and reality • Encourage participants to consider and develop personal goals around the learning and the topic • Pre-teach some of the concepts to save time in the workshops • Have participants reflect and prepare to build individual accountability further
Workshop(s)	• To provide a shared understanding of core concepts • To deliver practical tools • To share experiences • To surface, discuss and address barriers to application • To build further a sense of group as well as individual accountability	• Communicate core concepts • Provide an opportunity for skills building where participants can practise; • Engage in discussion to ensure that relevant issues are raised and addressed and that there is a shared understanding and agreement on priorities for action
Support	• To define and agree the support needed for participants to maximise the chance of success • To agree the ground rules and mutual responsibilities surrounding such support • To recognise that behaviour change and mindset shifts need time	• Identify what can be provided by way of ongoing internal support (eg, partners mentoring and bringing support and challenges, internal business development roles and responsibilities in working with participants, etc) • Provide additional touch-points (possibly through webinars, coaching, etc) to support behaviour change
Follow-up	• To hold participants accountable for taking action • To learn what adjustments need to be made to the programme going forward • To maximise the return on investment	• Use 'before and after' surveys • Arrange meetings with partner sponsors or internal business development staff to build personal accountability and bring a focus to individual actions • Identify key successes and opportunities for additional activity or focus • Check the validity of the needs analysis – were all of the barriers identified and addressed? If not, what else needs to happen?
Share success	• To build momentum • To recognise progress • To support further mindset shifts in the wider participant population	• Help participants recognise that they can change and improve in this important area • Show future participants that change is possible – build motivation and belief • Reinforce and encourage the role of senior stakeholder support and involvement

4.4   Build the 'why?' and address any mindset issues

We have touched on this topic previously in this chapter, but believe that it is so important to the success of a business development programme that it warrants specific attention when planning a programme.

A supporting mindset is critical to achieving a sustainable behaviour change with regard to business development, because mindset affects behaviours, which, in turn, impact on result.

Figure 3: The impact of mind-set

As part of the needs analysis phase of a programme, you must identify the mindset of the community that you are looking to develop. We often do this through anonymous surveys to encourage an open and honest response to questions relating to feelings about business development, and we frequently make distinctions between different aspects of the business development process which are helpful when we work with groups. The responses to mindset-related questions will help you identify how much work needs to be done to address this in the programme.

Managing a mindset is possible only once you are aware of it. Then the training can help you recognise the impact of that mindset and identify alternative, more positive, outlooks that can also be true. This is often about adding value to the client or achieving long-term career aspirations. But it is also about recognising what business development in a professional firm really is, and the distinction between that and what participants might view as selling. If lawyers feel that business development is about being pushy, about forcing your firm and yourself on your clients and using slick manipulative techniques to close the sale, then, understandably, they will want nothing to do with it. If, however, you identify that business development in a professional firm is more about influence, about helping people to buy (rather than about selling), about adding real value and solving client problems, then participants are able to consider it differently. Changing your perspective on something unlocks more possibilities and can dramatically increase your chances of taking action.

Linked with the issue of mindset is the need to establish a clear and personalised 'why?' – the motivation that will encourage an individual to take action and to keep taking action.

Connecting individuals with the benefits of engaging in business development and the consequences of not engaging is a helpful start point. Helping people identify their personal vision – what are their career aspirations – and how business development will help achieve this will often bring a personal 'why?' into focus.

Once there is a felt need, individuals are open to learning – but until they have that need, training is unlikely to stick and turn into sustainable action.

4.5 Focus on practical content

The content to be covered will develop from your programme objectives and needs analysis, and may focus on one or more aspects of business development, including:

- winning new work from new clients;
- winning new work from existing clients; and
- effectively managing key client relationships.

Each of these aspects presents its own specific challenges, priorities and needs, which is why it is critical to have a clear and specific view of what the desired programmes are before you look at content.

While this chapter's aim is not to provide detailed programme content, it might be helpful to list here some high-level questions that participants might have concerning each of the aspects of business development mentioned above.

(a) *Winning new work from new clients*

What is effective business development for me in my role?
How do I improve my pitch/win ratio?
Why should I do this? Can I do this? Do I want to do this? What if I do not do this?
How do I build my network strategically to support my business development?
How do I engage in a first meeting with a prospective client? What do I say?
How do I differentiate myself as a lawyer and as a firm?
What should my priorities be in terms of activities?
How can I encourage others to cross-sell me?
How do I make the time?

(b) *Winning new work from existing clients*

How do clients test the relationship?
How do I continue to differentiate myself?
How do I influence effectively?
What is 'value adding' in my context?
What should my relationship priorities be?
Why should I cross-sell people whom I do not know?
What do clients want from the relationship/what frustrates them?

(c) *Effectively managing key client relationships*

What is the right model for managing relationships?
How important is team working in relationship management?
How can I best leverage and utilise my internal BD resource?
What are my key relationship management priorities and actions?

Content to help answer these questions needs to be backed by research – intellectual rigour is important – but also needs to be pragmatic. Lawyers increasingly want the 'how to', but they are only going to be open to training when they engage with 'why' it is important and can be satisfied that what you are telling them is backed by research.

We also favour the use of client panels or what we call 'nearly clients' (see section 4.6 below) within business development training. Once lawyers have been exposed to research and approaches for business development, it is helpful for them to be able to test this input with clients and to be able to ask questions to confirm what they have been learning and to deepen their understanding.

4.6   Encourage 'practice at the edge of discomfort'

In *The Talent Code*, Daniel Coyle identifies the important factors that contribute to learning a new skill quickly. His studies show that it is the way that people practise the new skill that determines to a large extent the speed at which they get the new skill 'in the muscle'.

In the early stages of learning a new skill you are likely to feel uncomfortable when applying the skill, unlikely to get the perfect result and likely to question whether you are ever going to master the skill. With other priorities prevailing, there is a high risk that you will try a couple of times before reverting to what you were doing before.

This is a real challenge when looking to build business development skills and Coyle's research suggests that focusing on 'practice at the edge of discomfort' is a big part of the answer. Programme leaders should encourage the lawyers in the programme to try the new techniques and then, when they achieve a probably less than perfect result and feel both uncomfortable and less than confident engaging in the new activities, encourage these individuals to keep going with the new activities.

The extent to which we can encourage lawyers, who often equate competence with confidence, to persevere will help them develop the new skills quickly. Any training that fails to encourage its participants to use the newly learnt skill is likely to result in an initial burst of energy followed by some disappointment and then a reversion to how the participants acted before the development programme. With their critical minds, lawyers will also tend to say to themselves, "See, I knew that would not work for me" – they may pay attention only to the limited initial data and generalise this into a limiting belief about their business development ability.

Encouraging 'practice at the edge of discomfort': it starts in the training itself by recognising and acknowledging how lawyers may feel whilst learning and applying these skills. Covering this in a workshop environment will prepare them for the feelings and give a logical explanation for them.

Once you have surfaced and addressed this, you can focus on creating experiential learning opportunities through role plays and simulations and making these as realistic as possible. Traditionally, business development programmes include some element of skills practice – whether it be simulating a first client meeting or expanding the relationship and setting yourself out as an adviser rather than just a legal technical expert. These sessions often use colleagues or actors to facilitate the practice, but we have seen significant benefits from the use of nearly clients. 'Nearly clients' are individuals who either hold or have held senior positions in business (chief financial officer, managing director, etc) and, therefore, do not need to role play: they simply act as themselves. This brings a new and powerful dynamic to the training environment. Lawyers interact with individuals whose position they can respect, and whose perspectives and feedback they feel more open to. Nearly clients can be used in a number of ways to add the client perspective to any workshops, but the real benefit is that participants see their views as relevant and valuable. We have even been involved in training where general counsels were so impressed with individual lawyers that they hired them on to their panel!

While role plays are often the least looked-forward-to aspect of a training event, lawyers often report them as being among the most valuable afterwards.

Setting activity-based goals after the training will help foster the specific activities that you want to see. It is important then to provide the support and encouragement to continue to practise. A useful approach here is individual review and coaching conversations after the workshops. During these conversations you can focus on the experiences of applying the approaches and skills, and provide support to continue.

4.7   Build accountability for action and share successes

Once training has been completed, the focus needs to shift to building individual accountability for taking action. Action planning at the end of a workshop is insufficient on its own to guarantee change. When participants return to their desks, the real world of telephone messages, matters to progress and meetings to attend will work against making the required discretionary time for business development.

The job of building accountability starts before the workshop, is re-enforced during the workshop and is supported after the workshop. By aligning the pre-workshop conversations about vision and business development goals with the workshop content and practice, you can then focus on specific activity-based goal-setting after the workshop. You need to consider what form the support will take, how much support will be needed and how you will provide it (eg, through internal resource or external help?). It is likely that support will have a number of ingredients tailored to your specific participant and firm needs and reality.

Approaches that we have seen work include those listed below.

Business development coaching: this is less like the traditional non-directive coaching and more akin to a mentoring approach where an individual receives 1:1 sessions that combine coaching, to build responsibility and awareness, with some input and advice based on the business development coaches' expertise in the field. This is helpful to keep an individual's focus on the right things, encourage 'practice at the edge of discomfort' and recognise progress against key business development metrics.

Video: short, targeted video clips are used increasingly often as a reminder of key techniques, approaches or priorities for different aspects of business development. Video can help keep the learning alive after a workshop by drip-feeding reminders of concepts covered, and provide a just-in-time resource for individuals who might, for example, be going into a business development meeting and want to know what their key priorities or planning should be.

Webinar: webinars can be an effective way to connect with people in different locations either to review progress or to cover specific key topics to add to their knowledge base.

Learning groups: creating an opportunity for small groups of participants to meet – perhaps with a structure for the agenda – can be a straightforward way of helping build momentum and accountability. Light touch often works best here, but the format provides an opportunity to share what they have done, discuss results and have others challenge their assumptions about future actions.

Articles and books: as part of a self-directed learning element, participants can be led to specific written resources and asked to consider how they can apply what they read to their own business development situation.

5.   Summary

While business development is something that most firms would like to improve on, very few invest their time and energy in the right things to ensure success. For firms to realise benefit from any investment they need to know:
- what, specifically, they want to achieve from any programme;
- what the real barriers are to success and be prepared to address them; and
- that behaviour change for lawyers in this area directly relates to their mindset.

A successful business development programme is not just about the participants: it is about recognising that business development activity is often discretionary, and that means that the firm as a whole – its systems, support and culture – should ideally be aligned to support the behaviour change that you are looking for.

By challenging the real need upfront and being clear on what achieving sustainable behaviour change will require and gaining the buy-in from all connected, you pave the way for a programme that will deliver on its promises. Any programme must recognise the importance of surfacing and working with mindsets, and this requires thought on how lawyers can be motivated to want to engage in business development activity and supported to help them build the necessary skills, rather than trying something once and reverting back to previous behaviours. Closing any knowledge gap is relatively easy, but approaching business development assuming that knowledge gap is the issue would be a big mistake.

Small changes can lead to big results. It would be easy to let perfect be the enemy of good when creating a programme, but by focusing on the programme design and ongoing participant support, you can make a real difference to behaviours and start to change the culture of the firm.

Making the sale, clinching the deal – the case for a business development team

Thorsten Zulauf
Law Firm Change Consultants

1. Introduction

Business development has long been part of lawyers' careers and law firms' cultures in many ways. In times of increased competition among firms, a structured approach to getting the right kind of clients with the right kind of work is essential for long-term prosperity. In this chapter, 'business development' refers to the existence of a team of business support personnel qualified to assist lawyers in getting that process up and running. Since the market for legal services can be structured into different kinds of service provider, ranging from traditional law firms (domestic/international, specialists/generalists, small/large) to alternative legal service providers,[1] such as AXIOM, Integreon or Xenion, there is no 'one size fits all' approach. The only thing in common to all parties involved is the clients' need for premium legal services at the best possible quality, speed and price.

The variety of sizes, structures and cultures means that each law firm has to find the approach best suited to its set-up and purpose.

2. Variety of structures and approaches to business development

The integration of the business development function in a law firm is mainly dependent on the size, market position, organisation, geographic spread, number of legal practices, culture and history of the firm. Most law firms follow a standard approach where business development is closely aligned with the firm's legal practices, while marketing communications is considered a central function. As stated above, law firms differ widely from each other, but this approach can be a starting point for reviewing the current set-up with a view to establishing a new function.

The approach to business development focuses on enhancing the law firms' market standing in a sustainable and efficient manner. The business development team is playing a critical role here, but so do the partners who enable the success of this function. To avoid common mistakes, the partnership needs to find answers to the following questions:

- Do we need professional support?
- Do we want to invest time and money?
- Does the partnership want to participate actively in the change process?

---

1 David Barnard and Miriam Herman, "Trends in the legal industry: a US perspective", in: Christoph H Vaagt, *Law firm strategies for the 21st century* (Global Law and Business, 2013), p 73.

3. Sole practitioner/small practice v large international practice

Sole practitioners[2] and smaller law firms need to ask the same questions: the former to find answers (in instances with professional external support) for themselves, the latter to find a consensus in the partnership group on how to move forward.

One of the main questions is the definition of the target market and how fast the firm can penetrate this market. A sole practitioner should have a very clear view of the market, the clients and the service which he can offer, although he may be tempted to engage in various matters to generate revenue. A sole practitioner, for example, can serve a high-volume market with lower margins or a low-volume market with higher margins, the former focusing on a lower number of clients for whom he is handling all legal matters, the latter requiring exceptional technical qualities and personal standing (eg, insolvency or trial lawyers). The consequences for the development of his business differ significantly, especially when building a professional reputation, which takes considerable time.

The same applies to an international practice planning to enter a new geographic market, targeting a new client group or opening a new legal practice. Most firms undergo changes during their history out of necessity and/or a planned reshaping of the strategy; the better planned and executed the change, the higher the success rate. This can lead to a focus on certain practices, as seen among global law firms where corporate M&A and finance practice dominate, while commercial practices such as IP, trademark or non-corporate law work are spun off, or certain geographic regions are no longer served while investments are made instead in growth regions such as China or Asia in general.

Another important question concerns the growth rate and the investment time/money needed to manage that growth. A single practitioner is limited mostly by the time that he can invest in building new client relationships, increasing his market reputation and developing the practice's offering while servicing his existing clients. He can leverage his practice by joining a legal network to receive referrals or work together with like-minded lawyers. It is recommended to get advice from a business development consultant to validate the chosen approach and adjust it accordingly to maximise the potential for success.

International practice is facing similar decisions on how to tackle growth besides an organic growth scheme, when facing joint ventures or mergers with law firms/integrating partner teams active in the area of interest, be it in a specific location, with a specific legal practice, a specific industry or with portable client contacts. A business development function can help to organise the transition, foster the integration and implement best practices to increase the probability of the new venture's success.

4. Domestic client v global client

The expectations, structures, interests, motivations, processes or ownership structures of each potential client are unique; thus, any law firm needs to learn and understand as much as possible about the client in order to manage the relationship

---

2   Laurie Young, *Marketing the Professional Services Firm* (John Wiley & Sons, 2005), pp 41–43.

successfully. The opportunity to work for new clients or to win new matters from existing clients lies within a framework of both social and economic interaction managed through a so-called 'pitch process' – a process focused on determining if law firms understand the client and the task at hand – to increase the competition between law firms and get the best value for money.

Figure 1: Relationship between client and law firm[3]

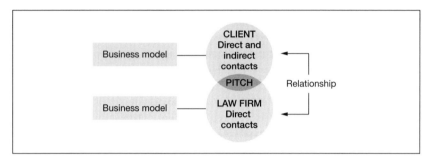

The business development team needs to be aware of, and the partnership has to be prepared for, some notable differences between domestic and international clients. Domestic clients tend to work with a relatively stable number of law firms, pitches for new work are rare, social contacts are crucial and competition is low. The business development function can deliver the most value by helping the partnership to leverage and nurture contacts (direct and indirect) as much as possible and by outlining the value that the firm is delivering with each assignment. The higher the level of trust between the client and the partner, the more robust the relationship, the less price matters for decision making and the higher the barriers are for competitors. This may change over time – for instance, through a merger or a change in contacts with a different perspective on law firms – but the more direct and indirect contacts can be established and developed between the client and the law firm, the lower the risk of losing the client. This is why we see sole practitioners or smaller, local law firms serving this kind of client without a special business development unit: the social interaction with the client, and the less formal relationship, enables the lawyer to gather the information needed to service the client and to build a high degree of trust. However, also with mid-size companies, the costs of outside legal counsel have risen so much that these companies have started scrutinising legal costs, starting either to recruit in-house counsel or to invite the procurement or the finance department to look after it. This process will be accelerated in the future; this is why we suggest that understanding the business development process is just as relevant for these smaller firms as it is for large international law firms.

International clients, by contrast, tend to switch between law firms for certain tasks to keep the levels of competition and engagement high, using pitches for major

---

3   Source: Law Firm Change Consultants.

work pieces/panels for certain areas of work (eg, by legal practice, type of work or geographic location). Executive contacts often change, and compliance regulations in assigning work to law firms strictly apply.

Most industry clients experiment with different purchasing methodologies – for example, online auctions, third-party providers managing the purchasing process or different sources for different kinds of work, such as sourcing standard legal work to alternative service providers because of their efficient processes and sophisticated legal work in comparison with traditional law firms.

The most common process, however, consists of an invitation either to pitch for an individual piece of work or to become part of a panel of law firms assisting the company in predefined areas of legal work according to the law firms' specialisation. The business development function, in contrast to the support needs of a domestic client relationship, must both cover a different set of tasks and put a slightly different emphasis on them. A key difference is the preparation for pitches: to begin with, they frequently have to start without sufficient information about the law firms' knowledge and problem-solving capability for a client-defined problem. The business development function can provide significant intelligence in translating the client requirements to the lawyers and advise on how to resent the legal and commercial issues in the offer. With the client's acceptance of the written submission, the second pitch to the client decides which among the remaining law firms will be assigned the work. Business development can help prepare for the meeting – for instance, through matching the participating client representatives with corresponding law firm representatives (eg, international background, gender, expertise, actual project lead) or through preparing commercial scenarios to address questions by participants from the purchasing department. Panels have become increasingly common with international clients, reducing the number of law firms that these clients are working with, to achieve higher quality and better commercial deals. The business development function can help to prepare for panels through intelligence gained from existing panels and industry trends; it can further advise on the panels where the law firm requires to be listed in order to be taken into consideration for high-profile work. Business development can support the communication to the client contacts and provide the partnership with the right messages to deepen the relationship and allow the contacts to excel internally, so that the firm can stay on the panel.

5. The role of technology in the business development process

The advances in communication and information technology can help the law firm to improve its relationships with clients and differentiate itself from its competitors. Technology is having a great impact on the way lawyers and lawyer support functions are working today and will work tomorrow.[4] It is clear, though, that in some areas we will see a disruption.[5] This affects areas like e-discovery or virtual due diligence through sophisticated artificial intelligence, but also knowledge

---

4   Iltanet, www.iltanet.org/downloads/ltfh-report.pdf.
5   McKinsey Global Institute, www.mckinsey.com/insights/business_technology/disruptive_technologies.

management or legal research, as here the technology will transform the way in which these activities are handled. If new technologies are to be implemented, they are supposed to assist (eg, enhance the market reputation or win new clients), but they may be needed just to maintain the competitive position among peers and mirroring developments on the client side.

The business development process will be affected by all of the above and can play a pivotal role in improving both the client experience and the way client data is organised and used within the organisation. In terms of client experience, the closer the connection to the client, the better – for instance, through real time project status, billing information, shared work platforms or the frequent push provision of customised legislative and industry know-how. Client data, by contrast, covers more than integrating contacts in a joint database; it is about bringing together all the bits and pieces on client information accessible for all relevant parties in one place. A common technological platform to achieve this is a customer relationship management (CRM) system, but, crucially, the implementation must be accompanied by a cultural change in the organisation. If information about clients (eg, current matters, strategic developments, contacts, financials) is not documented and shared openly within the CRM system, then there will be some disappointment over the client development potential not being utilised. Worse, it can damage the firm's reputation in the market by implying that the firm does not care about the clients' needs despite marketing claims to the contrary. It does not necessarily permanently damage a relationship, but in times of intense competition, the law firm may get neither the opportunity nor the time to repair that relationship.

The operational side of the process-supporting technology centres on established standards (eg, business development materials, pitch templates, publishing templates, CVs) and its availability for all legal personnel. The technology ensures that only the most up-to-date materials are used to prepare information for client purposes and that the business development team focuses on consulting the partnership in client-related activities.

The impact of social media has come into sharper focus with the continuous success of platforms such as Twitter, Facebook, LinkedIn, Google+ and the like. In order to leverage the potential positive impact, the law firm needs to decide, with the help of the business development team, which platforms it should be active on, the type of content to publish and the individuals to present (partner reputation building). A similar decision is to be made regarding all blogging activities, and to control/manage responses from the public/clients. Even with all such publishing activities, it is not guaranteed that the valuable content will reach the targeted client group, but the chances of success can be increased by correctly indexing the content in order to obtain a prominent listing in search engines.

6.   Selling a product v establishing premium law advice

The legal market has seen a strong commoditisation of legal services, such that legal advice is increasingly perceived as a product, similarly to consumer goods. To avoid these analogies, law firms are trying to establish their services as premium law advice where the perceived client value is high and the margins are healthy. Clients give high-value work to those law firms seen to be able to deal with these types of work, while assignments considered of lower value go to law firms in a different market segment; hence, it is the choice of the law firm for which type of work it wants to compete.

Figure 2: Value pyramid of legal services[6]

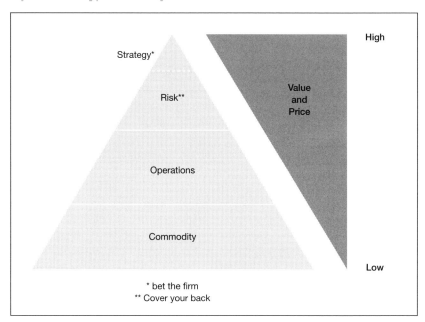

Figure 2 outlines the various types of legal service, as well as the perceived value and price of each service. The commodity-type service is the lowest in the pecking order of law, while covering the needs of both private and corporate clients. Typical commodity services are trademark or patent applications, standard work contracts, standard commercial contracts (general business terms and conditions), private wills or insurance claims. While some of these can elevate to standard operations such as work contracts for managing directors/board members or licensing contracts/ contracts under company law/supplier contracts, these areas of service have three things in common: pressure on price, a need for efficient processes and a need for high leverage.

At the top of the service pyramid, with strategy and risk being the most relevant, price and value are the highest possible.

The risk type of services can typically be summarised as professional and organisational practices that serve to protect oneself from legal and administrative penalties or other punitive measures. This applies to work such as corporate merger and acquisition, real estate and private equity, where selecting the right firm (with

---

6   Figure 2, Law Firm Change Consultants.

huge credentials as a perceived market leader) protects the decision makers to a certain degree. Another type of work deals with major insolvency cases like the one seen during the recent financial crisis with Lehman Brothers[7] where some 30 law firms assisted in the bank's wind-down.

Strategy-type services can typically be translated as 'bet the firm' services. In recent years, this has applied to white-collar crimes such as business fraud, corruption or unfair competition like the compliance work that Debevoise & Plimpton undertook for Siemens[8] without which the future of the company was uncertain. Strategic M&A projects can be added to the same cluster; if a merger is not properly legally and commercially advised, the future existence and/or success of the company is at risk.

Both risk and strategic legal services require the following:
- extensive in-depth experience;
- business-mindedness;
- outstanding quality;
- integration; and
- excellent back-up personnel.

A business development function can help to understand into which sections current and past engagements fit, and assist in moderating a process with the partnership to draw the relevant conclusions. If a law firm feels comfortable working in a commodity/operations environment, the client roster should enable high volumes in these services so the established processes in the organisation are fully utilised. The focus of these types of specialised law firm is on selling a legal service product processed with the best tools, the right people and the right organisation.

By contrast, law firms engaged in risk/strategy type of work are well known to corporations long before an incident/merger and acquisition takes place and are regarded as working with utmost confidentiality since few engagements make the broader news (also partly because they are subject to specific regulations for publicly listed companies). Business development can help the partners understand which requirements must be fulfilled to put their law firm in first place to secure an engagement when a potential client faces a company-threatening situation. To be successful, partners should be in an elevated position from which they can act as trusted advisers in strategic discussions. The focus of these types of law firm is on establishing a premium law service where outstanding lawyers in a client-centric organisation of the highest quality can mitigate most problems that a client may face.

7.   An international perspective on business development

To be successful internationally, a business development function requires good knowledge of the regions/countries in which it is operating or planning to operate. A simple export of existing practices, such as success in the United States to

7   CNN, http://money.cnn.com/2013/09/13/news/companies/lehman-bankruptcy-fees/.
8   Debevoise & Plimpton, www.debevoise.com/insights/news/2008/12/debevoise-conducted-siemens-internal-investigation.

continental Europe, will lead to frustration for all parties or a delayed start at best. A law firm should begin by understanding the region/country from an economic, historical and cultural viewpoint. The legal environment and the applied business practices should be taken into consideration as well. The recent departure of firms from the Arabian Peninsula (eg, Dubai, Saudi Arabia, Qatar, the United Arab Emirates), where these firms had opened offices to get their shares of developing markets, shows that not enough diligence was applied before opening.

From a strategic perspective, each law firm has to decide how to cope with business restrictions, such as those in place in China where foreign law firms are not permitted to practise Chinese law; thus, they need either to cooperate with a domestic firm to do so, or to focus their services on English law, such as outbound merger and acquisition. In the Middle East, law firms tend to underestimate some cultural aspects, such as the approval for opening an office being dependent on whether the said office will be staffed with a sufficiently high number of local lawyers to show respect for the leading sheikh. Business in the Middle East is generally done on a more personal basis; for instance, decision makers must be contacted personally – a process sometimes assisted by local consultants. Some aspects (eg, paying third parties for arranging contacts, giving presents to the relevant decision makers/bureaucrats) may contravene the compliance standards that the law firm is following.

Law firms need to find ways of dealing with some of these elements embedded in local culture or business practices. The corporations active in these markets are often not as independent as their western counterparts, so the mix between governmental and private influence has to be reflected in the business development approach.

The business development function can help to gain an understanding of how lawyers can be successful in the respective markets recognising the way business works there. Furthermore, it needs to establish proper communications with central management to foster a sensitivity to local matters, selling internally the potential that the region offers (and help deliver it!) and mitigate risks upfront.

8.   Business development is changing how you work

Building a unique and effective business development strategy is one of the keys to sustained success in the market for legal services. The change in the market[9] and the shift in clients' buying habits[10] are in many ways permanent, as is the pressure both from competitors – traditional as well as non-traditional service providers – and from the clients themselves through corporate law departments taking over workload, partly assisted by procurement departments. Legal work mostly originates from two sources: existing clients and corporations that law firms approach seeking a specific type of work.

The change that law firms have to initiate and act upon is thinking in advance about which kind of legal work, with which value propositions, they intend to acquire

---

9   Altman Weil Flash Survey 2015, *Law Firms in Transition*.
10   Thomson Reuters Legal Executive Institute, http://legalexecutiveinstitute.com/why-is-the-demand-for-legal-services-shifting/.

from which clients. This change requires a process where the business development department and the partners must cooperate in defining the necessary steps to acquiring the right type of legal work for their firm with its specific capabilities and (financial) needs. In the course of the process, the tasks and responsibilities are increasingly often split between business development and the partners, allowing each to leverage each other's expertise in the best possible manner. While the concept in itself is easy to understand, the change from a partner's perspective has to be taken seriously (accepting support, assigning tasks to non-fee earners, etc) and is to be positively addressed and supported through the law firm's management.

9. An executable strategy

The core of success is the definition and proper execution of a strategy valid for the individual law firm. Firms need to define, based on their current position, in which markets they should be active, with which clients and offering which services. This process is driven by the firm's partners, and the degree of success increases through jointly made decisions and true ownership by individual partners.

Figure 3: Strategy planning process[11]

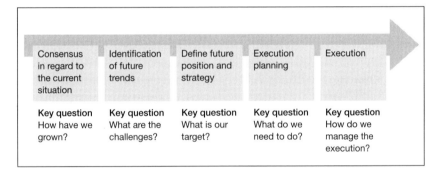

The process of deriving an executable strategy can be guided by five questions, coming from a joint conclusion on where the firm is situated today and a view of the challenges ahead, such as the impact of digitalisation on the offered services. Formulating a 'to be' position and strategy to become, for example, the leading European firm for intellectual property and trademark necessitates the formulation of an action plan and proper management to execute the plan.

The business development function can help partners by moderating and coordinating the process in order to derive a well-formulated but realistic strategy, which is the starting point of a successful business plan. A business plan in that sense is more than a document outlining a sales pipeline (client lists tend to be long and all too often ignored), but a strategy on how to develop further an existing client through new customised offers and winning new clients addressing or shaping their imminent/future needs.

---

11   Law Firm Change Consultants.

10.   Deepening your client knowledge

Apart from a suitable strategy, the focus of a law firm's activities should always be on the client and helping it by solving its problems. The firm is positioned well when it can demonstrate a deep understanding of the client's situation, its industry and business environment, or if the firm is happy to invest time in gaining this understanding. The business development strategy can help you to pinpoint the specific areas where you can make a true difference, compared to your competitors, and communicate these in the best possible manner.

The more you know about your clients, the better you are positioned to increase their loyalty to your firm, which in turn will help to improve the financial situation and allow you to invest time/money into deepening the relationship. Loyalty here works both ways, either preventing clients from moving to competitors because of high switching costs (money and loss of reputation) or motivating them to stay associated with your firm due to the exceptional legal and commercial guidance provided by your firm.

Figure 4: Strategic account management[12]

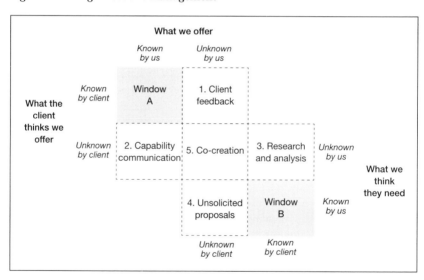

You can approach your service offering from Window A in Figure 4 above towards the middle, and the client needs to head from Window B towards the middle. Each window can be expanded through feedback, research and analysis, capability communication and so on in order to extend the client relationship to new levels. The master class is described in the middle where your firm and the client jointly develop innovative solutions.

Therefore, you need to ask yourself when was the last time a client complimented your firm for its exceptional understanding of its business and the

---

12   Barolsky Advisors, *Relationship capital*, June 2013, http://relationshipcapital.com.au/2013/06/.

excellent advice given, and if you cannot remember such an occasion, approach your client in order to find out what is needed to receive such feedback.

11.   How to develop a client-oriented firm

Most law firms position themselves as client-centric, in the business of serving the clients' needs and helping them become more successful, but how many firms live up to those high standards? Does client-oriented mean 24/7 availability, high quality at reduced costs, close partner attention or presenting practical solutions compared to theoretical papers?

The concept of client-orientation goes much deeper than service buzzwords. A legal service provider, either a law firm or a corporate law department, will always engage the client first to gain its view on how the services are supposed to be rendered. There will be instances where different viewpoints arise, but client-orientation means starting a discussion on how to proceed further together. Client-orientation means listening to your client and not trying to enforce a standard approach or being condescending to the client because the law firm has "so much experience in doing this type of business". In a discussion with the client, the firm will always learn something new, providing a better grip on the culture and understanding how the organisation works, the way that a client can look good internally, the spectrum of personalities and behavioural patterns involved, the commercial approach on services and so on. The implementation of client-driven processes enables the firm to seek input from clients to improve the quality of service delivery. The valuable information gained needs to be reflected in the firms' knowledge management so that each time that the client contacts the firm, the partner/lawyer is aware of the clients' specifics and can update the information himself if he learns something new.

McKinsey has claimed that the client should come first, the company second and self third. That sequence pretty much summarises client-orientation. The spotlight is on the client, not on the law firm or individual partner/lawyer. It is therefore important to stress this continuously and actively seek client feedback in order to understand and excel in meeting the client expectations. With that in mind, you can protect your reputation with the client and grow your business as a firm that truly understands the clients' needs.

12.   How to leverage your resources

The sourcing for business development can be based on two pillars: support personnel, such as business development managers/staff, and fee earners, with a focus on partners/senior lawyers. In order to use the fee earners' time as efficiently as possible, it is recommended to leverage your business development/marketing team for fee earner support. The leveraging can happen in areas like market intelligence, competitor research, commercial client reviews, pitch support, pricing strategies, client interviews, marketing credentials, track records, legal directory submissions, product or brand development, to mention some areas of expertise. Leveraging also means that to be effective, a business development professional depends on the time that he spends with fee earners, for instance to discuss legal developments (eg, new/changed laws, upcoming regulations, legal events) and the possible impact on the individual client or industry. This can help the business development team to define and propose actions to present the firm's problem-solving capability in the market, to inform existing/new clients on legal developments, and to raise the profile of the partners/firm in the market.

It is, however, challenging to know all your clients in such detail as to allow strategic development of all. In order to use partner time as efficiently as possible, it is recommended to establish key accounts for clients that are economically and strategically relevant to your firm (eg, those accounts whose loss would have a significant impact on your numbers and/or market reputation). Figure 5 provides an example of how to segment your client portfolio according to current economic potential and future economic/strategic potential. Key accounts are recommended for star clients and potential clients, while silver clients need attention to nurture/maximise revenue with as little partner time as possible.

Figure 5: Client segmentation[13]

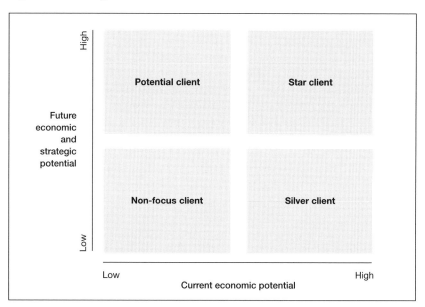

13. Delivering a superior client experience

The client experience in receiving the service is the key to a successful client relationship aside from the actual service delivered. It is relevant to identify how each client assesses its experience of the service and how you tailor your services accordingly. A superior client experience can vary in the legal scope from the structuring of work contracts to mitigating the firm's legal problem in order to secure the client's future. One client may value the technical expertise over speed of

---

13   Law Firm Change Consultants.

delivery, another the practical approach with an executive summary outlining the decision to be made over a legal analysis covering all options possible without offering a recommendation. It all depends on how the client wishes to be serviced.

This approach places the client's experience at the core of the service delivery. The client may perceive the service received rather differently from how the service was delivered by the firm.[14] A standard service delivery approach is counter-productive since each client is different, and the law firm needs to identify the differentiators that the client is looking for in order to tailor its services accordingly.

The firm can set standards, affecting the legal market as such and, thus, acting as a barrier for new entrants/competitors, which have yet to rise to that standard while your firm is further developing its own.

14. Communication with markets and clients

The communication with markets and clients is a core discipline within the business development/marketing communications function. There is a clear theoritical distinction between both, but in reality, depending on the functional evolution, there is often a mix, not least due to limited resources. While business development as a function focuses on the development of existing clients or winning new ones, and the development of legal products, marketing communications covers the broader interface with the clients/markets in order to secure/enhance the market reputation.

The distinction between the functions can be illustrated via the scope of a legal newsletter:

- Marketing communication would put together a newsletter for all clients (existing/prospective) showing the upcoming legal developments, sent by the marketing communications team.
- Business development would put together a customised newsletter for selected clients putting the legal development into perspective for the individual client situation, sent by the client relationship partner.

In terms of demand generation, the marketing communications function plays an important role in enhancing the market reputation targeted at a continuous business intake. In order to be successful, it is vital that the law firm understands its competitive reputation in the market and identifies mechanisms that it can utilise to enhance this reputation.

In this context, the branding of a law firm becomes increasingly critical, even if your firm is unaware of it. Your firm is nevertheless associated with a market image, be that generalist, niche player, overpriced, distinctive, authentic, pragmatic, etc; in order to maintain an image, it is essential to live up to its aspects. So the better the law firm can be positioned in the market with messages supporting its brand (eg, client testimonials or partner blogs), the sharper its image remains.

It is fair to say that a legal service is not the same as a car or a software product or a smartphone, but developments such as the commoditisation of legal services

---

14   Young, note 2 *supra*, p 296.

will lead to an increased importance of branding as experienced in the consumer world. The intensified usage of the Internet and social networks for information-gathering lead to better informed clients intending to use this knowledge to select the right firm.

15. Conclusion

This chapter has sought to provide a guide on how business development from both process and functional points of view can support the development of a law firm. By jointly developing a strategy, both business development and the lawyers can gain valuable insights into each other's way of thinking and working. Both can see where they can add value in the process and how the cooperation can lead to a productive, targeted and, ultimately, client-focused firm.

Business development can help to structure the legal services provided and define, together with the lawyers, the service needed to improve the firm's competitive stance and market reputation from the clients' perspective. Since the starting position of each firm is unique in terms of size, geographical reach or scope of legal services provided, there is no 'one size fits all' solution to the right business development organisation or technological infrastructure. Nonetheless, one aspect is common to all of them: the partners accepting the change of culture needed to implement a successful business development function and its underlying processes.

A day in the life of a head of business development

Christine Liæker Lindberg
Advokatfirmaet Wiersholm AS

1. Introduction

At a time when disruptions, change and innovation dominate the legal industry, business services leaders must adopt a visionary commercial strategy and implement supporting processes and infrastructure to drive efficiency and effectiveness.

Clients used to come to lawyers on their own accord, and the clients were mostly happy with long, complex answers regardless of the matter at hand. Business development, marketing and sales were never in the picture. The 'new normal',[1] though, is about the changes occurring in the delivery of legal services. Clients' newfound power has changed their views on what good legal advice consists of, as well as their criteria for client satisfaction. Their willingness to pay the asking price has also diminished.

The distinct trends[2] that law firms need to address include electronic discovery, social networking, legal process outsourcing, globalisation, virtual law firms, alternative billing models and alternative legal service models. Will the new normal affect the role of business development? Yes, of course. The changes in clients' attitude and in market conditions have forced law firms to rethink their business model, behaviour and culture. The business development team can be an important contributor in these change processes if management sees the services that the team offers as adding value to key areas such as marketing, project management, client management, strategy and innovation. Business development must comprise specific value-added activities that the rest of the firm workforce cannot tackle.

This chapter takes a close look at the business development function's day-to-day work and how business development specialists can add value to a law firm. Business development exists in every sector with different set-ups and objectives. A challenging task is to set up and use business development in a way that adds the most value in the areas that are vital to the firm in the new normal. This chapter highlights a set-up that should cover the needs of most law firms, with detailed thoughts on roles and responsibilities, the methodology for achieving the objectives and what a day in the life of head of business development looks like. To conclude, I will consider how the business development role is likely to evolve.

2. The overall goal of business development

The business development team works to improve the law firm's market position and

---

1 The New Normal Blog, *ABA Journal* (www.abajournal.com/topic/the_new_normal).
2 Sally Cane, "10 Trends Reshaping the Legal Industry", About.com.

achieve financial growth. The team defines long-term organisational strategic goals, builds key client relationships, identifies business opportunities and maintains extensive knowledge of current market conditions. It is its job to work with the sector teams, marketing staff and other managers to increase sales opportunities and thereby maximise revenue. To achieve this, the team needs to find potential new clients, and will also help manage existing clients and ensure that they stay satisfied and positive. Three important areas in which the business development team can add value and secure success for the firm are:

- sales and marketing – by implementing high-quality sales processes towards new and existing clients, structure and follow-up on important pitch processes towards new and existing clients, which include proactive research of clients and the market for potential leads;
- communication and public relations – by developing and executing a clear communication strategy, providing support to the overall firm strategy, using social media to increase awareness of the firm and position the firm's lawyers as thought leaders in their practice areas; and
- strategy and innovation – by creating structured client management programme and new service lines through the development, follow-up and measurement of customised activity programmes towards segmented client groups (ie, key clients). The team will explore new ways of serving the clients knowing their issues and needs, and supporting these ideas with relevant technological systems backing up the workflow.

The business development team is assigned to lift the firm in areas where the lawyers lack the necessary commercial skillset or particular expertise, such as marketing, communication and project management. The head of business development needs to define which activities to pursue and at what level (competence) these activities are most likely to add value. The team must be built accordingly, by hiring clever people. Good people mean good money – so the head of business development needs to be able to demonstrate payback for the investment.

3. Organisation and set-up

3.1 Structure, roles and responsibility

There are endless ways to organise the business development operations in a law firm depending on the size, market position and overall goals for the firm. In large jurisdictions such as the United Kingdom and Germany, business development teams and separate teams of marketers have been built over several years. The first business development teams in larger UK-headquartered international law firms such as Allen & Overy LLP were put in place in the mid-1990s.[3]

A competent head of business development will make sure that sales and marketing, communication and public relations, and strategy and innovation will

---

3   HR department in Allen & Overy LLP, London.

join up on the most important and critical tasks with relevant expertise. Platforms and tools will support the three dimensions of workflow in the best manner. I have too often seen support functions work in silos and not putting their minds together to explore holistic solutions. It is surprising how many business development professionals fail to engage with the firm's customer relationship management (CRM) system. In these people's view, this activity belongs to either the CRM team or the marketing department. Close cooperation within the non-lawyers team is crucial, however, as it contributes to developing an even stronger professional input to the firm. There are similarities in the set-up of the support functions within the same jurisdictions, but when differences occur, the common basis is the management team's confidence in the business development role adding to the firm's revenue. Firms that have an innovative and long-term outlook with a tireless eye on client satisfaction appreciate the head of business development taking the lead on initiatives and execution of these matters. They see what the business development team brings to the table, and include it in management and strategy processes. Successful law firms see the need for a more professionally managed service firm.

Figure 1: Structure, roles and responsibility for the business development team

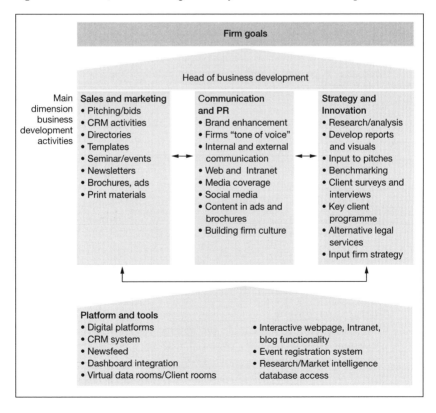

The roles of each function in this organisation model are discussed in more detail below.

Sales and marketing: the sales and marketing team is responsible for the pitching work, which is often the main sales activity in law firms. Sales and marketing bridges input from the lawyers for solutions, from the communication team on certain topics related to policy and it calls for the strategy and innovation team when it comes to customised and advanced input, such as the client's needs, concerns and objectives. The chief financial officer is involved when it comes to pricing. Other key activities are:

- identifying potential clients and the decision makers within the client organisation, providing the lawyers with sufficient background information, analysis and marketing material, and conducting research and building relationship with new clients;
- developing and engaging the legal team to use the CRM system to measure the marketing efforts, as well as tracking and recording activity on accounts;
- follow up on pitches and their need for relevant marketing material, etc;
- arranging and participating in internal and external client debriefs;
- preparing marketing material – print, web, presentations; and
- planning and executing events and publications.

Communication and public relations: this function is all about creating relevant and high-quality content in the right communication channel – both internally and externally. It promotes and protects the brand, making the department a key contributor to what and how the firm communicates to its various markets and stakeholders by:

- creating a communication plan with clear messages and a uniform content – this to make it easier for the lawyers to adapt to the firm's tone of voice and its strengths and objectives;
- attending industry functions, such as association events and conferences, and providing feedback and information on market trends;
- presenting to, and consulting with, mid- and senior-level management on business trends with a view to develop new services; and
- using knowledge of the market and benchmarking of competitors to identify and develop the firm's unique selling propositions and differentiators. It sells the firm's story – that is, why the firm should be the client's preferred legal adviser.

Strategy and innovation: this team leads the analytical aspects of business development, and is responsible for leading larger projects, such as key client programmes, new service lines, advanced market research, client's surveys, advanced reporting to management, input to the firm's strategy and complex pitches. These types of activity represent high value for the firm, and require skills that are often lacking among the firm's lawyers. The team's activities include:

- developing, following up on and measuring key client programmes;

- submitting weekly progress reports and ensuring that data is accurate;
- ensuring that data is accurately entered into and managed within the company's CRM or other sales management system;
- forecasting sales targets and ensuring that the client team meets them;
- participating in complex pitches – advising on solution/service;
- providing business development training to lawyers; and
- researching and developing a thorough understanding of the client's people and capabilities.

Platforms and tools: technology and digital platforms supporting sales and marketing, communication and public relations, and strategy and innovation are managed by the head of business development, but hosted by the IT department. The main function is to make sure that the firm takes advantage of the digital opportunities to enhance its services to the clients (client rooms, market intelligence, web, blog, etc) and streamlines internal services. It is instrumental to ensuring that the digital arm of the business remains part of the core organisation structure of the company, rather than being an independent silo on the side. The ability both to share the firm's complete knowledge of its clients – through live updates – and to make easy use of its best practice templates is crucial to deliver on demand. Advanced technology as an important tool for developing legal services, and offering more for less requires that business development take responsibility for being on top of IT usage in the firm in order to innovate with new service lines.

Head of business development: that person plays a key role in the set-up depicted in Figure 1, being responsible for all four dimensions. Defining long-term organisational strategic goals, building key client relationships, identifying business opportunities and maintaining extensive knowledge of current market conditions are the fundamental hands-on activities that the head of business development needs to master. This person is a part of the firm's senior management – an enhanced and central position in the new normal in delivering legal services. It is the head of business development's job to create seamless interaction with the relevant staff within the business development team and other stakeholders to increase sales opportunities and thereby maximise revenue.

3.2 Important stakeholders

In a firm with different professions working closely together towards the same goal, smooth cooperation is paramount. Sharing the same vision and understanding of how you can contribute to your co-workers' success is crucial. Engaging your stakeholders by informing, including, demonstrating added value and appreciating their involvement are key elements in the relationship. Your success depends on what you can do for others and what others can do for you. Please see Figure 2 for examples of important stakeholders.

3.3 A day in the life of the head of business development

Bearing in mind the structures, roles and responsibilities described above, it will

Figure 2: Important stakeholders

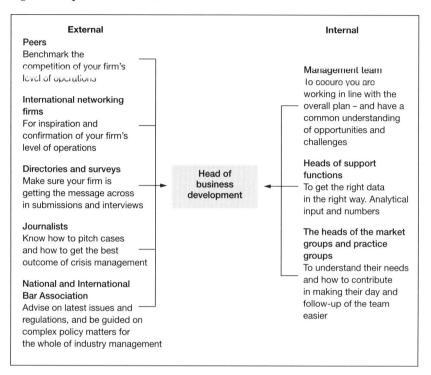

come as no surprise that there are no ordinary days in the life of a head of business development. It is not just that the tasks and responsibilities are weighing on your shoulders; you're enthusiastic, bright and impatient colleagues are too.

This is because law firm professionals are bound by the onerous task of tracking every minute of their time in order to bill it to a client. Law firms frequently impose high monthly and yearly billable hour requirements upon partners, associates and paralegals, making law firm employment among the most demanding professional service environments. Indeed, to understand the life of a head of business development, it helps to understand the life of the people surrounding the business development team – namely, the lawyers. In addition to the pressure stemming from both a competitive environment and exacting billing quotas, high expectations, irregular hours, steep learning curves and strict academic and experiential requirements all contribute to creating a busy and hectic working environment in high-end law firms.

However, the central tasks of a head of business development will include those outlined below.

Management meeting and preparation: the head of business development is usually a member of the management team, which means frequently reporting on project progress, client programmes, sales and new assignments for the business development team. Preparation is essential to serve the management team efficiently.

Follow-up on marketing teams/practice groups (both consisting of lawyers): the structure of law firms varies, but often consists of marketing teams, practice areas or business sectors. An important task for the head of business development is to follow up the progress in these groups by guiding, motivating and assisting them. Experience shows that there are different levels of engagement in these groups. The head of business development is responsible for coordinating efforts and securing best practice and progress on the various projects.

Key client programmes: many of the larger law firms have a dedicated key client programme, whereby a dedicated team approaches the most important clients with specific activities, follow-up and extras. The relationships with these clients, the activities undertaken and the revenue generated are closely monitored by a CRM system and the financial system. Business development is responsible for gathering the information in easily understandable reports for evaluation and status updates. These efforts are time consuming, and the need for specific information is most commonly *ad hoc*. The head of business development is often involved in the sector group meetings and must be ready to:

- inspire, motivate and engage;
- follow up – both teams and clients;
- prepare for client evaluation meetings;
- link activities towards revenue;
- show progress;
- evaluate the programme;
- evaluate the teams/partners; and
- present reports, analysis and statistics.

Pitching/quoting, writing proposals: increased competition has given clients more power. They are less loyal and now request quotes/proposals for every matter – especially from panel firms. Thus, support is needed with regard to:

- pricing, team available, approach, focus (ie, value for the client);
- relevant experience and proof thereof;
- research on sector, client and competition; and
- templates available.

Sporadic follow-up on projects and drop-ins, this covers:

- internal projects – on and off;
- follow-up of team on operational tasks;
- completion of own tasks;
- personal issues with team members;
- inquiries/late emails as lawyers tend to handle internal tasks after client work/in the evening; and
- sporadic project progress depending on the capacity of the lawyers involved.

Thus, a typical day in the life of a head of business development could be illustrated by the figure below.

Figure 3: A day in a life of a head of business development

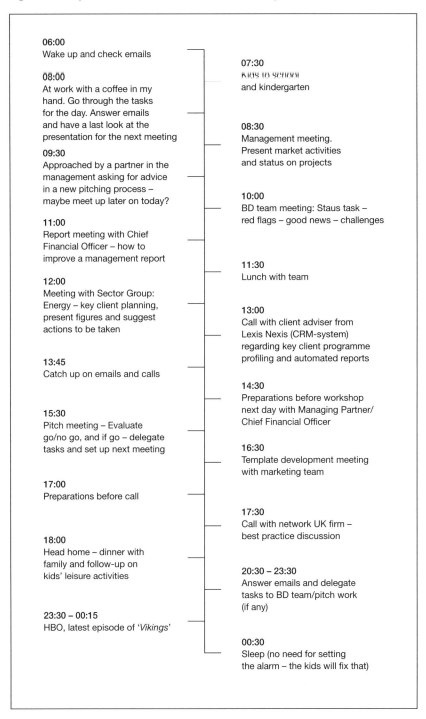

06:00
Wake up and check emails

07:30
Kids to school
and kindergarten

08:00
At work with a coffee in my
hand. Go through the tasks
for the day. Answer emails
and have a last look at the
presentation for the next meeting

08:30
Management meeting.
Present market activities
and status on projects

09:30
Approached by a partner in the
management asking for advice
in a new pitching process –
maybe meet up later on today?

10:00
BD team meeting: Staus task –
red flags – good news – challenges

11:00
Report meeting with Chief
Financial Officer – how to
improve a management report

11:30
Lunch with team

12:00
Meeting with Sector Group:
Energy – key client planning,
present figures and suggest
actions to be taken

13:00
Call with client adviser from
Lexis Nexis (CRM-system)
regarding key client programme
profiling and automated reports

13:45
Catch up on emails and calls

14:30
Preparations before workshop
next day with Managing Partner/
Chief Financial Officer

15:30
Pitch meeting – Evaluate
go/no go, and if go – delegate
tasks and set up next meeting

16:30
Template development meeting
with marketing team

17:00
Preparations before call

17:30
Call with network UK firm –
best practice discussion

18:00
Head home – dinner with
family and follow-up on
kids' leisure activities

20:30 – 23:30
Answer emails and delegate
tasks to BD team/pitch work
(if any)

23:30 – 00:15
HBO, latest episode of 'Vikings'

00:30
Sleep (no need for setting
the alarm – the kids will fix that)

4. The methodology – how to get things done

A clear methodology in how to achieve the goals set out for you is crucial. The main elements of such methodology are:

- to have a clear understanding of both your responsibilities and your operational set-up;
- to make sure that you invest in the right people based on the tasks at hand and your planned activities;
- to have an overall business development plan that supports the overall strategy of the firm – and to split it into intermediate goals (you will need wins along the way); and
- to show the firm, and especially your Managing Partner and management team, that you and your team are adding value. Elaborate on the effects of your initiatives and deliverables. This will also build trust in you as the right person for the job.

4.1 Investing in competence – an analytical approach

Many law firms strive to see the value in investing in the business development team. To illustrate the added value of investing in specialist competence, we need to look at the specialist's role in reference to value for the firm and the lawyers' competence for the activities in question. Within the new normal, considering the business development teams as advanced secretaries coordinating the sales activities is insufficient. The new normal requires support staff (business development) to drive the processes and initiatives to get things done and add real value for the firm.

An interesting and useful exercise is to evaluate what activities drive value for the firm and the investment needed from the business development team to fill the gap between activities with high value for the firm and the lawyers' low competence in that area.

The business development team needs to put its efforts into the four areas depicted in Figure 4 and further detailed below.

1. Standardisation: the activities are useful for the firm, but do not have high value. The lawyers have low competence in these activities, and the business development focus will be to standardise these processes.

2. Capacity and coordination: the activities are useful for the firm, but do not have high value. The lawyers have high competence in these activities, but it would make more sense financially to use business development team members rather than lawyers to fulfil these tasks.

3. Investing in specialists: these activities have great value for the firm, but the lawyers lack the competence to make them a success. This is a window of opportunity for the business development team to show real value for the investment. Closing the gap means investing in business development specialists to ensure that goals are reached, and show that you are adding value.

Figure 4: Investing in competence/an analytical approach

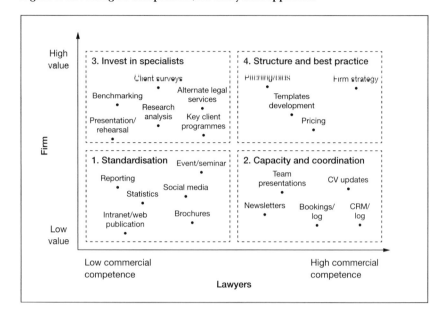

4. Structure and best practice: these activities have great value for the firm, and the lawyers will be interested in sharing their knowledge. The business development focus will be to work closely with the lawyers and develop a solid template/experience database for the firm in order to understand, structure and develop best practice for these processes.

4.2   **Short-term planning and execution – with long-term focus**

Succeeding in a partner-structured firm where time is money for great, ambiguous, hardworking and perfectionist minds is always a challenge. There are always important, and urgent, tasks ahead. Being a non-lawyer in this environment and, at the same time, being responsible for bringing results to the table based on efforts you have pushed the lawyers to make, is not easy.

To succeed in a law firm, business development requires to pay particular attention to the key elements listed below (in addition to being extremely enthusiastic about law firms and lawyers, and being dedicated to making a difference in how the firm as a whole relates to its clients – and in how you can make each lawyer adapt to the new normal).

An overall business development plan that supports the overall firm strategy: this requires a solid understanding of the firm, its goals and expectations from its business development activities. It also requires:

- to be relevant and add value. Make sure that your projects and activities are directly connected to what drives revenue and client satisfaction. Focus especially on projects;
- have a plan for the next six months and a longer-term strategy for the next

year or two. Make sure that you develop this together with your managing partner/management team;

- be realistic and innovative when setting up the tasks ahead with clear and measurable goals; update your plan every six months and the long-term strategy accordingly; and
- ask your team for input on what to focus on in your plan – ask relevant stakeholders/lawyers what they think. Avoid asking too many, though, as expectations grow with every person that you include in the process.

Figure 5: Short term planning and execution/long term focus

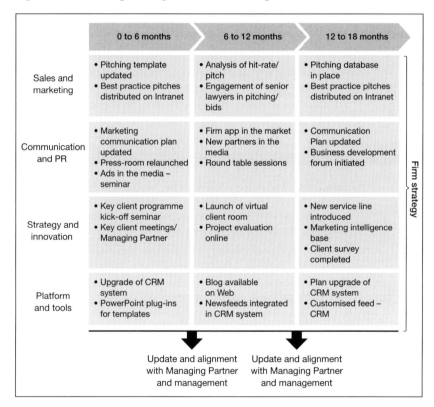

	0 to 6 months	6 to 12 months	12 to 18 months
Sales and marketing	• Pitching template updated • Best practice pitches distributed on Intranet	• Analysis of hit-rate/ pitch • Engagement of senior lawyers in pitching/ bids	• Pitching database in place • Best practice pitches distributed on Intranet
Communication and PR	• Marketing communication plan updated • Press-room relaunched • Ads in the media – seminar	• Firm app in the market • New partners in the media • Round table sessions	• Communication Plan updated • Business development forum initiated
Strategy and innovation	• Key client programme kick-off seminar • Key client meetings/ Managing Partner	• Launch of virtual client room • Project evaluation online	• New service line introduced • Marketing intelligence base • Client survey completed
Platform and tools	• Upgrade of CRM system • PowerPoint plug-ins for templates	• Blog available on Web • Newsfeeds integrated in CRM system	• Plan upgrade of CRM system • Customised feed – CRM

Firm strategy

Update and alignment with Managing Partner and management

Update and alignment with Managing Partner and management

Excellent project management: this is essential to achieve the goals set out in the overall strategy and six-month plan. In summary, a great project manager's plan will manage and handle details in a way that lets others relax. This requires:

- to be agile. Make a short and to-the-point project plan with clear and measurable goals, preferably in Excel or PowerPoint so you can easily share your status and updates with your team and management;
- to prioritise. Set aside time every week to update your project plan with status and make sure that you progress every week;
- to work with a sense of urgency; and

- to communicate along the way as the next best thing to good news is early warning of bad news. Make sure that you communicate progress and possible delays as soon as possible. This will reassure your subordinates that you are on top of the situation and can manage it.

Good writing and presentation skills: this requires proficiency in the key presentation tools and templates used by the firm. It also involves:
- ensuring that your presentation is relevant for the setting, and that you highlight what you want to be the key takeaway;
- sticking to the time given and be relevant when you comment on and answer questions; and
- initiating reports/slides/set-ups that easily give an overview of your projects' status and show results that make a difference.

Excellent time management: this involves a number of tasks and qualities:
- Get an early start. Take the first 30 minutes of every day to plan your day. Do not start your day until you complete your time plan. The most important part of your day is when you schedule your time.
- Be tough when prioritising. Learn to say no. Do not give people your immediate attention unless it is absolutely crucial to your activity. Politely decline additional tasks if you think that you are already overloaded with work. Take a look at your 'to do' list before agreeing to take on extra work. As long as you say no with a smile and advise where help can be found, your colleagues will understand and learn what your responsibilities are, and that you might not be the right person for these tasks.
- Delegate. Most of us take on more than we can handle. This often results in stress and burnout. Delegating is not running away from your responsibilities, but is an important function of management. Learn the art of delegating work to your subordinates according to their skills and abilities.
- Schedule time for interruptions. Plan time to be pulled away from what you are doing. Especially in a busy and large law firm, there will be *ad hoc* activities, and you must always be available for urgent requests from a client, team or your boss.
- Put up a 'do not disturb' sign when you absolutely need to get work done. Interruptions will delay important work, so do not be afraid of stating that you need time to finish up. People will understand and respect that, as long as it does not become a habit.
- Remember that it is impossible to get everything done.
- Look forward to going to work.

Business development in a law firm is not for everyone. Passion and dedication for the role are essential. Finding really good business development people is difficult because not only is the role in itself extremely demanding, not least because of the high responsibilities that it carries, but the organisational set-up also adds a layer of complexity – and the sense of urgency attached to the tasks at hand is permanent.

4.3 Accomplishments – show the added value

Personal public relations is not as bad as you might think. It is certainly a necessity for business development professionals, to ensure that colleagues are aware that the business development powers are directly linked to performance.

The head of business development must tell the rest of the firm what the team has done, and highlight the effects that it has on the firm. This also gives colleagues an understanding of what the team does all day. Sharing accomplishments will require that the head of business development follow these instructions:

- Create an understanding of why you do it – explain why the firm profits from what you do. If it has no value for the firm, reassess the activity.
- Remind and update – start every management meeting by saying, "Good morning, let's look at what we have done since last we met…" Use the same format so your colleagues get used to the concept and you can illustrate improvements.
- Measure added value – measure effects on your initiatives in terms of cost saving or value for money.

5. The future of business development in law firms

Being successful today and not feeling under real pressure to change is not a good place to be in. "Nothing fails like success," said Arnold Toynbee (in reference to complacency). The firms that sustain success are those that constantly adapt to changes. Ultimately, innovation requires a culture that accepts failure, whereas the fear of failure will prevent sustainable change.

The outlook for law firms is ever-more-demanding clients and executives that are looking for ways to streamline and protect their business. Technology will increase the value of knowledge management, lead the reorganisation of standard legal services, advance market intelligence and create new ways of communicating with our clients. Clients expecting more for less will make law firms improve their workflows, enhance investment in their key client programmes and introduce new service lines. Specialists will turn into commercial advisers – a significant shift for many lawyers. The lawyer's role has changed and the demands for additional skills are evident in relation to advanced technology, project management, communication skills and commercial nous in delivering service to clients. And who knows? Maybe the business models for law firms with partner structure will come under pressure too.

The future role of business development depends on the changes made by the law firms and how they develop. The new normal adds to the importance of having a solid business development team with specialists in sought-after disciplines – of getting things done. For high-value activities where lawyers lack competence, investing in business development specialists will more than pay for itself when these specialists close the gap and release value.

Many organisations have seen the enormous advantages of digital technology; yet, we find the process of integrating platforms, people and planning a constant challenge. Even so, the challenge is not that we do not have the answers, but that we do not know the questions to ask.

A good piece of advice to law firms exploiting the value of business development[4] is to understand that your business needs to be curious about technology and its impact on client behaviour. Test, learn, and get close to the technological future. Define your competitive context and then imagine different scenarios in the time to come. That said, nothing can substitute the chemistry that a personal relationship creates. No video conference, FaceTiming, Lync meeting, email or telephone call can replace the effect of sitting around the same table, discussing and sensing the atmosphere and adjusting your strategy along the way to close the deal. The main job of a head of business development is to get the lawyers to that table – through marketing, public relations, sales, communication, strategy and innovation – all on the right platforms, and that is indeed adding value to the firm.

---

4   Deloitte, *Harnessing the "bang" – Stories from the digital frontline.*

Marketing through good HR

André Andersson
Mannheimer Swartling

1. Setting the scene

The career paths of lawyers and law graduates are different in different jurisdictions, and it comes as no surprise that each legal market has its own peculiarities. This chapter discusses how you, by seeing and treating law students, applicants and associates as future clients, can market your firm to them and establish a strategic long-term position for your firm in the local legal market. How you do this will, to a large extent, depend on the market in which you operate.

The ideas and recommendations set out here could thus fall flat in circumstances that differ from those that exist here in Sweden. Having said that, many legal markets are similar to Sweden and the general premise is relevant in all markets.

Just under 10 million people live in Sweden. Virtually all lawyers in firms operating in Sweden have Swedish law degrees. The same is true for lawyers working in-house. Six Swedish universities offer law degrees that then qualify their holders to become members of the Swedish Bar Association. About 1,200 law graduates come onto the market each year. Most in-house lawyers started their careers in law firms. Most larger corporations employ in-house lawyers who are responsible for selecting and retaining law firms.

Well over 90% of the Swedish law graduates get relevant legal employment almost immediately after graduating. Most of them continue with legal work throughout their career, although of course a few move across to the commercial side or pursue other career paths. Few Swedish law graduates work abroad for more than a limited period of time.

The legal market in Sweden is therefore, to a large extent, a self-contained ecosystem. This can give rise to tremendous opportunities, especially for a large firm that is willing to make long-term investments in marketing through good human resources (HR). The rest of this chapter describes strategies that can be implemented in this type of environment in order to market your law firm to some of your future clients.

2. First impressions

First impressions are always very important and will often last a lifetime. It is easy to think that employer branding is just what it says that it is, but that is not the whole story. By focusing your efforts and contacts at universities exclusively on the law students who are potential recruits for your firm, you risk repelling a large group of individuals who will, in a self-contained ecosystem, go on to become your potential future clients.

Your marketing at recruitment fairs and at universities will often naturally be aimed at finding and recruiting the right law graduates. That is why you are there and there is of course nothing wrong with that. But even if you focus your efforts on potential recruits, it costs very little to be inclusive rather than exclusive. By holding some broader university events and also taking time to present your firm to the law students at large, you are controlling the first impression that they form of your firm. You can be assured that there will be an excess of gossip and stories about the major law firms circulating among the students, but at least you have done what you can to draw an initial fair picture.

One human tendency to keep in mind is to rationalise and make a virtue out of necessity. A law student whose grades are not good enough or who otherwise lacks the qualifications to apply to a particular firm is likely to see that firm as less attractive – "it's just a sweatshop" or "they're just a bunch of snobs". This means that a large proportion of the student population is inclined to see a top law firm in a less-than-favourable light. To counter this effect as an elite law firm, you will need to go out of your way to be extraordinarily nice and accessible, which may not always be that easy. However, it is important to remember the built-in biases that you are facing and to do what you can to explain carefully your business model and how you select applicants to the students whom you are not interested in recruiting.

To prevent students from believing that they know who you are and what you stand for based on university gossip, you will need to start presenting your firm to students as early as possible – preferably during their first years on the law programme, rather than just before they graduate. This also means that you will have more time to build the picture that they will have of your firm when they start their legal career.

It may seem daunting to take such a broad approach to recruitment activities, but in a market such as Sweden it requires only a little extra effort to present and market your firm to most lawyers coming into the market. For Mannheimer Swartling, it means that we have to be continuously visible at the six law faculties around Sweden – a manageable task.

3. The recruitment process

The next step to consider is the recruitment process. How do you deal with applications and how do you conduct interviews? This area is even more sensitive than general employer branding, since you are dealing with law graduates who want to join your firm, but the vast majority of whom will be rejected.

At Mannheimer Swartling we receive well over 400 applications each year. We interview about 120 graduates and in a normal year we recruit between 40 and 50 new lawyers. It means that one-third of all law graduates in Sweden will go through our recruitment process and that we will reject almost 90% of them. Since we are an attractive employer and since students know that they need good grades to be considered by us, it is safe to assume that the applications that we receive, on the whole, come from the best students in each year. We know that the graduates whom we reject will primarily go on to other law firms, and over time many of them will end up as in-house lawyers and thus potential clients. Just imagine what it would do to our long-term standing in the Swedish market if these students got a bad impression of the firm from the recruitment process.

I certainly remember my first job interviews, even though they took place almost 30 years ago, and I am sure that this is true for most people. I have some very good friends who have subsequently been immensely successful in their legal careers, but who still remember and talk about their interviews with Mannheimer Swartling and how they were rejected.

It is extraordinarily difficult to avoid some degree of resentment among those who are not offered jobs, but it is important to do all you can to minimise it. For those who are rejected without an interview, it is primarily a question of dealing with the applications efficiently and to be forthcoming if they call you during or after the process. Among other things, we have learned that it is best to avoid too formal a tone in written communications with them.

For those who make it to at least the first interview stage, there are much better possibilities for damage control. The first thing to remember is that the interview will probably be their last contact with your firm for a long time, and that the outcome of the interview will give them a good reason to resent you. It is thus wise to use part of the interview to talk about the firm and for the interviewers to present themselves, preferably in a humble way. But most important is the atmosphere during the interview, which is what will give the candidate his lasting impression of your firm. For those you end up recruiting, the interview is irrelevant for the purposes discussed in this chapter. Their view of the firm will be determined by what it is like as a workplace, which I will discuss in the following sections of this chapter. But for those who are not offered a position, this one interaction is likely to stay with them forever.

Experienced interviewers can often assess early on in an interview whether the candidate will not make it to the next stage. Where that is the case, you should neither lose interest in the candidate nor cut the interview short. Instead, turn on the charm and use the last part of the interview to sell the firm subtly; thus, you will hopefully have created a long-lasting good impression of the firm that will not be too much tainted by the rejection to come.

Communicating rejection is always hard, but sending a letter in these circumstances will not create a good impression of your firm. If a candidate has come to one or more interviews, he deserves a telephone call from an empathic person who can convey this negative piece of news in a manner that will nevertheless leave the recipient with a mostly positive impression. The caller should take the time to give a credible explanation for the decision. The explanation should preferably be truthful, although a white lie may sometimes be called for.

4. The right mindset

The first sections of this chapter considered the recruitment process, but arguably more important is how you treat associates when they have joined the firm and when they subsequently move on from the firm. The remaining sections thus focus on the attitude that you should have toward your associates and how you should invest in personal relations with them, all in order to create long-term loyalty to the firm. This is obviously the most difficult part of the process, since it by necessity involves all partners in the firm and requires an active buy-in from them.

Historically, most firms have seen their associates at best as future partners and at worst as cannon fodder that will be replaced from time to time. That the latter view is devastating if you want to market your firm through good HR requires no further explanation, but even the former view is highly illusionary these days. In our firm, over nine associates in 10 will not make partnership; the figures are probably similar in most major law firms operating in mature legal markets. What we should all do is to see our associates as future clients, because that is what a significant number of them will become, at least if we treat them well.

To shift attitudes so that this view permeates the entire firm will require time and sustained effort, but it is achievable. Partners should always keep in mind that the associate in front of them is a future client and should be treated accordingly. You do not treat a future client badly or unfairly. You listen to a future client and explain what you do and why you do it. Not least, you try to establish a personal relation with a future client.

Another equally important aspect is how you treat your clients and talk about them in front of your associates. The way that your associates see you dealing with clients is the way that they will expect to be dealt with as clients in the future. This means that you should never talk disparagingly about clients or the service that you provide to them. On the contrary, you should make your associates feel that you go out of your way to assist and provide a top-class service, always in the client's best interest rather than your own. This may often require that you take some time with the associate to explain your thoughts and considerations in the matter at hand.

Last but not least, there is the question of fees and invoicing. All law firms around the world are under price pressure from clients. The time to counter this pressure is when the future client is still your associate. Many partners (including many in our firm) think that associates should be as little involved in invoicing as possible. I argue the contrary. A senior associate will have a full insight into what has gone on in the matter, the amount of work that has been required and the work products that this has resulted in. What you should endeavour to do is to make your senior associates appreciate all of this and be proud of what they have participated in creating. Based on this, you should involve them in the determination of the fees so that they feel that the client is paying a fair price for the services provided, a price that they can justify and defend in their own minds as being reasonable. You must never internally give the impression that you have got away with a hefty uplift or over-charged an unwitting client.

What is true for invoicing is of course equally true for providing fee estimates. In this situation it is even more obvious how you, in collaboration with a senior associate, can discuss and establish what is a fair price for a certain matter. This is perhaps the ideal situation, where you can take time to educate an associate about what high-quality legal services should cost and why that is so.

While the attitudes of individual partners as discussed above are the most important by far when it comes to treating associates as future clients, the attitude of the firm's management is also important. When future clients are still associates, the firm has the opportunity to sell its strategies and business model to them much more easily than after they have left the firm. Consequently, the managing partner and others involved in the marketing of the firm should also direct some of their efforts internally so that the associates get the same marketing message as clients. Additionally, internal communication to associates should include the clients' perspective whenever possible, not just the employees' perspective.

5.   Optimal attrition

All good things come to an end, and if only one associate in 10 makes partnership, it means that nine associates will have to leave the firm over a period of time, unless there is an alternative career path available. When should this happen? Do we want associates to stay with the firm until they knock on the metaphorical partnership door? The perceived wisdom has always been that the longer they stay, the better. This is not necessarily true. Optimal attrition is something different.

Looking at the careers of our former associates reveals that those who leave us during the first six years primarily go to in-house positions, while those who leave us at a later stage tend to go to competing law firms. On the whole, those who leave us earlier tend to have a better long-term relationship with the firm than those who leave us at a later stage. Different factors can explain this. For instance, those who stay longer are likely to be more interested in a future career as legal consultants, and those who have invested a longer time with us are more disappointed if they do not make partnership.

Nevertheless, there is some merit in encouraging associates, who could have been useful to retain, to move on from the firm at a stage in their career when they are more likely to become future clients rather than future competitors. It should also be in line with the associates' best interest to give them a fair and honest assessment of their partnership prospects at a stage when they have more career options open to them. Having said that, the partners working with good associates will always want to keep these associates for longer rather than let them go at the optimal time from the associates' perspective. So constant monitoring and enforcement will no doubt be necessary to implement this strategy.

The other aspect to consider is the associates' professional development pattern. An associate who is developing professionally tends to be happy. Likewise, the firm tends to be happy with the associates as long as they can perform the tasks relevant to their seniority well enough. When an associate has plateaued professionally, everything suddenly becomes more difficult. The associate will feel that he is no longer developing and the partners will feel that it is becoming increasingly difficult to utilise the associate. The result is likely to be that the associate gets too little to do, becomes alienated in the organisation and increasingly bitter and resentful. This should, in an ideal world, never happen. If this associate is instead encouraged the leave the firm at an early enough stage, he may very well end up becoming a happy and grateful future client who had a short but worthwhile period with the firm. So, again, the laziness of the organisation and the inclination to retain people for too long could create unnecessary resentment.

6.   Creating happy leavers

In the old days, an associate leaving a firm was seen as either a betrayal or a failure, sometimes both. This was, and sometimes still is, the case despite everybody knowing that not all associates can become partners. So the first thing is to treat an associate leaving the firm as the natural career progression that it is. This is not always easy, particularly when associates have been very close to becoming partners. It has to be signalled throughout the organisation that the firm really wishes the former associate well in his future career, and that the partners are grateful for the time that the associate has spent with the firm.

But creating happy leavers is not just about giving the former associates a good send-off. It is more about the small details in connection with the termination of employment. Unless the circumstances dictate otherwise, it should be 'business as usual' during the termination period. The associate should be expected to put in the hours and in return he should not be cut off from the information flow and should continue to participate just as actively in the life of the firm.

It is far too easy to be mean to associates who are about to leave the firm. Many years ago, our firm decided not to pay a bonus, in relation to the previous calendar year, to associates who had given notice of termination before the bonus was paid out. One particular associate, who had given notice before the bonus was to be paid out, thought that he deserved his bonus, having worked diligently the entire previous year. We stuck to our principles and did not pay him a bonus – to his great dismay. That associate is now general counsel at one of the major Swedish corporations and still bears, in my opinion rightfully, a certain grudge against our firm. Our short-sighted decision may over the years have cost us lost fees amounting to hundreds of times the amount which we thought that we had saved. We have, however, learnt the lesson and now apply more generous principles.

Another example is how you deal with salary increases for associates who you want to leave the firm. We used to be rather brutal and stop salary increases to reaffirm the signal to such associates that it was time to move on. As with bonuses, this policy tended to create less-than-happy leavers and we are now very careful before we make any such decision.

7.   Maintaining an alumni network

Maintaining an alumni network is now standard procedure in most major law firms. However, this can be done in different ways, some good, others less so. What is important is to have your heart in it and the entire organisation behind it. The partners should be involved and appreciate that the firm's alumni are an important resource.

Regular events to which you invite alumni back to the firm are a good starting point. This is an opportunity for the alumni to keep in touch with the firm and each other, and to be informed about new developments at the firm. However, you should not forget to keep them informed and market the firm to them also between these events. Even the alumni who do not work for potential clients will be a first port of call for information about the firm in their respective networks. So marketing the firm to them will indirectly reach potential clients, even if the alumni are not themselves potential clients. This is equally true if they are your competitors.

It may be even more efficient if you, in addition to a more general alumni programme, can maintain sub-networks of alumni on an industry or practice group level, since there will be more interaction within the specialist group and between the alumni and the corresponding practice group within the firm.

Also in your general relationship-building with, and marketing to, clients and potential clients, it is a good idea to identify your alumni and focus on them. They will already know the firm well, and will hopefully as a consequence appreciate the qualities of the firm and thus be more receptive to your messages. Ensuring that they are invited to seminars and made to look good in their respective organisations will secure them as well-informed ambassadors for the firm. As a general rule, you should make sure that your alumni are informed about, and invited to, all relevant client events. By helping them to be successful wherever they are, you are creating goodwill that will make them more inclined to recommend and use the firm. A free piece of advice over the telephone will often turn out to be a very good investment.

8.   Continuous career management

As a part of your work with the firm's alumni network, you could also become actively involved in career management for your former associates. Unfortunately, this is not something that can be arranged on a firm-wide level, but is rather something for each partner to do in relation to his protégés. While it is initially about making sure that these protégés move to good positions when they leave the firm, preferably with clients or potential clients rather than competitors, it is also about keeping your eyes open for future career opportunities for them. Ideally, it should become so widely known in the market that you do this that your clients, and others, will call you for a recommendation when they want to recruit a lawyer.

This is an area where you really can create a win-win situation. You help your former associate to a good job, but you also help the relevant organisation to find an able lawyer who will fill their requirements. So absolute honesty and integrity are necessary. If it does not work out well, you will have failed on two counts and you may not get a second chance to recommend a lawyer to that organisation.

Making sure that your former associates are well placed stems from both offensive and defensive strategies. If you have followed the programme described earlier in this chapter, these associates will be positively inclined to the firm and likely to use its services and pay adequately for them. But by placing them in the right positions you will also prevent these positions being filled by lawyers with a different background and a different attitude to the firm.

9.   Conclusions

This chapter describes strategies that have worked for Mannheimer Swartling, based on our position in the Swedish market. These approaches will hopefully work equally well in other markets with similar characteristics. However, what will work well everywhere are the following two fundamental ideas: treat all associates as future clients and make sure that all associates who move on from your firm are happy leavers.

These strategies, taken as a whole, may appear cynical. Nothing could be farther from the truth. Implementing similar strategies requires a genuine intention to treat students, candidates, associates and alumni well. Only thus will you create the goodwill necessary to market your firm successfully through good HR. The standard to apply is best described in *Matthew* 7:12: "Do unto others what you would have them do unto you."

What to do when your clients involve legal procurement

Silvia Hodges Silverstein
Buying Legal Council; Fordham Law School; Columbia Law School

General counsel and legal departments are no longer the only buyers of corporate legal services. In more and more companies around the world, legal procurement – the purchasing department or corporate function responsible for acquiring goods and services – is quickly gaining importance in sourcing legal services and managing relationships with law firms.

The involvement of legal procurement is one of the side effects of a power shift to clients. Procurement applies business discipline to legal services. It is generally much less focused on relationships with trusted firms than the legal department. It compares and contrasts law firms, uses data and develops evidence-based rationale to reduce legal spending substantially.

For years, legal services were largely spared the intense cost scrutiny that other business units and functions have been facing for years. The recent financial crisis acted as a catalyst and sped up the process for the adoption of legal procurement, particularly in large corporations. Publicity about billing practices, big-ticket spending and profit pressure is at the root of this seismic shift. The pressure to cut costs is ever-present, not only in companies pressured by activist investors.

The number of *Fortune 500* companies and major international corporations with dedicated legal procurement personnel has been quickly increasing over the past few years. While there is no reliable data available on the exact number of procurement professionals in the legal category, the legal procurement trade organisation *Buying Legal Council* (www.buyinglegal.com) estimates that today two-thirds of the *Fortune 500*, as well as a growing part of multinational companies, employ dedicated legal procurement professionals.

This chapter briefly discusses why procurement is involved and what changes for law firms when legal procurement is involved in selecting and managing law firms. It then suggests which requests for proposal (RFPs) – a popular procurement tool – you should compete for and reviews some best practices for winning RFPs. It also advises on what you and your firm should consider regarding the delivery of legal services and how best to partner with your clients. Many of the presented suggestions are taken from Buying Legal Council's *Legal Procurement Handbook*.

1. Why procurement?

In most companies, top management brings in legal procurement to apply business discipline to sourcing legal services and managing relationships with law firms. Legal spend has become a line item that few chief executive officers (CEOs) and chief financial officers (CFOs) can ignore. According to studies of the Buying Legal Council, the main drivers to bring in procurement are the desire to:

- manage cost/reducing supplier spend;
- ensure that the company buys goods and services in compliance with company policies;
- make sure that the company gets good products and services from reputable suppliers;
- achieve more objective comparisons of legal service providers through measuring and benchmarking outside counsel's value;
- streamline operations;
- improve efficiencies;
- find better ways to structure fee arrangements;
- budget more reliably; and
- increase predictability and transparency.

Why legal procurement? Could the legal department itself not apply business discipline? Yes. However, many CEOs and CFOs believe that the legal department benefits from procurement's core competencies in getting better value from its suppliers. Top management is convinced that legal procurement can make value-added contributions that go beyond what any functional department like legal could accomplish by itself. Involving procurement in the sourcing of services has worked in other functional areas and there is no reason to believe that this will not hold true for legal.

Pharmaceutical companies, financial services institutions and other highly regulated industries such as energy and utilities were among the first to embrace legal procurement. Long before companies with significant legal spend started to involve legal procurement in the early/mid 2000s (the earliest legal procurement activities date back to the mid/late 1990s), procurement started sourcing other complex functional areas. Procurement's involvement significantly changed the way that these professional services are bought. Procurement got involved in sourcing engineering and architectural services in the late 1980s, marketing, public relations and advertising services in the mid/late 1990s, accounting, auditing and tax services in the early/mid 2000s. Each professional service area was reportedly appalled by the notion of procurement sourcing their respective area. The reaction was similar to those of lawyers today: "How can procurement possibly know anything about [engineering/creativity/etc]? This is ruining our profession." Despite the protests, it is common for procurement to be involved in sourcing these professional services today. It is unlikely that it will be any different for legal services. In other words, there is no evidence that would suggest that legal departments will once again choose law firms without any involvement from procurement. There is no 'back to normal': this is the new normal.

Not everything is entirely new, though: legal departments have been using some procurement tools for over two decades. For example, chemical giant DuPont spearheaded the convergence trend in legal services back in 1992. Many legal departments have since adopted the DuPont Model. It is based on the ideas of reducing the number of suppliers to facilitate management of outside counsel and increasing purchasing power to obtain lower rates from outside counsel. According to the model's website (www.dupontlegalmodel.com), the "DuPont Model has provided a solid, dynamic, integrated approach to providing services to the DuPont Company since 1992. The Legal Model's competitive edge has been derived by applying business discipline to the practice of law." The recurring key word is the application of business discipline to legal services.

Most multinational corporations today have business people involved in selecting and managing outside counsel. Law firms are advised to adjust their marketing and business development accordingly. Many law firms have hired business people such as pricing directors, as well as process improvement and project management experts who are the natural counterparts for procurement.

Lawyers often lament procurement's lack of understanding of the legal profession's complexity and idiosyncrasies. It is certainly true that the sophistication and effectiveness of legal procurement is influenced by the maturity and experience of the procurement professionals involved, their awareness and understanding of the distinction of legal services and of the quality of the legal work product. As legal procurement is becoming more common, however, it will be less and less of an issue. It is also influenced by the way procurement professionals are being measured and rewarded, and by the level of collaboration between the company's procurement professionals and in-house lawyers. Needless to say, there is still a lot to be done and improved, but the trend appears to be favouring more collaboration: when consulting firm Altman Weil asked chief legal officers for its 2010 *Chief Legal Officer Survey*: "Are procurement/purchasing/strategic sourcing professionals in your corporation involved in outside counsel selection decisions?", 81.4% answered "never", 17.4% said "sometimes", and 1.2% answered "always". By contrast, in 2014 73.9% answered "never," 16.6% "sometimes", 3.6% "usually" and 5.9% "always". This is a significant shift for companies to include procurement in the sourcing of legal services and promises rapid growth in the future.

Often without dedicated human resources for legal procurement, some companies have started to hire specialised consultants to help manage legal spend. How legal procurement consultants support corporate clients can vary, however, they can bring tested procurement methodologies successfully applied elsewhere (usually in other complex/professional services), as well as procurement tools customised for the legal marketplace. There is even talk of legal procurement consortiums to achieve greater buying power and lower spend.

2.   Working with procurement: what should law firms do?

What should law firms do when their clients and prospects involve procurement? I can suggest a few different ways, including partnering with clients, focusing on the delivery of legal services, careful planning and scoping of legal work. First, let us discuss best practices for RFPs. RFPs are now commonly used for legal services, in particular when legal procurement is involved in the purchasing decision. RFPs can be used to select firms for a panel or individual matters. While legal procurement managers may not be the final decision-makers when selecting law firms and typically do not award a contract or assignment to a firm single-handedly, they unquestionably can disqualify or promote your firm at different stages, in particular early on. So how can you maximise your firm's chances to win RFPs?

2.1 Which RFPs are worth competing for?

The first step is to decide which RPFs to participate in and how best to compete in the RFPs. You are advised to qualify rigorously and not feel compelled to participate in every RFP that your firm receives. Establish very clear rules about which RFPs you want to participate in and stick to your rules. In his article "Bidding to win: six winning moves" in the *Legal Procurement Handbook*, bidding expert John de Forte warns that you should not waste resources on RFPs which you cannot win or which are unsuitable for you and your firm. Focusing on the most appropriate opportunities is critical to achieving and maintaining a decent win rate. For example, do not hesitate to decline to participate in an RFP if you have no existing relationship with the organisation issuing the RFP and the opportunity at hand does not appear to be a good fit, and/or if you have no access to forge a relationship with procurement, preventing you from developing a proper understanding of the opportunity.

Again, be sure to formulate a clear qualifying policy and get everyone in the firm to adhere to this policy. De Forte warns that if the qualifying criteria are too vague, they will be easy to overlook and ignore. If they are too rigid, fee earners will say that bureaucracy stifles their entrepreneurial spirit. De Forte recommends applying four qualifying tests before jumping on the next RFP opportunity. He believes that you should participate in an RFP only if it passed all four tests:

- The strategic test: does the opportunity fit your firm and will it advance your growth strategy? Is the work offered in the RFP your core business? Is it in your target (industry) sector? Is the client issuing the RFP your target client? Proceed only if the answers to these questions are "yes".
- The tactical test: do you have an existing relationship with the client? Do you have access to the client during the RFP? Do you think you are competitive price-wise for the work at hand? Some RFPs are effectively tire-kicking exercises: the company issues an RFP to test the market and to understand current prices better, without necessarily intending to change its current providers. If you have an inkling that this may be the case, you may want to think twice about participating in that RFP 'opportunity'.
- The logistical test: do you have the resources available for the work offered in the RFP? In other words, do you have enough capacity or bench-depth to do a good job? Do you have the resources for participating in the RFP itself? Do you have enough and the right people to handle it?
- The commercial test: does competing in the RFP make good business sense for your firm? Calculate whether the RFP opportunity is likely to be profitable. In fact, you should consider measuring your return on investment for RFPs in general. It will help you decide which pursuits merit your attention and how best to deploy your resources. To do this, take into account the estimated contract value (how much money will the client pay

you over the life of the matter?), your opportunity cost (how much could the team you are likely to propose make on other engagements?), intangible benefits (how else does your firm benefit from taking on this client or this matter? Does it gain in prestige? Does it get additional, valuable insight from the work? Will it help attract other clients or laterals?), as well as overhead cost attributable to the work. Also understand the risks involved and consider your costs for participating in the RFP. You can quantify the cost of participation in the RFP by quantifying the number of hours your fee earners and staff spend on the RFP multiplied by their hourly rates appropriately discounted to reflect current utilisation levels. Add to this the contribution of the firm's pitch department – business development and pricing professionals – expressed as an hourly rate based on overhead cost plus any hard costs (eg, design and print cost or consultants' fees). The value of a winning tender can be treated as the estimated fee income that will accrue as a result of it over a one-year period. If the assignment is a recurring or long-term appointment, you can multiply this figure (but it is best to do so on a reasonably conservative basis).

According to de Forte, many lawyers have a tendency to chase too many targets without being clear about what makes most strategic sense. Full-service firms are often more prone to skip careful qualifying than boutique firms, in his experience. Participating in all RFPs can lead to wasting time and resources. As mentioned before, it is useful to calculate the return on investment of your RFP participation. Track the time and resources involved in your RFP. You might be surprised by how much money your firm spends on answering RFPs.

2.2   How to win RFPs

Once you decide to participate in an RFP, what will enhance your chances for winning? Business development professional Melania Wenstrup shares best practices in her article "Bidding to win: Before, during, and after the RFP process" in the *Legal Procurement Handbook*.

Before the client issues the RFP: According to Wenstrup, clients usually signal large-scale opportunities long before they issue an RFP. To be able to pick up the information, it is important to build a relationship with procurement and not just interact with them during an RFP. Get to know your clients' and prospects' procurement teams. You should see procurement as your partner, not your adversary, recommends Wenstrup.

Make an effort to get to know your key clients' and prospects' legal procurement team. Learn how they evaluate law firms. How do their criteria differ from the company's in-house counsel's criteria? Understand how procurement's involvement drives the client's purchasing strategies. If at all possible, help procurement managers define the business requirements for a given legal situation and make suggestions regarding the parameters of the specification before an RFP is issued. Demonstrate your understanding of their organisations' internal and external environment, and inform the legal procurement team about relevant changes in the law, particularly as it pertains to their industry. Arrange meetings to discuss developments in their business and make sure that your informal relationships are fresh in case you are not allowed to contact those involved in the RFP when a new RFP is issued.

When preparing the written material for the RFP, aim to create tailored propositions that show the business side of your approach, rather than creating a credentialing brochure. Clients and prospects expect the RFP to be tailored to their organisation's requirements. You and your partners will need to invest time in thinking through the issues affecting the client and developing a response that specifically addresses these issues. This highlights the importance of having an existing relationship with the organisation, or at least access to decision-makers during the RFP: without a genuine understanding of the organisations' objectives, the expectations that it has of its legal advisers, the issues and challenges that it faces, you cannot develop the necessary tailored RFP answers.

It is important that you understand the client's or prospect's assumptions and are clear about the scope of work: delivering legal services in a high-quality but cost-effective way requires careful planning and scoping of matters. So what does legal procurement expect from you? What do they see as important parts of the matter at hand? What do they think they are purchasing from you? What are their assumptions? Both you and the client or prospect have to agree on what happens when the situation presented in the RFP changes significantly. Will it still be covered under the current agreement? Also, what is the outcome that the client desires? You will need to know this to be able to set a robust budget. Clients today expect firms not only to come up with a number, but also to be able to explain the number that they present. In addition, understand how your client or prospect perceives the work: is it bet-the-company type work, commodity work or somewhere in-between? Do they believe that many law firms or other legal service providers could get the job done? Naturally, commodity work is significantly more price sensitive than bet-the-company type of work. Also, what is at stake for the client?

Also find out what procurement is trying to achieve with the RFP. Procurement's goals may differ significantly from the legal department's goals. But beware, you cannot assume that procurement is only about price reduction and the legal department is only about the legal advice irrespective of the cost. Other than 'winning the matter' or 'closing the deal', what is the main driver for the client choosing the firm? Is it absolute cost? Is it value for money? 'Value' is often referred to in RFPs, but what 'value' actually means may not be well defined. It can mean different things to different clients, but typically it is about the right balance between price and quality. When you participate in the RFP, ensure that you understand how to articulate the value that you offer to your clients and prospects. Wenstrup recommends doing this by discussing the idea of value with your client or prospect and articulating tangible examples of value that you offer. How can you showcase how you offered value to other clients or prospects in the past? Perhaps offer your client or prospect a visit of your offices to give them a feel for how you and your team operate. Also try to quantify the economic benefits of your quality. To be able to do this, you need to discuss with your clients what it is exactly that they measure.

Although cost will likely be critical when dealing with procurement, there will be other key drivers. Ask procurement questions so that you can demonstrate how your RFP will help them achieve their goals. For example, what if procurement is looking for service quality? Aim to help procurement benchmark your quality against other firms. Quantify the economic benefits of your quality and convert this to what is meaningful to procurement. Communicate in a way that works for procurement. What's more, offer sample key performance indicators for quality. If the client or prospect focuses on risk management or mitigation, offer a review of draft terms early on, consider an umbrella services agreement to apply to all contracts between you and the client or prospect, and offer procurement a direct link to your contracts team.

You will also need to understand your own cost basis, as well as market prices. Understand whether you and your firm are truly competitive. What areas do you want to focus on? What margins are you striving for? How good is the opportunity that the client or prospect is presenting you? If necessary, are you prepared to accept a narrower margin in exchange for other concessions or do you have the confidence to walk away and focus on opportunities with higher returns?

What would also increase your chances of winning the RFP is using 'price-to-win' (PTW) methods, believes bidding expert de Forte. He stresses that you need to have a clear conception of what the winning price will be. Companies bidding for large contracts in the defence, IT and outsourcing sectors have adopted PTW. It is now increasingly used in professional services. PTW involves in-depth competitor analysis, including pricing estimates based on competitors' past performance and likely approach to the solution. A common technique is the appointment of a 'black hat' team to second-guess competitors' pricing strategy. Another critical element is setting work-streams a price target and incentivising them to undershoot it. Using the PTW approach, firms need to adjust the way that they allocate bid resources. De Forte suggests that firms should spend at least 10% of the overall budget on competitor analysis and a similar amount on strategic pricing.

To achieve the best results when bidding, involve a partner experienced in RFPs to act as a counsellor who is not part of the proposed team. His role is to provide a more objective and independent perspective on all key decisions, including the selection of the leader and other members of the service team, proposing the fees, and whether to proceed with the bid in the first place. Presentation teams should rehearse in front of the counselling partner and others not involved in the RFP. Their primary role is to ensure that the team comes across as a cohesive, unified unit – something which may be difficult to judge for the team itself, but will have a great impact when presenting to the client.

During the RFP: Procurement typically aims to ensure a level playing field among bidders. They do so by providing the same level of access to decision-makers and sharing the same information with all bidders. New firms should have the same chance of winning as incumbents. Do not try to circumvent legal procurement to get a leg-up with the legal department. This approach can badly backfire and you might get disqualified from the RFP.

When you fill in the RFP document, make sure that you answer every element of the question. Even if you believe that you have answered a question already in an earlier section, never cross-refer to other answers. ("As answered in question 33 above…" is not the way to go.) Be patient and answer it again. Keep in mind that different sections of the RFP may be read by different people who may or may not have access to all your RFP answers. It is also possible that the questions are similar only at first glance. Try to understand what nuance the client or prospect is looking for. Always stick to the format that your client or prospect provides. If the RFP requires you to put your response in the client's template, use their template and do not change it in any way. Provide evidence to back up what you are stating in the RFP (we will discuss this further in the section on delivering the service, project management and process improvement). Showcasing examples and providing evidence will likely distinguish you from your competitors and makes the evaluators feel less subjective when scoring your submission (and hopefully more likely to give you a higher score). Do you have examples or case studies of how you helped a client with a similar issue? If so, say so. Pay attention to word limits (which may include wording on diagrams) and do not try to trick the system by adding long attachments. It is possible that they will not be looked at and/or that you receive negative points for not following the outline. In brief, colour within the lines when participating in the RFP.

During the RFP process, Wenstrup recommends that you:

- get your pitch teams in touch with procurement (unless the RFP itself prohibits it). Make an effort to ensure that your client or prospect understands the value that you and your firm can add and how your service is different from your competitors';
- be a resource for procurement, be collaborative and understand procurement's challenges (not just that they need financial quantification), and help them with their issues and challenges;
- put yourself in legal procurement's shoes given the situation at hand (what would you like/dislike from your suppliers? What would you expect from them?); and
- uncover what legal procurement is really trying to achieve and the challenges hindering them from realising these goals.

After the RFP: You won the matter/the panel place? Congratulations! Do you know what made them choose you? If you did not win, do you know why you lost? Whether you lost or won, it is important to find out why. Seek feedback from legal procurement and communicate that you want to be true partners. Most procurement teams are more than willing to give firms feedback on RFP participation. They know that it is the best way to improve the quality of future RFPs.

It would be wrong to assume that if the firm is not appointed, the exercise has been of no value. Apart from likely training benefits (RFP participation gives your team experience and improves their pitching skills), a decent bidding performance may be the building block for winning work from the organisation next time. Anything that you can glean from legal procurement's scoring process and any marginal elements of the decision can help you pitch more effectively next time. Cultivate relationships with your client's and prospect's legal procurement teams and ensure that they receive invitations to knowledge-sharing events, relevant publications, newsletters and any trends and issues that are critical to their success.

3. Delivery of legal services

Let us now talk about the delivery of legal services. As mentioned before, procurement's involvement in the sourcing of legal services is about applying business discipline to all parts of the organisation, including the legal department. Using tools like Lean Sigma, project management and process improvement helps demonstrate your firm's commitment to efficiency, quality and continuous improvement. 'Project management' is a role and skill set that ensures that for a particular engagement, we use our best process appropriately and actively manage schedules, staff and deliverables throughout this matter. It ensures that everything is on track, delivered how and when the client expects it. Processes are the way law firms can create and deliver value to their clients. They embody the knowledge of the law firm, department, practice group or team.

In her article "Deliver value through Legal Lean Sigma & project management" published in the *Legal Procurement Handbook*, Catherine Alman MacDonagh says that, ideally, a firm's processes should be based on best practice. As today's best practice may not be tomorrow's best practice, firms should use process improvement to ensure efficiency, excellent quality of work and service, high probability of successful outcomes and predictability.

Using a process-driven approach also gives firms a sense of how much effort it takes to deliver a particular kind of work. This information is essential for pricing exercises that legal procurement often requires. Clients, in particular legal procurement, expect firms to be able to put a price tag on matters, as well as on different phases of a matter. MacDonagh says that from the client's perspective, "it is inconsistent to be told that a firm has decades of deep experience handling a particular kind of matter and then in the next breath have it explained that there is no possible way to predict how long something should take, the costs and impacts of what could happen at each step, and how much the whole project will cost".

In addition to project management and process improvement that help manage the work and determine the best way to carry it out, law firms can also use other tools like Lean and Six Sigma to make themselves more appealing to legal procurement when pitching for work.

Lean centres on lowering cost. Developed by Toyota in the 1980s, it focuses on eliminating waste, on making obvious what adds value by reducing everything else. It accomplishes this through simplifying processes, reducing waste – that is, the number of steps – maximising process speed and improving productivity. In brief, Lean is about doing the right things. While it was designed for manufacturing, the idea has been successfully applied to legal and other professional services.

Six Sigma is a set of techniques and tools for process improvement that Motorola developed in 1986. A six-sigma process is one in which 99.99966% of all opportunities to produce some feature of a part are statistically expected to be free of defects. Motorola set a goal of six sigma for all of its manufacturing operations, and this goal became a byword for the management and engineering practices used to achieve it. Six Sigma is about creating quality standards and optimising one's output through reducing and controlling variation. The idea of Six Sigma is to have best practices for doing things rather than treating every matter as an entirely unique situation. In brief, Six Sigma is about doing things right.

The combination, Lean Sigma, is about deciding the best way to do something and then always doing those things correctly. To use Lean Sigma correctly, your firm needs to understand which activities your clients see as value-adding – that is, something the client is willing to pay for – rather than non-value-adding – that is, activities that take time and resources, but do not create additional value for the client.

According to MacDonagh, firms who have employed tools like Lean and/or Six Sigma experienced that most of their processes can be improved and fall short of their potential. Improving these processes will benefit both the client and the firm.

What's more, the above tools will provide you and your firm with metrics and results that you can communicate to your clients and prospects, and are particularly popular with procurement professionals. You will be able to differentiate yourself from your competitors by showing how you approach complex matters efficiently and effectively, and how you are able to add value to their business.

MacDonagh says that firms that ignore Lean, Six Sigma, process improvement, project management and other efficiency tools do so at their own peril, particularly when procurement is involved in the purchasing process. She believes that clients can see immediately whether a firm is serious about cost containment, efficiency and being the best value provider for its clients. She reminds that firms able to demonstrate their efficiency to a client are significantly more compelling than firms that merely tell the client about their efficiency. Procurement professionals want to see evidence.

Pioneering firms started to embrace these efficiency tools in the mid 2000s. They now have robust programmes with teams of Lean and Six Sigma practitioners, and skilled project managers, as well as many completed projects that showcase critical improvement benefits and savings for their clients. In addition, says MacDonagh, these firms can speak the language of continuous improvement with their clients, many of whom have employed the methodologies for years and have cultures in which Lean Sigma plays a central role. Many clients today ask firms to describe their project management, process improvement and Lean and/or Six Sigma programmes in their RFPs. They want to know what the firms do to become more efficient and expect firms to provide recommendations as to how they can help the client. As the use of these tools is increasingly prevalent among firms, not using them and hence not being about to show the use of efficiency tools may quickly disqualify a firm: think of an RFP response that is a cobbled-together paragraph of text about how efficient a firm is compared to another firm's response that contains a clear approach with specific metrics, graphs and process maps. Procurement professionals typically are process experts and many are certified in project management and process improvement themselves. They appreciate the benefits that these tools bring and have trouble believing that any firm can operate efficiently without using the tools.

Here are examples of questions clients may ask. You may have come across similar questions in recent RFPs in which you participated. What is your firm's answer?

- We are interested in your ideas on the topics of cost reduction, transparency and efficiency.
- What changes could [Company] implement to make your work for us more cost-efficient?
- Please describe your approach to process improvement and project management.
- We ask you to illustrate how your firm ensures the highest quality outcome for our matters while guaranteeing the most efficient use of our resources.
- How do you measure your performance against our business requirements?
- Our company uses process improvement methodologies such as Six Sigma and Lean. We expect our suppliers to use equally efficient techniques. Please explain your firm's methodologies.

By learning and adopting Lean Sigma tools, firms can have discussions with procurement about the steps, milestones, variables, key deliverables and decision points that can be anticipated at different stages. To win an RFP and keep work when procurement is involved, firms must be able to make a compelling case that includes detailed and ongoing analysis of accurate and timely data, as well as a comprehensive exploration of processes. The goal is to establish processes that employ the lowest cost resources which are capable of doing each task in a way that delivers exactly what the client wants, when and how the client wants it.

## 4.	Partnering with clients

To ensure ongoing success, law firms are advised to develop stable, long-term relationships with their clients and focus on real teamwork and cooperation. In her article "Procurement & outside counsel: The benefits of partnering" from the *Legal Procurement Handbook*, Colleen Nihill suggests partnering with clients throughout the legal engagement lifecycle: beyond the RFP process, from the initial risk assessment, to negotiation and budget preparation, to the post-mortem relationship review.

For example, companies regularly undergo internal risk assessments to mitigate issues that could adversely affect corporate performance, such as regulatory, reputational, human resources-related and technology-related issues. Nihill suggests that law firms partner with their clients and add valuable input by helping clients identify both business and legal risks. They can do this as long as they are real partners and understand the business and culture of the client. Nihill believes that partnering on risk assessment benefits both procurement and outside counsel by:

- identifying potential risks and constraints to set reasonable expectations;
- providing an action plan for unforeseen events;
- identifying impact of successful and unsuccessful results; and
- providing a foundation for better future decision making.

Law firms can take a step towards partnering by closely working with their clients to anticipate clients' needs. Discussions with clients should centre on the delivery of the legal service, such as a summary of the project objectives, scope of work, key members of the legal team, a communication schedule, provisions for change requests, as well as feedback mechanisms and timing. Defining business goals and objectives help better inform legal strategy. Establishing the scope of work, key deliverables, timeline expected results are necessary to put together the most appropriate legal team and to set fee arrangements that reflect value and encourage a trusted relationship.

If designed correctly, a budget should reflect the costs associated with the legal engagement, as well as the type of fee arrangement that best encompasses the company's cost management rationale, according to Nihill. Poorly designed budgets do not take into account the business problem that the client is trying to solve. Firms must understand whether a client is interested in a litigation strategy that favours early case settlement or whether the client pursues a strategy to win at all costs, even if that includes a (possibly) long drawn-out discovery period to strengthen their position. Without such information, the firm cannot properly compose the team and project the timeframes for each phase of the matter. Additionally, taking into account the strategic objectives enables the budget to become the basis of a detailed project plan.

Nihill also recommends regularly conducting relationship reviews. Firms should use scorecards that include both quantitative and qualitative metrics to assess the relationship with a client properly. To avoid surprises, it is critical to identify and solve problems immediately. Do not wait, she commends, but conduct relationship post-mortems on each project of a predetermined size in addition to conducting a general performance review. For longer cases, (semi) annual reviews or reviews after reaching certain milestones may be more useful than (just) post-mortems. It enables the firm to identify quickly positive results and gaps, and allows outside counsel to adjust its course if the outcome is less stellar than anticipated.

5.   Conclusion

Legal procurement is not going away. It is part of the new legal industry make-up. Its business approach to selecting and managing law firms challenges law firms to deliver legal services in a cost-conscious, efficient way, and requires increased business discipline from law firms. Legal procurement expects law firms to do more than provide quality legal advice. They must add value to the client's business and the overall effectiveness and efficiency of the client's legal function.

You and your firm are well advised not to ignore the existence of legal procurement, but address the challenge of reconnecting value to costs for legal services. It is wise to get started now, before all your competitors have followed suit and you no longer have a competitive advantage. If you have not already done so, consider hiring experienced business development, pricing and project managers to work as your counterparts for legal procurement. Your firm will look eye-to-eye with your clients' and prospects' legal procurement professionals.

The marketing and advertising of legal services

Coordinators and editors:
Martin E Kovnats
Rachel T McGuckian
Carlos Valls Martinez
Professional Ethics Committee of the International Bar Association

This chapter contains responses to a survey on the regulation of marketing and advertising legal services from 13 countries around the globe. The participating jurisdictions include countries from Asia, Europe, Oceania, North America and South America, with roughly half of the countries basing their legal system on common law and the other half on civil law. The International Bar Association's (IBA) main objective behind the survey is to create a resource that includes a comprehensive comparison of how different countries around the world regulate the marketing and advertising of legal services, all in one place. This survey is particularly timely, given the many different ways of advertising that are being created around the world and which are being used to great effect by lawyers.

The questions posed to the contributors from each jurisdiction included queries on the regulation of lawyers' activities, generally, as well as more specific questions concerning certain types of marketing, such as handing out branded materials to clients or prospective clients. The answers varied greatly between jurisdictions; however, a few trends emerged once all the responses were compiled.

Interestingly, virtually none of the jurisdictions surveyed have legislation, rules or specific guidelines dealing with different treatment for advertising and marketing through old or new media. Some jurisdictions, like Canada, vary their rules for certain types of online marketing. However, by and large, the jurisdictions' general marketing rules and/or guidelines cover all forms of advertising, regardless of the medium. It will be interesting to see if this type of blanket regulation changes as new media, such as Twitter and Facebook, continue to develop and grow in popularity. The advertising rules have been changing in the past decades, from being an activity severely regulated, or even prohibited, to being in most jurisdictions fairly liberalised, with certain restrictions. India still maintains an extensive ban on lawyers' publicity – an important exception. Some jurisdictions, such as Brazil, explicitly specify what forms of advertising and marketing of legal services are banned, while most jurisdictions simply provide guiding principles to be applied to marketing and advertising materials.

In regards to questions referring to specific forms of advertising, such as that which includes references to past successes or explicit prices for services, the results were also mixed. Brazil and India bar both of the above methods of advertising, while Australia, Canada, Chile, Panama, and England and Wales allow references to prices or past successes in ads – though with certain restrictions and qualifications. Argentina, Japan, Spain, Luxembourg and Paraguay bar only one of the above methods, while permitting the other. It appears more difficult to provide complete responses to these questions for the United States, as the rules and regulations can vary greatly from state to state.

Most jurisdictions allow for lawyers or law firms to give out branded material to clients or potential clients, although many qualify the ability to do so by stating that such promotional materials should not be misleading. Some jurisdictions have no rules or regulations regarding this type of marketing at all.

The strictest jurisdictions surveyed concerning the advertising and marketing of legal services appear to be India, and then Brazil, while many countries connected with the Commonwealth appear to be more liberal in approach, yet with more detailed regulations (United Kingdom, Canada). By contrast, many civil law jurisdictions, which have more generally drafted and principle-oriented rules, seem also to follow a deregulating path but with less detailed rules and a more principled approach. Perhaps the most relaxed jurisdiction surveyed is Paraguay, which has few explicit rules or regulations regarding the advertising and marketing of legal services. Overall, apart from providing protection to prospective clients by requiring the content not to be misleading, or stopping marketing in distress situations (eg, Spain banning soliciting work at funerals or accidents), there is a general call for preserving the dignity of the profession. For example, there is a reported case in Brazil where publicity using glasses for marketing was reprimanded, as it was associated with drinking, which was considered to violate the seriousness of the profession. Perhaps the jurisdiction that makes the loftiest and more inspirational call is Luxembourg, when it requires "the dignity, the delicacy and the probity" of the profession to be upheld in advertising.

The editors of this chapter considered including an analysis as to how the range of restrictions of marketing for the legal profession may have developed in various jurisdictions worldwide. We wondered whether there were trends that might be discerned between common law and civil law jurisdictions, or between developing countries and developed countries, whether there was a linkage or causation regarding restrictions or limits between countries where foreign, or global, firms are permitted and those jurisdictions where such firms are not permitted. Are marketing restrictions or limitations aimed at protecting specific interests, and, if so, who or what is the target of that protection? Are there any trends with regard to which body regulates the marketing activity of the legal profession, as between the courts and law societies? Is one governing body more efficient than the other? More sophisticated than the other? More focused on client protection than the other? Make and enforce more and greater restrictions and limitations than the other? More susceptible to political or professional pressure than the other? Are there any trends to be discerned between jurisdictions where there is a concentration of ownership of media and other channels of marketing messages, and those jurisdictions where the ownership or control of channels of media and marketing are more diffuse? Does greater liberalisation of regulations associated with the marketing and publicity of law firms correspond to a more sophisticated legal system? Or does stricter regulation correspond with a more sophisticated legal system? The sample size of only 13 countries and space limitations in this chapter did not allow inquiry into these questions – although the three editors believe these and other questions to be important and interesting.

One thing seems to be clear in all jurisdictions: the behaviour of the legal profession in its promotion and publicity is a concern as it may affect the perception, and the confidence, of society in the legal sector.

1. Civil law countries

1.1 Argentina

1. **What is the basis for determining the rules governing professional activities in your jurisdictions?**
Is there a code of conduct promulgated by the profession? Is it a code of conduct promulgated by the courts?

Each province, as well as the City of Buenos Aires, has its own code of conduct. The code governing the activities of lawyers in the City of Buenos Aires is the Code of Ethics issued by the Bar of the Federal Capital (*Colegio Público de Abogados de la Capital Federal*, or CPACF).

In the province of Buenos Aires, the bar of each of the different departments into which the province is divided – for judicial purposes – has disciplinary authority over the lawyers registered and practising within that jurisdiction. Nevertheless, the different bars of the province apply the same code.

As the CPACF Code of Ethics was enacted almost 30 years ago, there is a consensus within the legal community that it should be amended both to reflect the new daily realities of the profession, as well as the new technologies, and to relax the strict two-year statute of limitation.

2. **Who enforces the code of conduct?**
Is enforcement commenced by regulatory/court authority in response to a complaint? Is the enforcement commenced by the regulatory/court authority upon its own instigation?

The CPACF Disciplinary Court enforces the Code of Ethics. Its decisions are however subject to appeal to the Federal Administrative Courts of Justice of the City of Buenos Aires.

Enforcement may be commenced through a complaint, by lawyers regarding their own conduct or by the Disciplinary Court.

In practice, the Disciplinary Court acts following complaints filed by clients against their lawyers. Complaints may be filed against a law firm, in which case the court has to pursue the case against the professional or professionals employed by the firm. Many complaints allege misleading advertising, or because the success and/or also a short timeframe to obtain results are guaranteed (eg, releases from prison in one day).

3. **Does your jurisdiction have rules regarding advertising and marketing by members of the profession?**

Yes – a number of specific provisions exist, including the prohibition:

- to post advertisements that contain misleading information;
- to offer benefits that are in violation of the laws in force, or violate professional ethics; and
- to use, whether directly or indirectly, paid intermediaries to obtain clients.

Other provisions exist in relation to more general terms – for instance, to compel lawyers to refrain from advertising their legal services without observing the moderation, seemliness and dignity of the profession.

As a general rule, institutional advertisements are allowed. The Court of Discipline will consider the purpose of the advertisement.

4. **Are members of the profession allowed to publicise historic success?**

It is allowed with certain restrictions. Court rulings that are subject to an appeal can be publicised, as long as the fact that they are not final is made clear. Moreover, confidentiality law and professional secrets must be in all cases observed, unless expressly waived by the client and/or all interested parties.

5. **Are members of the profession in your jurisdiction permitted to advertise fee arrangements?**

No. Advertising fee arrangements is expressly forbidden (Article 10(f) of the Code of Conduct).

6. **Are members of your profession in your jurisdiction permitted to market – for example, using social arrangements or giving away branded materials?**

Yes, but as a general rule these marketing practices will have to observe the moderation, seemliness and dignity of the profession.

7. **What are the potential consequences for breaching the rules and/or guidelines? Suspension, fine, disbarment?**

Sanctions for breaching the rules are as follows:

- a warning;
- a warning in the presence of the managing board of the Bar;
- fines (limited to the salary of a civil judge of first instance);
- suspension of up to one year; and
- disbarment in serious cases.

8. **In a few paragraphs would you please describe the policies applicable to the rules/guidelines regarding members of the profession advertising in your jurisdiction?**

There are no other applicable policies. Nevertheless, the Disciplinary Court is becoming more open to considering the guidelines of other organisations, such as the Buenos Aires Bar (*Colegio de Abogados de la Ciudad de Buenos Aires*) and even the IBA.

1.2   Brazil

1. **What is the basis for determining the rules governing professional activities in your jurisdictions?**
   Is there a code of conduct promulgated by the profession? Is it a code of conduct promulgated by the courts?
   In Brazil, the Lawyers Statute governs the activities of lawyers.

   Rules applicable to lawyers are also enacted by the Federal Council of the Brazilian Bar and, within their respective jurisdictions, by the local chapters of the Brazilian Bar. The most important in respect of marketing activities is the Code of Conduct.

2. **Who enforces the code of conduct?**
   Is enforcement commenced by regulatory/court authority in response to a complaint? Is the enforcement commenced by the regulatory/court authority upon its own instigation?
   The local bar council with jurisdiction over the territory in which an infraction occurs has the power to punish the lawyer who commits it, except if it is committed before the Federal Council. The process may be commenced by the court authority upon its own instigation, by any other authority or by any interested party. The trial will be conducted by the local Tribunal of Ethics and Discipline. In certain cases, appeals may be heard by the Federal Council of the Brazilian Bar.

3. **Does your jurisdiction have rules regarding advertising and marketing by members of the profession?**
   Yes. The main rules regarding advertising and marketing by lawyers and law firms are contained in the Code of Conduct, mentioned above, and in what is known as *Provimento 94* (Regulation 94).

4. **Are members of the profession allowed to publicise historic success?**
   No. Lawyers are not allowed to publicise historic success.

5. **Are members of the profession in your jurisdiction permitted to advertise fee arrangements?**
   No. Lawyers may not advertise fee arrangements.

6. **Are members of your profession in your jurisdiction permitted to market – for example using social arrangements or giving away branded materials?**
   The advertising rules do not address marketing using social arrangements or the giving away of branded materials. A local Tribunal of Ethics and Discipline has held that the giving away of branded trinkets to clients does not violate the principles of ethical conduct, as long as it is moderate and limited to clients and co-workers, and includes no contact information (telephone number, address or email). However, the giving away of drinking glasses was considered to violate the ethical principles and the seriousness of the profession.

7. **What are the potential consequences for breaching the rules and/or guidelines? Suspension, fine, disbarment?**

The penalties that may be imposed are reprimands, suspension and exclusion. Fines may be added to reprimands and suspension.

8. **In a few paragraphs would you please describe the policies applicable to the rules/guidelines regarding members of the profession advertising in your jurisdiction?**

The marketing of the lawyer's profession must be informative only and must be extremely plain and serious. In the lawyer's advertising or on the lawyer's business cards and office material which the lawyer uses, the lawyer must include his name or that of the law firm, and the bar admission number or numbers. The lawyer may make reference only to the academic degrees and the honours relating to his professional life, as well as the professional legal organisations of which the lawyer is a member, his areas of expertise, address, email, website, electronic page, QR [quick response] code, the firm's logo and the photograph of the offices, office hours and foreign languages spoken.

The sponsoring of events or publications of a scientific or cultural nature, as well as the release of bulletins, through physical or electronic means, on issues of interest to lawyers, is also permitted, as long as their circulation remains restricted to clients and interested persons within the legal area.

The Internet and telephones may be used as vehicles for advertising, including for the remittance of messages to specific addressees, as long as they do not imply an offer of services or constitute a form of attracting clients.

1.3 Chile

1. **What is the basis for determining the rules governing professional activities in your jurisdictions?**
Is there a code of conduct promulgated by the profession? Is it a code of conduct promulgated by the courts?

The bar associations, which are constituted in accordance with the law, shall be authorised to hear and determine the claims filed about the ethical conduct of its members. Interested parties may appeal the bar's resolutions before the Court of Appeals.

Articles 1 to 11 of the Code of Professional Ethics provide, among other things, that lawyers must:

- care for the honour and dignity of the profession;
- care for the institutions – lawyers must promote the trust and respect for the profession, the correct and efficient administration of justice and the validity and enforceability of the state of law;
- show loyalty towards their clients, while working with the clients' best interest in mind and respecting the clients' autonomy and dignity;
- act honestly, with integrity and in good faith, and not advise client to carry out fraudulent acts; and

- strictly respect their clients' confidentiality and require recognition for his right to professional secrecy (see Title IV of the code).

2. **Who enforces the code of conduct?**
   Is enforcement commenced by regulatory/court authority in response to a complaint? Is the enforcement commenced by the regulatory/court authority upon its own instigation?
   Various bodies, listed below, within the Chilean Bar Association play a role in the enforcement of the code:
   - the secretarial lawyer:
   - the instructor;
   - the vice president of the general counsel;
   - the Ethics Tribunal;
   - the Bar's general counsel; and
   - the Ethics Commission.

   The client has the inalienable right to file a claim against a lawyer's breach of professional ethics. Also, the lawyer who learns of a transgression of another lawyer is authorised to report it.

3. **Does your jurisdiction have rules regarding advertising and marketing by members of the profession?**
   Yes. Article 12 of the code provides that to build his clientele the lawyer may inform honestly and truthfully of his professional services. In particular, the lawyer is forbidden to:
   - promise results that do not depend exclusively on his professional conduct;
   - offer the use of means contrary to law;
   - imply that he has the ability to influence the authority personally or through third parties;
   - reveal privileged information;
   - inform the identity of his clients without their authorisation; or
   - rely on comparisons with other lawyers or firms founded on an unsubstantiated basis.

4. **Are members of the profession allowed to publicise historic success?**
   Yes. To build his clientele, the lawyer is authorised to inform honestly and truthfully of his professional services, which would include his historic success, so long as confidentiality is respected.

5. **Are members of the profession in your jurisdiction permitted to advertise fee arrangements?**
   While there are no express prohibitions on this matter, it is not generally done by lawyers.

6. **Are members of your profession in your jurisdiction permitted to market – for example, using social arrangements or giving away branded materials?**

There are no express prohibitions on this matter, other than what is stipulated regarding the direct or indirect solicitation of clients.

7. **What are the potential consequences for breaching the rules and/or guidelines? Suspension, fine, disbarment?**

The disciplinary measures available to the Chilean Bar Association are an oral reprimand, a written censure, a fine, suspension of the collegiate lawyer's rights and disbarment.

However, legal penalties may also apply if a lawyer breaches his duties as such, especially his confidentiality obligation towards his client.

8. **In a few paragraphs would you please describe the policies applicable to the rules/ guidelines regarding members of the profession advertising in your jurisdiction?**

Specifically regarding members of the profession advertising in our jurisdiction, the general policy applied is established in Article 12 of the code, which, as indicated above, requires lawyers who wish to advertise their professional services to inform their potential clients honestly and truthfully of their professional services. Moreover, Article 12 introduced several prohibitions on marketing for lawyers, in addition to the general prohibition of solicitation (see question 3 above).

1.4 Japan

1. **What is the basis for determining the rules governing professional activities in your jurisdictions?**

Is there a code of conduct promulgated by the profession? Is it a code of conduct promulgated by the courts?

Professional activities are governed by the rules promulgated by the Japan Federation of Bar Associations (JFBA) and the local bar associations. The JFBA is formed by practising attorneys and local bar associations in Japan. They enjoy a high degree of self-governance. They examine the qualifications of, and take disciplinary action against, attorneys and their activities. The activities of practising attorneys do not fall under the supervision of the courts, public prosecutors or administrative institutions. The JFBA also promulgates the Basic Rules on the Duties of Practising Attorneys to define both a code of ethics and a code of conduct for attorneys.

2. **Who enforces the code of conduct?**

Is enforcement commenced by regulatory/court authority in response to a complaint? Is the enforcement commenced by the regulatory/court authority upon its own instigation?

The code of conduct is enforced by the local bar associations and the JFBA. While practising attorneys in Japan do not fall under the supervision of the courts or any other government power, they are required to submit to the disciplinary authority of their local bar associations and the JFBA.

Attorneys are not allowed to practise law unless registered with both the JFBA and a relevant local bar association. Anyone may file a complaint against an attorney for disciplinary action with the local bar association to which the practising attorney belongs. When a complaint is filed, the bar association is obligated to initiate disciplinary procedures and have the matter investigated.

3. **Does your jurisdiction have rules regarding advertising and marketing by members of the profession?**
Yes. Advertising by practising attorneys is subject to the JFBA Rules on Attorneys' Advertisement. The JFBA also publishes the guidelines regarding the interpretation of the rules.

4. **Are members of the profession allowed to publicise historic success?**
Publicising a success rate is specifically prohibited. The publication of other descriptions of historic success will also be prohibited if they are inaccurate, misleading, disgraceful or otherwise against the laws and rules of the bar associations.

5. **Are members of the profession in your jurisdiction permitted to advertise fee arrangements?**
Generally, an accurate description of fee arrangements in an advertisement is not prohibited. Vague, inaccurate or incomplete reference to fee arrangements will likely fall within the scope of prohibited advertisements. For example, a statement such as 'we are prepared to offer a discount' is prohibited because it can be misleading.

6. **Are members of your profession in your jurisdiction permitted to market – for example, using social arrangements or giving away branded materials?**
No, except to the extent that they are socially accepted out of courtesy. For example, giving a calendar (featuring a firm's name) as a year-end gift to existing clients will likely be permissible. Giving existing clients a pre-paid card (featuring a firm's name) as a mark of the firm's 20th anniversary will likely be fine. Handing out such pre-paid card regularly to clients or on the street to passers-by is very likely prohibited.

7. **What are the potential consequences for breaching the rules and/or guidelines? Suspension, fine, disbarment?**
A bar association may order a member attorney in breach of the Rules on Attorneys' Advertisement to cease the activity, rectify the breach or take other appropriate measures to prevent recurrence of a breach.

A breach of the rules can also result in disciplinary sanctions. Four types of disciplinary sanction can be imposed:
- disbarment (loss of qualification for a period of three years);
- order to withdraw from the bar association (loss of status);
- suspension from the practice of law for up to two years (no impact on status or qualifications); and
- reprimand (no impact on status or qualifications).

8.   **In a few paragraphs would you please describe the policies applicable to the rules/guidelines regarding members of the profession advertising in your jurisdiction?**

Attorneys' advertisement used to be prohibited generally (permitted only under specified limited circumstances). Today, the general principle is that a practising attorney may advertise his services. This is because the principle of freedom of advertisement is viewed as important to provide information to the people and to improve people's access to justice.

At the same time, in order to maintain the trust of society and the general public, attorneys should not engage in any inappropriate advertising that will likely bring the profession into disrepute. To this end, an attorney's advertisement is regulated by the rules of the JFBA.

1.5   Luxembourg

1.   **What is the basis for determining the rules governing professional activities in your jurisdictions?**
    Is there a code of conduct promulgated by the profession? Is it a code of conduct promulgated by the courts?

The legal profession in Luxembourg is governed by the Law on the Legal Profession of August 10 1991.

The Grand Duchy of Luxembourg has two bars: one in Luxembourg City, where most lawyers are registered and one in the city of Diekirch, in the north of the country, where approximately 10% of Luxembourg lawyers practise.

Each of these bars has elected its own president (*bâtonnier*) and its own bar council (*ordre des avocats*), which in turn have set up their own internal regulations (*règlement intérieur de l'ordre des avocats*) according to Article 19 of the law.

There is no code of conduct for lawyers promulgated by the courts.

2.   **Who enforces the code of conduct?**
    Is enforcement commenced by regulatory/court authority in response to a complaint? Is the enforcement commenced by the regulatory/court authority upon its own instigation?

The code of conduct is being enforced by the relevant bar council (*conseil de l'ordre*) represented by its president.

The president of the bar will first examine the complaint and then decide to close the file, issue a minor sanction to the lawyer directly or submit the case to the bar's Disciplinary and Administrative Committee (*Conseil Disciplinaire et Administratif*). The Disciplinary and Administrative Committee is set up pursuant to Articles 24 and 25 of the law and serves as an internal court for lawyers. It is made up of five elected members.

Any decision by the committee may be subject to an appeal before the Appelate Disciplinary and Administrative Committee, composed of two judges from the Court of Appeal and one elected member of the bar. The bar council will act only, according to Article 26 of the law, upon a complaint or upon a request by the prosecution.

3. **Does your jurisdiction have rules regarding advertising and marketing by members of the profession?**
Yes. General rules on marketing and communication with the media are laid down in Article 6 of the internal regulations.

4. **Are members of the profession allowed to publicise historic success?**
The lawyer may publicise cases only when:
- the client concerned has given its prior approval;
- the case is notoriously known to the public; or
- the client has already made the case public.

A case may be publicised without prior approval if it is sufficiently anonymous, and contains no confidential information.

5. **Are members of the profession in your jurisdiction permitted to advertise fee arrangements?**
No. Advertisement connected with special fee arrangements is explicitly prohibited.

6. **Are members of your profession in your jurisdiction permitted to market – for example using social arrangements or giving away branded materials?**
Yes, as long as the lawyer sticks to the rules of dignity, delicacy and probity. In this regard, sponsoring of *pro bono* events, legal conferences or surrounding a legal topic were allowed in the past.
Giving away branded materials under the conditions above is allowed.

7. **What are the potential consequences for breaching the rules and/or guidelines? Suspension, fine, disbarment?**
In general, the following sanctions can be issued:
- warning;
- reprimand;
- a fine up to €20,000;
- exclusion from the legal profession for a term not exceeding five years; and
- life-long prohibition to exercise the profession.

8. **In a few paragraphs would you please describe the policies applicable to the rules/guidelines regarding members of the profession advertising in your jurisdiction?**
Pursuant to Clause 6 of the Luxembourg City Bar's internal regulations, canvassing is forbidden, and advertisements are regulated. Specifically, advertisements are limited to objective facts, must be done with "dignity, delicacy and probity", must be sincere, and must comply with a lawyer's professional obligation of independence and secrecy.
Moreover, advertisements may not identify the clients represented, or the matters handled, by the lawyer or law firm.

1.6   Panama

1.   **What is the basis for determining the rules governing professional activities in your jurisdictions?**
      Is there a code of conduct promulgated by the profession? Is it a code of conduct promulgated by the courts?
      All attorneys are bound by the Panamanian Code of Ethics and Professional Responsibility, approved by the General Assembly at the 10th Annual National Attorney Congress on January 27 2011. The code was published in the *Official Gazette* (26796) on May 31 2011.
      The Code of Ethics establishes the rules governing the professional activities of attorneys and includes specific sections on advertising and marketing of legal services and similar dispositions in different sections.

2.   **Who enforces the code of conduct?**
      Is enforcement commenced by regulatory/court authority in response to a complaint? Is the enforcement commenced by the regulatory/court authority upon its own instigation?
      The Code of Ethics is enforced by the Fourth Chamber of the Supreme Court of Panama. Any presented complaint is investigated by an Honours Tribunal composed of five principal members.
      After the investigation is concluded, the report is sent to the magistrates of the Fourth Chamber who decide, by a majority vote, the validity of the case and the corresponding sanctions.

3.   **Does your jurisdiction have rules regarding advertising and marketing by members of the profession?**
      Yes. The Code of Ethics clearly states the parameters that can be used by lawyers in regards to marketing and advertising of professional legal services.

4.   **Are members of the profession allowed to publicise historic success?**
      As the Code of Ethics contains no specific provision on this matter, regular contractual law applies. Law firms and attorneys may publicise historic success as long as the client authorises the content and outlets of the publication.

5.   **Are members of the profession in your jurisdiction permitted to advertise fee arrangements?**
      The Code of Ethics does not address this matter. However, it is not the general practice to do so in any marketing or advertising material.

6.   **Are members of your profession in your jurisdiction permitted to market – for example using social arrangements or giving away branded materials?**
      The Code of Ethics does not address this matter specifically. However, it is the general practice to do so as it is not prohibited. Many law firms offer promotional (branded) materials such as pens, note pads, etc.

7. **What are the potential consequences for breaching the rules and/or guidelines? Suspension, fine, disbarment?**
    Sanctions for breaching the Code of Ethics can involve:
    - private reprimand;
    - public reprimand;
    - suspension, which consists in the prohibition to practise law for a term no shorter than one month nor longer than a year, when dealing with first time offenders; or
    - exclusion, which consists of the prohibition to practise law for a minimum term of two years for repeat offenders.

    If the actions constitute a crime, the Honours Tribunal will submit the case to the Public Ministry. The existence of a criminal process will not suspend the disciplinary sanctions imposed by the Honours Tribunal.

8. **In a few paragraphs would you please describe the policies applicable to the rules/guidelines regarding members of the profession advertising in your jurisdiction?**
    Attorneys must avoid any public declaration or publication in the media in relation to current cases or pending or future litigation, unless the counterparty does not comply with this principle and the attorney needs to publish any clarification to the general public.

    The Code of Ethics established that attorneys must not advertise in any outlet or in terms that go against the sobriety and seriousness of the profession. A lawyer may not present inaccurate facts or personal information, including the declaration of legal specialisations without the corresponding diploma or university degree. In addition, attorneys may not obtain customer leads through agents or brokers, promote or grant discounts in legal fees not authorised by law.

1.7 Paraguay

1. **What is the basis for determining the rules governing professional activities in your jurisdictions?**
    Is there a code of conduct promulgated by the profession? Is it a code of conduct promulgated by the courts?
    In Paraguay, the Supreme Court of Justice grants an authorisation (*matrícula*) to all new law graduates. This authorisation is not dependent on any qualification, it is only an administrative procedure.

    The Bar Association of Paraguay is a union body but membership is not mandatory to practise law in Paraguay.
    The Code of Ethics governs the activities of the members of the Bar Association, but it imposes moral sanctions rather than punitive ones.

2. **Who enforces the code of conduct?**
    Is enforcement commenced by regulatory/court authority in response to a

complaint? Is the enforcement commenced by the regulatory/court authority upon its own instigation?

The Code of Ethics is an element used by the Bar in cases of mismanagement of its members or as serious regulatory or ethical violations that warrant a moral sanction.

3. **Does your jurisdiction have rules regarding advertising and marketing by members of the profession?**

No. There are no guidelines either.

4. **Are members of the profession allowed to publicise historic success?**

This is not prohibited and lawyers often publicise their historic success in foreign law journals circulated worldwide.

5. **Are members of the profession in your jurisdiction permitted to advertise fee arrangements?**

This information is considered private and confidential.

6. **Are members of your profession in your jurisdiction permitted to market – for example, using social arrangements or giving away branded materials?**

There is no regulation on this matter.

7. **What are the potential consequences for breaching the rules and/or guidelines? Suspension, fine, disbarment?**

The sanctions of the Court of Ethics of the Bar are only moral sanctions.

8. **In a few paragraphs would you please describe the policies applicable to the rules/ guidelines regarding members of the profession advertising in your jurisdiction?**

Advertising issues relates to commercial conduct and laws require advertising to be transparent, clear and truthful, and neither misleading nor comparative.

1.8 Spain

1. **What is the basis for determining the rules governing professional activities in your jurisdictions?**

Is there a code of conduct promulgated by the profession? Is it a code of conduct promulgated by the courts?

Spain considers the activity of lawyers as a hybrid between the business and the profession. As a result, the legal profession is governed by two sets of rules: those which are general to the rest of business activities (eg, unfair competition) and those specific to the legal profession, access to which is regulated or restricted, which are based on the principle of self-regulation, and are under the authority of the national[1] and regional[2] bar associations, and – in some cases – of the local bar associations as well.

1   *Consejo General de la Abogacía Española* (General Council of the Spanish Lawyers).
2   For example, *Consell General de l'Advocacia Catalana* (General Council of the Catalan Lawyers).

The codes of conduct are therefore not enacted by the courts, as in certain other jurisdictions, but rather left to the professional associations.

2. **Who enforces the code of conduct?**

Is enforcement commenced by regulatory/court authority in response to a complaint? Is the enforcement commenced by the regulatory/court authority upon its own instigation?

The codes of conduct are enforced by their own promulgators, the bar associations, at their local level: the competent bar association to deal with an alleged infringement of the code of conduct by a lawyer is the bar association with which the lawyer is registered.

Any disciplinary proceedings start with a complaint from a client or from another lawyer (sometimes even *ex officio*, by the bar association, in particularly notorious cases). It is also possible for professional disciplinary proceedings to be initiated by a judge, even though the civil law on procedure gives judges other means to punish bad-faith behaviour from attorneys (eg, direct court sanctions).[3]

The complaint against a lawyer for infringement of the code of conduct is filed before the relevant local bar association, through the corresponding disciplinary commission (*comisión de deontología*).

The decision (which must be reasoned) and the sanction may be reviewed in turn in most Spanish regions by the regional council of the local bar associations and subsequently by the ordinary courts (at two further instances, the last being the Supreme Court).

3. **Does your jurisdiction have rules regarding advertising and marketing by members of the profession?**

Yes. In addition to the general rules regarding advertising and marketing which affect the rest of activities and professions (eg, the General Law on Publicity, the Law on Unfair Competition, the Law on the Defence of Competition, etc), the codes of conduct include certain rules on specific restrictions on advertising and marketing for lawyers.

These rules have been in force since 2001.[4] The general rule is the freedom to market and advertise with certain limited restrictions based fundamentally on the need to preserve the dignity inherent to the profession, and the capacity of clients to decide objectively on the appointment of lawyers in particular circumstances (eg, no adverting after accidents, at funerals, etc).

4. **Are members of the profession allowed to publicise historic success?**

While the 2001 Spanish National Code expressly prohibits the publicisation of historic success, the first page of the code as it appears on the website of the General Council for the Spanish Lawyers expressly states that there is a debate on whether to reform the code, including Article 7 on publicity.

---

3   Article 247 of the Law on Civil Procedure.
4   The Spanish National Code, approved by Royal Decree 658/2001, which can be consulted at www.abogacia.es/wp-content/uploads/2012/06/codigo_deontologico1.pdf, as at November 25 2015.

The outcome may be not so much a question of total prohibition not to publicise historical success, but how this historical success is put into context so as not to mislead potential clients, or breach professional secrecy.

5. **Are members of the profession in your jurisdiction permitted to advertise fee arrangements?**
No. There is not an express ban specifically on the publicity of fee arrangements.

6. **Are members of your profession in your jurisdiction permitted to market – for example using social arrangements or giving away branded materials?**
Yes. There is certainly no restriction to giving away branded materials or having special events for potential contacts or clients, other than the very general principle of dignity of the profession.

7. **What are the potential consequences for breaching the rules and/or guidelines? Suspension fine, disbarment?**
Sanctions depend on the respective local or regional bar associations. A good reference may be the Catalan Regional Council Code, where sanctions for breach of publicity rules can include temporary disbarment (*inhabilitación*) of up to one year, or fines of up to €5,000. There is a possible complementary sanction of having to return the economic profit obtained with the infringing behaviour.

8. **In a few paragraphs would you please describe the policies applicable to the rules/guidelines regarding members of the profession advertising in your jurisdiction?**
Since the late 1990s the general principle has been one of free competition with specific exceptions due to the nature of the legal profession. These exceptions will be interpreted taking into account the relevance or extent of the impact or reach of the publicity and of its breach, which in turn will affect the type of sanction, which can be considered serious (*grave*), unless it represents a breach of the duty of secrecy. A minor (*leve*) offence cannot lead to temporary disbarments, but mostly only written caution or smaller fines.

The fact that disciplinary proceedings and decisions at bar level are held behind closed doors and come into the public sphere only if they are subsequently appealed reduces the number of decisions that are accessible.

Bar associations may take a stricter view when dealing with new media due to its potential impact and reach; however, the subject has yet to be considered to its full extent.

2.   Common law countries

2.1   Australia

1.   **What is the basis for determining the rules governing professional activities in your jurisdictions?**
Is there a code of conduct promulgated by the profession? Is it a code of conduct promulgated by the courts?
The ethical duties and professional conduct obligations of lawyers are derived from three sources:
- the courts through the common law, with legal practitioners being officers of the court charged with the duties of upholding the rule of law and promoting the administration of justice;
- a code of professional conduct prepared and adopted by the legal profession (known as the Australian Solicitors' Conduct Rules (ASCR)) or equivalent rules; and
- the same professional conduct rules adopted by the legal profession (the ASCR or equivalent rules) being promulgated as statutory rules in the state and territory jurisdictions.

2.   **Who enforces the code of conduct?**
Is enforcement commenced by regulatory/court authority in response to a complaint? Is the enforcement commenced by the regulatory/court authority upon its own instigation?
Subject to oversight and enforcement by the courts and by the designated state and territory regulators of the legal profession, which are systematically shared between statutory regulatory bodies and the local bars and law societies.

Enforcement action can be commenced by the regulatory authority, either upon the making of a complaint or at its own instigation. Enforcement action can also be commenced by application to a court by a client or former client or by another affected party seeking to restrain the actions of a law firm or legal practitioner, or prevent a breach of fidicuairy duty and the code of conduct.

3.   **Does your jurisdiction have rules regarding advertising and marketing by members of the profession?**
There are limited restrictions upon advertising of legal services in Australia, such as restrictions included in consumer and competition laws and laws relating to personal injuries proceedings; and in the codes of professional conduct. The ASCR provide that any advertising of legal services must not be false, misleading or deceptive, offensive or prohibited by law.[5]

---

5   Law Council of Australia, Australian Solicitors' Conduct Rules: Rule 36 (www.lawcouncil.asn.au/lawcouncil/index.php/divisions/legal-practice-division/australian-solicitors-conduct-rules).

4.   **Are members of the profession allowed to publicise historic success?**
Provided that the publication of historic success rates would not breach the restrictions on advertising and marketing imposed by the ASCR and/or relevant legislation, there is no specific restriction on publicising historic success. However, given the restrictions on advertising or marketing which is misleading and deceptive, and the real risk that advertising historic success rates may be taken by consumers to be representations of the likely result of their own matter, publicising historic success rates is regarded as unwise.[6]

5.   **Are members of the profession in your jurisdiction permitted to advertise fee arrangements?**
Similarly, there is no specific restriction on publicising fee arrangements.

6.   **Are members of your profession in your jurisdiction permitted to market – for example using social arrangements or giving away branded materials?**
Yes, provided such marketing does not breach the restrictions on advertising and marketing.

7.   **What are the potential consequences for breaching the rules and/or guidelines? Suspension, fine, disbarment?**
The penalties may include suspension or cancellation of a practising certificate and cost orders. It may also include orders against a practitioner or law firm to cease acting for a client.

In some states, a breach of a restriction on seeking personal injuries work is punishable by a fine.

8.   **In a few paragraphs would you please describe the policies applicable to the rules/ guidelines regarding members of the profession advertising in your jurisdiction?**
Advertising of the provision of legal services is permitted in Australia but may not be false, misleading or deceptive, offensive or otherwise prohibited by law.

The restrictions applying to the advertising of legal services also commonly specify constraints on advertising which may describe or claim that a practitioner or firm is a specialist in a particular field of legal practice.

2.2   Canada

1.   **What is the basis for determining the rules governing professional activities in your jurisdictions?**
Is there a code of conduct promulgated by the profession? Is it a code of conduct promulgated by the courts?
In Canada, every province and territory has its own self-regulating law society,[7]

---

6   See Julia Zivanovic, "Advertising Legal Services – the guidelines" [1997] BalJINTLawSoc 186; (1997) 7 Balance: *Journal of the Law Society Northern Territory* 8,(www5.austlii.edu.au/cgi-bin/download.cgi/cgi-bin/download.cgi/download/au/journals/BalJINTLawSoc/1997/186.pdf.

established by the legislature of each province,[8] that is responsible for setting rules or codes of professional conduct.

Canadian courts have no formal role to play in the governance or regulation of the legal profession.

2. **Who enforces the code of conduct?**
Is enforcement commenced by regulatory/court authority in response to a complaint? Is the enforcement commenced by the regulatory/court authority upon its own instigation?
Enforcement of the rules governing the legal profession is usually triggered by a complaint filed with the appropriate law society against a member lawyer by an individual or another lawyer.

Complaints can also be filed by a judge or other adjudicator and regulatory staff. If a lawyer's advertising were characterised as misleading, he could be subject to proceedings under Part VII.1 on deceptive marketing practices of the Competition Act of Canada.

3. **Does your jurisdiction have rules regarding advertising and marketing by members of the profession?**
Yes. The Canadian Bar Association is a voluntary association for lawyers and often develops guidelines and recommendations that may be adopted by provincial or territorial law societies.

4. **Are members of the profession allowed to publicise historic success?**
Yes. Lawyers are allowed to publicise past successes so long as those claims conform to the rules on advertising.

5. **Are members of the profession in your jurisdiction permitted to advertise fee arrangements?**
Yes. Lawyers are permitted to advertise fee arrangements. Most jurisdictions provide that "a lawyer may advertise fees charged for legal services if the advertising is reasonably precise for each service being quoted, the ad states whether other amounts, such as disbursements and taxes, will be charged in addition to the fee, and the lawyer strictly adheres to the advertised fee in every applicable case".[9]

6. **Are members of your profession in your jurisdiction permitted to market – for example using social arrangements or giving away branded materials?**
Yes. Lawyers are permitted to arrange social functions or give out branded materials

---

7   In Nova Scotia, the governing body of the legal profession is called the Nova Scotia Barristers' Society. For simplicity (and economy), reference will be made only to law societies.
8   There are 10 provinces in Canada and three territories. The latter are mostly self-governing entities established by Parliament. For the purposes of this chapter, they can be considered provinces, though they do not have constitutional standing as provinces with assigned powers under the Constitution Act 1867. The Province of Québec has two professional associations of lawyers, the *Barreau du Québec* and the *Chambre des Notaires du Québec*.
9   Rules of Professional Conduct (Ontario) and Code of Professional Conduct (Nova Scotia), Rule 4.2–2.

as part of their marketing efforts. This type of marketing must conform to the particular law society's rules. Ontario, British Columbia and Nova Scotia have no specific rules related to this issue.

7.   **What are the potential consequences for breaching the rules and/or guidelines? Suspension, fine, disbarment?**
Possible consequences range from a reprimand to disbarment, though disbarment would be likely only if there were repeated violations and the lawyer were characterised as "ungovernable". Sanctions at the lower end are likely for breach of the rules governing advertising.

8.   **In a few paragraphs would you please describe the policies applicable to the rules/ guidelines regarding members of the profession advertising in your jurisdiction?**
In Ontario, British Columbia and Nova Scotia the content and format of rules related to marketing all require, with slightly varying language, that "the activities [described] must be true, accurate, verifiable, not capable of misleading or confusing, and in the best interests of the public".[10] Ontario and Nova Scotia add the caveat that marketing activities must also be consistent with a "high standard of professionalism".[11] The law societies also provide commentary related to their rules, setting out examples of marketing practices that may contravene them.

In Ontario and British Columbia, a lawyer cannot advertise that he is a specialist in a particular field without being so certified.[12] In Nova Scotia lawyers are prohibited from describing themselves as specialists or experts in any field of law. In all three jurisdictions, however, lawyers may advertise that they practise or have a particular proficiency in particular areas of law. All representations must be accurate and demonstrably true.

2.3   England and Wales

1.   **What is the basis for determining the rules governing professional activities in your jurisdictions?**
Is there a code of conduct promulgated by the profession? Is it a code of conduct promulgated by the courts?
The Law Society of England and Wales is the approved regulator of the solicitors' profession and had delegated this role to the Solicitors Regulation Authority (SRA), which is described as an independent regulatory authority.

In terms of professional behaviour and ethics, the SRA sets and monitors standards that are contained in the *SRA Handbook*. The handbook is published on the SRA website[13] and contains all of the principles, outcomes, rules and regulations

---

10   Rules of Professional Conduct (Ontario) and Code of Professional Conduct (Nova Scotia), Rule 4.2–1 and (British Columbia), Rule 4.2–5.
11   Rules of Professional Conduct (Ontario) and Code of Professional Conduct (Nova Scotia), Rule 4.2–1(c).
12   Rules of Professional Conduct (Ontario), Rule 4.3–1 and Code of Professional Conduct (British Columbia), Rule 4.3.
13   www.sra.org.uk

which are required by the SRA. In terms of personal behaviour, and in respect of the topic of publicity, the starting point is a consideration of the SRA Principles and the SRA Code of Conduct 2011.

Courts are aware of the professional behaviour that is required of solicitors and have the discretion to advise the SRA if they feel that an individual is failing to meet these standards.

2. **Who enforces the code of conduct?**
Is enforcement commenced by regulatory/court authority in response to a complaint? Is the enforcement commenced by the regulatory/court authority upon its own instigation?
The SRA has the power to enforce compliance with regulatory requirements. It is a risk-based regulator and determines a proportionate response to a breach by reference to the impact that this may have on meeting the regulatory objectives in the Legal Services Act 2007, reputational impact (to it as an approved regulator under the LSA and to the solicitor's profession) and to the detriment of the client.

The SRA obtains information which may trigger the need for enforcement action from a variety of sources: from solicitors and other individuals employed in law in compliance with the duty in some circumstances to self-report; from clients; and from third parties, such as the courts and the Legal Ombudsman. They may also gather intelligence from scrutiny of the media.

3. **Does your jurisdiction have rules regarding advertising and marketing by members of the profession?**
Yes. Solicitors must observe a number of legal requirements on advertising. The SRA Code of Conduct 2011 provides that all solicitors, and others working in SRA-authorised law firms, must comply with all legislation relevant to their business.

The SRA has published several regulator guidelines and restrictions.

4. **Are members of the profession allowed to publicise historic success?**
Yes. Publicising historic success is considered to be publicity and would need to comply with the SRA Principles and the SRA Code.

Outcome (4.1) in Chapter 4 of the SRA Code of Conduct (Confidentiality and Disclosure) is relevant and must be achieved in these circumstances: "you [must] keep the affairs of clients confidential unless disclosure is required or permitted by law or the client consents".

5. **Are members of the profession in your jurisdiction permitted to advertise fee arrangements?**
Yes, but subject to compliance with the SRA Principles and the SRA Code of Conduct. In this regard, the outcomes in Chapter 8 are relevant, but it is also necessary to consider the regulatory requirements relating to client care and interaction with the client.

6. **Are members of your profession in your jurisdiction permitted to market – for example using social arrangements or giving away branded materials?**

Trinkets are sometimes used by law firms as advertising vehicles. While this is not prohibited, it would need to be considered compatible with the SRA Principles (eg, Principle 6 and the duty that "you [must] behave in a way that maintains the trust the public places in you and in the provision of legal services") and the SRA Code outcomes in Chapter 8.

7. **What are the potential consequences for breaching the rules and/or guidelines? Suspension, fine, disbarment?**

    The SRA has a range of enforcement and disciplinary powers which can be used against solicitors, and others working in SRA-authorised entities, and against the entities themselves. The SRA investigates concerns about standards of practice and compliance with the regulatory framework, where necessary taking regulatory action such as reprimanding a solicitor. When necessary, the SRA also has powers to place conditions on an authorised firm's continuing authorisation or to close it down if this is deemed a proportionate response to the duty to protect clients and the wider public. In the worst-case scenarios involving individuals, the SRA will make referrals to the independent Solicitors Disciplinary Tribunal and deal with the prosecutions. The tribunal has powers to strike a solicitor from the roll of solicitors (ie, disbarment) or to place orders on other individuals preventing their employment in law firms.

8. **In a few paragraphs would you please describe the policies applicable to the rules/guidelines regarding members of the profession advertising in your jurisdiction?**

    As with all regulatory policies relating to the conduct of solicitors, the SRA has regard for compliance with the regulatory objectives and professional principles in the Legal Services Act 2007. The regulations relating to publicity are designed to ensure that the profession's reputation is not tarnished by publicity techniques that are commonplace in other businesses, such as cold-calling. The publicity policy is also steeped in values arising in respect of the traditional solicitor-client relationship.

2.4   India

1. **What is the basis for determining the rules governing professional activities in your jurisdictions?**

    Is there a code of conduct promulgated by the profession? Is it a code of conduct promulgated by the courts?

    The legal profession in India is governed by the Advocates Act 1961 and the Rules framed by the Bar Council of India (the BCI Rules) under the act. Part VI of the BCI Rules provides for the standards of professional conduct and etiquette (the Code of Conduct), which an advocate must strictly adhere to in the practice of his profession.

    The BCI and the state bar councils established under the act seek to facilitate independent regulation of the legal profession in India. Various functions are undertaken by the bar councils for effective regulation of the profession.

2. **Who enforces the code of conduct?**
Is enforcement commenced by regulatory/court authority in response to a complaint? Is the enforcement commenced by the regulatory/court authority upon its own instigation?
The Code of Conduct is enforced by the BCI Disciplinary Committee and the disciplinary committees of the state bar councils. When a state bar council, on the basis of a complaint by any person or on its own instigation, has reason to believe that an advocate on its roll has been guilty of professional or other misconduct, it shall refer the case to its disciplinary committee. The BCI Disciplinary Committee also has the same powers in respect of advocates not on the rolls of any state bar council.

The BCI Disciplinary Committee has the power to transfer to itself any disciplinary proceeding pending before any state bar council's disciplinary committee. The BCI Disciplinary Committee may also hear appeals from the decisions of the disciplinary committees of the state bar councils. Further, the Supreme Court of India may hear appeals from the decisions of the BCI Disciplinary Committee.

3. **Does your jurisdiction have rules regarding advertising and marketing by members of the profession?**
Rule 36 of Chapter II of Section IV of Part VI of the BCI Rules prohibits advocates from directly or indirectly soliciting or advertising in any manner.

However, Rule 36 was slightly relaxed in 2008 and advocates are now allowed to provide basic information about themselves on their websites. That basic information includes their name, address, telephone numbers, email address, academic and professional qualifications and areas of practice.

4. **Are members of the profession allowed to publicise historic success?**
No. Publication of historic success is impermissible.

5. **Are members of the profession in your jurisdiction permitted to advertise fee arrangements?**
Rule 36, as stated previously, prohibits direct and indirect advertising in any manner. Therefore, even a passive tactic such as advertising fee arrangements may be construed as flouting Rule 36.

6. **Are members of your profession in your jurisdiction permitted to market – for example using social arrangements or giving away branded materials?**
As stated previously, advocates in India cannot advertise themselves in any manner. Therefore, it would be impermissible to promote themselves by distributing any branded objects.

7. **What are the potential consequences for breaching the rules and/or guidelines? Suspension, fine, disbarment?**
Advertising in violation of Rule 36 may amount to professional misconduct. If an

advocate is found guilty of professional misconduct, the BCI Disciplinary Committee or relevant state bar council disciplinary committee may reprimand the advocate or suspend him from practice for a specified period or disbar him.

8. **In a few paragraphs would you please describe the policies applicable to the rules/guidelines regarding members of the profession advertising in your jurisdiction?**

    Although advocates in India may be restrained from promoting themselves, practice shows that they have devised other means to make themselves visible. For instance, various law firms during festive seasons send greetings and gifts to their clients. The packages of these gifts are aesthetically appealing and bear the name and logo of the law firm.

    Many lawyers are also active on social media, and use this tool to market themselves. Many others also appear on television channels and often get quoted in the press. The BCI has not as yet considered this and whether this amounts to advertising.

    In conclusion, although there are strict rules, which have been enforced on occasion, the more savvy members of the Indian Bar seem to manage a significant amount of promotional activity.

2.5   United States

1. **What is the basis for determining the rules governing professional activities in your jurisdictions?**

    Is there a code of conduct promulgated by the profession? Is it a code of conduct promulgated by the courts?

    The United States is a federal system with attorney regulation at the state and territorial level; these regulations and laws form the basis for governing professional activities, with limited exceptions.

    Lawyers are subject to the rules of professional conduct, promulgated by the local jurisdiction's regulatory body, which include advertising and solicitation. In addition, though, a lawyer may be sanctioned by a state regulatory authority or court if that lawyer engages in conduct in a state where the lawyer is not admitted, provided there is personal jurisdiction over that lawyer. The American Bar Association, a voluntary association of lawyers, also issues so-called 'Model Rules' that are often the basis for the various states' adoption, either in whole or in part.

2. **Who enforces the code of conduct?**

    Is enforcement commenced by regulatory/court authority in response to a complaint? Is the enforcement commenced by the regulatory/court authority upon its own instigation?

    With limited exceptions, generally attorneys are licensed and regulated on a state-by-state basis. While certain federal courts may permit admission before them notwithstanding the absence of admission before the state authorities in which the federal court is located, and certain safe harbours for specified types of transient practice, lawyers are generally permitted to practise only in the states in which they are licensed. When marketing and ethics are considered in the United States, then they are considered in terms of the applicable jurisdiction's particular rules.

3.   **Does your jurisdiction have rules regarding advertising and marketing by members of the profession?**
Yes. Marketing and business communication may be in many forms: electronic, oral, hard copy and so forth. The US Supreme Court has recognised that lawyers have a First Amendment right to advertise their services as commercial speech. However, it is not unlimited, and the Supreme Court has recognised competing public interest concerns, and issued subsequent opinions setting down standards with regard to advertising and solicitation.

4.   **Are members of the profession allowed to publicise historic success?**
It varies by state, with some older opinions precluding any such references, but most allowing some reference with varying degrees of disclaimers and contextual reference, subject to the general overall rule that the statements must be accurate and not misleading, and not constitute a promise of future success.

5.   **Are members of the profession in your jurisdiction permitted to advertise fee arrangements?**
The American Bar Association's Model Rule 7.2 permits advertising subject to Rule 7.1's admonitions, and certain restrictions on "direct contact with prospective clients" as set forth in Model Rule 7.3, but restricts a lawyer from paying (in money or in kind) for recommendations, except for reasonable advertising costs and usual charges for certain legal service plans or qualified referral services, or paying for a law practice as permitted under Model Rule 1.17, and under such other non-prohibited arrangements.

6.   **Are members of your profession in your jurisdiction permitted to market – for example using social arrangements or giving away branded materials?**
Generally, yes, but subject to the above-noted standards and rules governing client solicitation. Each state's rules must be consulted.

7.   **What are the potential consequences for breaching the rules and/or guidelines? Suspension, fine, disbarment?**
It varies by state and will depend on severity of violation, past violations by the attorney, and other factors. Some states may also utilise public or private reprimands. It also depends on whether the breach was singular or other ethics rules were involved.

8.   **In a few paragraphs would you please describe the policies applicable to the rules/guidelines regarding members of the profession advertising in your jurisdiction?**
It is not possible to provide a comprehensive discussion of all the nuances involved.

Different states have varying levels of specificity and restrictions far beyond those of the Model Rules.

Disclaimers may and should be used to make clear that legal advice is not being given and that there is no intention to be practising law in any other than the lawyer's authorised jurisdiction. Websites, like any other lawyer communication, must not be misleading. Lawyers also need to be careful to avoid creating attorney-client relationships through careless blog posts or other communications in the guise of advertising, which may be construed as legal advice.

The IBA would like to thank the people listed below for their contributions (listed alphabetically by country):

Argentina: *Alberto Navarro*

Australia: *David W Marks and Steven Stevens*

Brazil: *Eduardo M Zobaran*

Canada: *Martin E Kovnats, Angela Swan and Liam Tracey-Raymont*

Chile: *Camila Kutz and Claudio Undurraga*

England and Wales: *Tracey Calvert*

India: *Akil Hirani*

Japan: *Seiichi Okazaki*

Luxembourg: *Joram Moyal*

Panama: *Patricia Villanueva*

Paraguay: *Hugo Berkemeyer*

Spain: *Carlos Valls Martinez*, with invaluable help from *Begoña de Urbiola* of the Deontology Commission of the Barcelona Bar Association (*Comissió de Deontologia de l'Il·lustre Col·legi d'Advocats de Barcelona*)

United States: *Steven Richman*

Communications and public relations in law firms – connection and contradiction

Chris Davis
Freshfields Bruckhaus Deringer

The role of communications – and particularly external communications – varies substantially from one firm to the next. Where roles like business development and knowledge management benefit from generally larger teams, and in turn a broader sense of orthodoxy across the sector, the communications function remains poorly defined by comparison.

Historically, the communications function has been subject to a piecemeal approach from firms – oftentimes the responsibilities being spread across a combination of marketing, business development, internal communications and even IT professionals.

This is in part due to the size of firm required to support a dedicated communications function – in small firms, communications often sits with the partners directly. This confined approach is further exacerbated by a lack of clarity as to the methods and benefits of communications within the legal sector.

However, as law firms continue to globalise and enter into a broader range of markets and legal disciplines, the demand for communications professionals, and a better understanding of communications methodology, has increased.

This is coinciding with an increasingly competitive global legal sector, and a group of consumers who are accessing information more disparately. Users of legal services can educate themselves about, and engage with, the legal market in more diverse ways than ever before. Accordingly, the impetus on law firms to communicate with 'the outside world' is now greater than ever before as well.

1. The case for communications in law firms

In some respects, external communications about the work of a law firm is anathema to the habits and professionalism of legal practitioners – who rightly treat client confidentiality and commercial sensitivity as sacrosanct.

In turn, one of the great challenges that law firms face is convincing themselves of the very need to communicate outside of the four walls of the firm in the first place. For an industry that is trained to assess, understand and mitigate risk, communications mishaps (and particularly public relations disasters) represent a wasteful exposure to risk for the prospect an often unmeasured or unrealistic reward.

However, with very few exceptions, commercial realities demand that external communications are at the core of any law firm's business development and client engagement strategy in the modern legal market.

Law firms occupy a rare space in the modern marketing world in that their expenditure on traditional marketing techniques, like advertising, is extremely low. Beyond sponsorships and event marketing (seminars and conferences), law firms are often reticent to consider advertising as a means of external communications.

Despite that reluctance, law firms are not immune from the need for brand awareness in their market segment of choice. In some respects, law firms are more dependent on a strong brand than other sectors, because the firm brand is equally crucial in recruiting top-level talent to the firm as it is in generating work from clients or advocating on issues of interest in the public arena.

One of the great challenges which law firms of all scales and scope face is a fundamental marketing challenge: differentiation in a crowded marketplace, whereby all providers essentially sell the same core product. It is difficult to persuade people of the superiority of something as intangible as advice. Effective external communications – leading to a strong 'brand build' in the long-term – can predispose legal buyers, and potential recruits, to one firm's quality compared to that of a competitor.

Beyond the most superficial brand recognition that effective communication generates for firms, it can also play a vital role in educating new and existing clients, as well as other stakeholders, on current or future legal issues that they face. When done well, this is genuinely beneficial for the client and also serves to generate potential business for the firm. External communications can add value to the lawyer-client relationship and lead to a deeper discussion of the issues that confront the client.

At its best, effective communication can generate discussions between the firm and clients that would not have otherwise occurred.

Communications within a law firm is one of the few business services that can benefit all members of a partnership or firm in equal measure. The professional services environment has long grappled with the balancing act between the needs of the broader firm and that of individual practitioners, and this is often deeply felt in the marketing and business development function. However, awareness of a firm's brand is inherently applicable to every member of the firm – and in that sense, the communications function offers a rare synergy between the needs of all individual partners or fee earners, and the firm itself.

That 'full firm' benefit extends substantially into the recruitment realm. Whereas business development is often augmented by client history, personal relationships and technical expertise, the impact of a firm's brand is far more influential in attracting premium talent at the graduate level. As law firms invest progressively greater resources into campus recruitment, the prevalence and prestige of a brand is one of the few factors that can meaningfully elevate one firm as a potential employer over another.

The role of external communications has an ongoing influence in retention as well as recruitment. Indeed, a well-articulated brand in the public domain is an effective means of reinforcing internal engagement (firm pride) and bolstering internal communications initiatives. In general terms, people feel better about their organisation if that organisation is externally perceived to be a leader in its field.

This is, of course, a general assessment of the case for communications in law firms. The need for external communications will vary from firm to firm – for instance, plaintiff firms and niche firms will have very different communication requirements than multinational full-service firms. This also shapes the tactics and strategies available to them, which will be discussed subsequently.

2. Contextualising communications within the law firm – from traditional comfort zones to modern media management

External communications, as a function of a law firm, often suffers from an identity crisis. The scale of law firms means that external communications functions are typically very small – the very largest firms in the world would seldom have more than a dozen people in dedicated external communication functions – so there is a deficit of knowledge that exists in no other business services functions.

Anecdotally, many law firms do not employ their first dedicated external communications practitioner until the partnership has grown to more than two dozen partners. The total headcount, by this point, will typically be well into triple figures and many firms are only contemplating external communications for the first time. When compared to other industries of similar revenue and staffing levels, it is evident that the legal sector is a late starter in terms of initiating external communications.

A natural by-product of this 'institutional tardiness' is a lack of awareness as to where an external communications practitioner is best placed within the organisational structure, and what functions suitably fall within his purview.

The most immediate, and most common, placement of communications in a firm hierarchy is as an adjunct of the firm's business development function. There are similarities in purpose between the two groups – business development activities (eg, pitching) benefit from a well-known and strongly articulated brand, and external communications should complement those activities that the firm undertakes to market itself to clients.

There is a synergy of skills that will often benefit both sides of this alignment – for instance, business development teams will benefit from acquiring communications know-how (particularly business writing) and communications teams will benefit from the industry knowledge that business development professionals amass from their experience at the 'coalface' of client interaction and pursuing mandates.

Beyond this tendency to find the same starting point, the role of communications within the firm varies significantly.

This is due, in large part, to a lack of the same critical mass of practitioners that the legal sector has when it comes to other support roles – such as business development, information technology and human resources. By way of example, professional development for communications practitioners in law tends to be catered for by the large professional services marketing associations, as opposed to any dedicated communications organisation, despite a significant divergence in the skills and knowledge required of the two groups.

Consequently, the evolution of communications within a law firm is often driven by forces inside the firm – such as partner priorities and the strengths of individual communications professionals.

A result of this unpredictable use of communications professionals is that the discipline is sprawling and evolving within individual firms, or even segments of firms, in very different ways.

In many partnerships, the communications practitioner will take a leadership role in overseeing the communications channels that firms are most comfortable with namely, awards and directories. Indeed, the quantity of both has multiplied in recent years; oftentimes large, dedicated teams are employed simply to make sure that awards and directory submissions are managed punctually. In smaller firms, that function will typically be folded into the communications remit.

The rapid expansion of awards providers, though, means that the prestige of individual outlets is constantly under threat – and to some extent, the sheer volume of awards on offer to law firms now means that a great many of these awards are inherently devalued. Over time, this is leading to a recognition within law firms of the disproportionate levels of investment being placed in these 'comfort zone' communications channels as opposed to more mainstream methods.

In turn, a balanced approach to communications in law firms demands a much more diverse approach to reaching the outside world.

Law firms are becoming increasingly comfortable with media relations – or at least, conceding that the business case for public engagement through the media is a compelling one. It is in this realm that communications within law firms is reaching a new maturity.

3.   Impediments to media relations in law firms – digging the moat, building the bridge

The diversity of law firms – in terms of size, geographies and practice areas – creates equally diverse challenges and opportunities when undertaking media relations. However, firms of every stripe face the same fundamental hurdle: balancing client sensitivity and confidentiality against the business development and profiling needs of the firm. This is commonly the single largest impediment to law firms taking a more proactive approach to media relations.

This is exacerbated by historic restrictions around law firm marketing in some jurisdictions – where media engagement could have previously, or still can, run afoul of obligations to local law societies or other regulatory bodies. Many jurisdictions continue to have restrictions around the use of particular terms in law firm marketing – and, typically, firms seek to mitigate any risk by considering press commentary as being subject to these prohibited terms.

These theoretical concerns are sometimes confirmed by difficult personal experience. Law firms in many markets face extensive scrutiny from the niche legal media – itself a competitive media landscape where the pressure to find the next scoop is high. In turn, senior lawyers – many of whom will not have had formal media training – are often subject to their first experience of media in the heat of sophisticated and direct enquiry from talented members of the legal press.

In this context, the retreat away from media relations is understandable, but ultimately counterproductive.

Accordingly, there is growing demand within the legal sector for communications practitioners that have substantial experience in media management – where once the skillset most readily sought after would have been a background in directories research or the law itself.

Communications practitioners within law firms are increasingly tasked with managing the nexus between fee earners and the outside press. In many firms, the management of these relationships is relatively foreign to lawyers, and this is an area where communications professionals can add considerable value to the firm's operations.

Inherently, communications within law firms demands a degree of contradictory thinking. Opinion leaders within a firm need to be convinced of the value of proactive media engagement (something which struggles under the weight of its ephemeral rewards, to be discussed subsequently), and that the risk of 'doing media' is actually worth taking.

In turn, there is typically a need for the media relations personnel to be somewhat evangelical about engaging media in the first place. Their primary job, more often than not, is to get internal stakeholders excited about talking to journalists and sufficiently confident to run the gauntlet of media interaction.

Yet, paradoxically, the same media relations personnel must ensure that a robust system of checks and balances exists within the organisation to mitigate risks around confidential information, client sensitivities and obligations to regulators.

These systems inevitably vary according to firm size, structure and eagerness to participate in media relations. Fundamentally, the media relations function needs to be closely aligned with firm risk protocols to ensure that processes such as conflicts checks and liaison with relevant relationship partners are taken into account prior to any approach or response to media.

Often, these systems – when executed properly – will leave law firms with a diminished scope for media commentary, and this can occasionally frustrate journalists and lawyers alike. However, it is vital that firms implement clearly articulated media policies and rigorous systems to complement those policies – as it is the existence of both that ultimately gives lawyers within the firm enough confidence to comment in the public domain without a fear of inadvertently damaging client relationships or airing confidential matters.

Ultimately, these same processes give individuals dealing with media on behalf of the firm certainty in articulating boundaries to enquiring press clearly and quickly. Even if the process determines that no comment can be made publicly, it allows for the quick arrival at that conclusion, and an efficient interaction with journalists that can help build long-term relationships which are beneficial to the firm.

By and large, journalists – themselves familiar with the complexities of handling sensitive information – understand the nuanced position in which lawyers are placed when faced with questions regarding specific deals or client matters. It is more fruitful for both parties if a firm is able to respond quickly to enquiring media representatives – even if the answer is "no comment" – than to prolong these exchanges.

The potential for tension between media relations needs and client sensitivities, while challenging, should not deter law firms from utilising media as part of their marketing and brand mix. Asides from the commercial demands of profiling that were alluded to previously, it is this tension – and the fact that many legal professionals shy away from press because of it – that gives firms an opportunity to gain mileage in the media landscape quickly.

Fundamentally, the role of the media relations professional in a firm – be it a partner or dedicated business services resource is to build a bridge between journalists and the intellectual capital of the firm (typically, senior lawyers). This function is critical to the interactions between journalists and lawyers, in that the media community will generally respect any moat that a firm builds around its people, so long as a reliable bridge is also in place. That is to say, if you are genuine in your exchanges with the media about what is and is not possible, the media will respect obligations to client confidentiality and commercial sensitivity.

4.   Finding the fit – the coalescence of law and news value

A common narrative in recent years has been the global decline of newspapers – and in turn, an inferred decline in the very idea of news.

There is truth to the assertion that newspaper circulation is in sustained decline, and in many markets that decline looks beyond arrest. By way of example, research from the Pew Research Center paints a picture of major US newspapers commonly suffering year-on-year declines in readership and advertising revenue. While the move to digital news consumption has gathered speed, the divergent nature of the digital space means that new advertising revenues from the online world are not compensating for losses in the print world.[1]

However – the idea that news is suffering a similar decline is a misinterpretation. The market for news is splintering as sources, particularly online, proliferate – but not declining. The result is demand for more customised news and high-quality journalism in an expanding number of niche and technical topics – the sum total of which is equivalent to previous readership sizes in traditional print media and more. The rise of business blogs, for example, is testament to the demand for niche insights and coverage.

There is less demand for generic news, as defined by the era of traditional media dominance – but a much greater demand for tailored, sophisticated news as sought after by individual readers and viewers. Increasingly, news consumers – including legal buyers – are a self-curating group of consumers that have the tools (search engines, social media), resources (both economic, as the cost of news declines, and personal, as mobile devices create new time in which to read news), and willingness to seek out the news that is most directly relevant to them.

All of this culminates to create an environment in which the legal profession has more news sources to deal with than ever before. Even within the very specific legal media space, there is a fracturing of news sources – dozens of websites and publications, often with internationally based journalists, catering for everything from in-depth market commentary to case analysis, deal reporting, lateral

---

1   Barthel, M (April 29 2015). Newspapers: Fact Sheet. Retrieved September 24 2015, from Pew Reseach Center (www.journalism.org/2015/04/29/newspapers-fact-sheet/).

movements and industry gossip. This same horizontal proliferation of news is occurring even more significantly within general and business news beats.

For lawyers seeking to engage the media, this is a mixed blessing. The downside of this boom in outlets means that the cost of media relations is increasing; a lawyer's phone is more likely to ring because there is more demand for expert commentary and this takes time to manage. However, the opportunity should far outweigh the burden. If a lawyer or law firm genuinely has a story, there is usually someone willing to publish it. This is especially relevant for practitioners in more technical, or inaccessible, areas of practice that previously may have struggled to find a home in print outside of technical or academic journals. In the modern media landscape, there is cachet in highly specific content that did not exist previously.

The changing shape and size of news reporting means that different lawyers and firms can interact with the media in very different ways. There is no 'one size fits all' for media relations in the legal sector, however, there are some broad themes which permeate the interaction between journalists and lawyers.

In many respects, the single largest factor in determining the nature of this relationship is the size of the firm itself. Larger partnerships will implicitly struggle with larger conflicts footprints – this means that the cases and companies that they can discuss will typically be more constrained. Smaller law firms, less confined by these considerations, are often well positioned to leverage the media in ways that larger players cannot. Individual lawyers and smaller firms are often able to move nimbly to generate media opportunities from the work of their larger counterparts (to be discussed later) by way of commentary.

The nature of the work undertaken by a lawyer or firm has a direct impact on the nature of the media relations that they can reasonably undertake. There are areas of practice that simply have broader news value or more outlets to choose from when looking to gain coverage.

Plaintiff law firms are one group which the broader sector can draw guidance from. While the content of media driven by plaintiff law firms will be greatly different to that of their corporate cousins, the tactics and strategies are largely applicable across both groups. Plaintiff firms – driven by different economics from commercial firms – have aggressively pursued media coverage for decades, and often while contending with greater constraints in terms of restrictions from governing bodies.

Plaintiff firms, and those firms working in practice areas that are applicable to 'everyday' experience – such as employment and consumer law – can be readily visible in mainstream media (ie, tabloid newspapers and evening news broadcasts) with the right internal preparation. Firms which work in areas of law that can have a direct impact on the general public, such as personal injury, class actions, employment or medical negligence, often have a rich array of resources that arouse media interest – most notably the clients.

In this respect, the law is at its most interesting to the mainstream media when it translates to the lives of its readers. In the contentious space, this is most often limited to class actions (in applicable jurisdictions) and disputes involving household names – namely, prominent people and brands. Plaintiff firms in particular have been very successful in promoting the stories of their clients to the press – both for the purposes of advocacy (ratcheting pressure on opposing counsel) and promotion of the lawyer or firm themselves.

Lawyers and firms at the more commercial end of the spectrum – such as those driven more by transactional work – should not discount the value, and suitability for media, of their clients. The value of client-specific commentary is most often demonstrated by those firms not directly related to legal matters of interest to the press; it is common to see a lawyer demonstrate his expertise by commenting on the intricacies of a deal or dispute that he has no direct connection with. He implicitly demonstrates his own expertise by commenting on the practical experience of a competitor and client that he has no experience with.

While, for those lawyers working on a specific matter, issues around client sensitivity and confidentiality make it more difficult to discuss client issues in the public domain, clients can still serve to be fruitful sources of media coverage in the abstract.

Indeed, one of the areas where the law has fallen behind other comparable sectors – such as corporate accounting – is a willingness to discuss the business of clients in a 'big picture' context. Generally, accounting and consultancy firms have a far greater appetite for commentating as an expert on business as opposed to merely accounting or management issues. As the globalised world brings greater interplay between regulators and markets, lawyers have a greater stake in the discussion of these issues than ever before – yet the sector is, in general terms, far more reluctant to enter the public discourse – despite its relevance and expertise.

This is one of the great challenges for communications practitioners within law firms – helping identify newsworthy topics for and with lawyers. The technical nature of the legal profession means that lawyers encounter matters and problems that seem commonplace to them, but are actually highly novel or interesting to the outside world (and journalists as a function of that world). An effective communications practitioner is, in that respect, a dual-advocate – he is advocating the views of his lawyers and firms to the journalists, and simultaneously representing the interests and curiosities of journalists to the lawyers themselves.

5.   Outside the four walls – media tactics in the law

A great bulk of the time that goes into producing media content within a law firm is spent first identifying topics for promotion and then confirming that those topics are suitable for public discussion. This process is complicated by the diverse and nuanced nature of partnership structures under which most law firms operate – by their very definition, they include considerably more stakeholders and decision-makers than traditional corporate structures.

At a micro level, reaching approval is a watershed moment in the communications process. Tactics and execution are relatively conventional by comparison.

Media relations in law firms – as with any business – can be achieved in a wide variety of ways. Every external communications practitioner will have different methods and habits in how he communicates – be it media, advertising or digital –

but there are certainly particular tactics which are generally applicable to all lawyers and law firms.

These methods – given the impediments to media in a law firm – are best discussed in the context of control. As a rule of thumb, the more controlled a piece of commentary can be, the more palatable it is within the legal setting.

Opinion pieces are often a first port of call for the legal profession. The defining characteristic of opinion pieces is that they are fully within the author's influence – every word in an opinion piece has been written, reviewed and approved by the lawyer and/or their firm. The scope for faux pas related to clients, or inadvertent misreporting by a journalist, is dramatically narrowed. This comforts legal and communications professionals alike, in that the likelihood of a mishap is reduced to near zero. The trade off, though, is that opinion pages are relatively scarce (and hotly contested) in the print world and command relatively small readerships. The reward is often commensurate with the risk.

At the other end of the spectrum, the least controllable engagement with media is the face-to-face interview or press conference – in that the final product is often unseen until a story is printed or broadcast. Interviews can represent a difficult proposition for many lawyers in that they are compelled to provide an immediate response. If the questions go toward a matter affecting clients, or take a lawyer outside of their primary expertise, they can cause great discomfort and anxiety.

Increasingly, though, lawyers and law firms are coming to grips with the reality of modern news gathering. Interviews are a powerful tool with which to build journalist rapport and the most effective way to insert oneself into the media – the majority of stories are still reliant upon quotes from experts in a given field, regardless of the medium.

Within the most prestigious publications in business and mainstream press – daily broadsheets, for instance – the interview remains the primary means of gathering information for coverage. While the risks in an interview are self-evidently higher than that of an opinion piece or self-published commentary (client briefings), the rewards are much higher as well. An insightful quote in a prominent story is a powerful communiqué to clients and colleagues alike. So long as interviewees are being sufficiently prepared for interviews, and a robust vetting process has been undertaken, this should be the primary media output of law firms.

Sitting somewhere in the middle of these two extremes is the vague and habitually abused concept of 'thought leadership'.

While defining such a vague term could itself be a source of many scholarly works, in the day-to-day reality of law firms, 'thought leadership' could aptly be used to describe the observations and insights that lawyers have every day – presented to the public in an accessible way.

This is a rich source of media content for firms – particularly firms large enough to fund and produce meaningful research, built to sidestep their conflicts footprint. Often, thought leadership material comprises research that a law firm is uniquely placed to conduct – such as inward-looking analysis of their own casework and matters (the macro-level trends being sufficiently large that individual client privilege is maintained), industry-wide data analysis or legal white papers. When executed thoughtfully, all of these forms of collateral are highly relevant to various elements of the media and equally newsworthy.

There is an added value to this sort of media relations compared with the other methods discussed – there is typically greater scope for complementary business development and communications activities. In the course of assembling thought leadership material, lawyers are inadvertently building a cache of content that can be easily repurposed for client conversations, events, digital communications and direct marketing.

The drawback in pursuing thought leadership-led media tactics is that the burden of quality is high. This is a hotly contested area of media relations – one that is dominated by other professional services, like accounting – and a great deal of time and money goes into the resulting collateral. Journalists are rightly sceptical of content that has been too manicured by advisers, such as lawyers and accountants, and the risk of 'survey fatigue', for instance, among media outlets is significant. The investment in thought leadership can be costly and there is considerable risk of the material not resonating with journalists if it lacks genuine insight or commentary. Too often, commentary from law firms sets out to avoid strong opinions and this can dampen journalist interest – the exhibition of expertise tends to demand strong views to be compatible with media interest.

The possibilities and permutations in media tactics, even in the tightly controlled legal environment, are too plentiful to list in full – but these three examples (opinion pieces, interviews, thought leadership material) give some idea of the variety of control and depth of content that is available in pursuing media coverage. Ultimately, there is no universal template for proactively approaching the media, other than recognising that the needs and capabilities of every lawyer are different, and to plan accordingly.

6. **Identifying success – measurement in legal media**
One of the great challenges facing every law firm in their external relations generally, but particularly media relations, is measuring success and the value added to the firm. Defining success (and in turn, return on investment) is a problem inherent to public relations – outside of the realm of crisis management – and an issue that dominates a lot of discussion in PR scholarship and the industry itself.

In many respects, it is the most critical role of the communications operative within the law firm – the costs associated with brand building can be significant, but the results are often indirect; it is a rare thing for a client to email a fee earner with a new mandate and admit to doing so because they saw the firm's name in that morning's business paper (though it does happen).

The demonstration and measurement of reputational growth is as important as the growth itself. In organisations as complex as law firms, and in a climate of ever-increasing drives for efficiency, the pressures on expenditure not directly related to winning or doing work can be very high. Therefore, it is vital that the person or people responsible for communications within the firm set clear benchmarks that speak to their firm's business needs and pursue accountability.

Setting a benchmark that reflects the firm goals for brand also sets a strategic tone in the firm's communications. While it was once enough merely to count the number of times that a lawyer or firm was named in the relevant press, assessment techniques have rightly become more strenuous. No single approach is universal, but firms are right to give consideration to a number of different metrics.

For instance, the persuasive qualities of media coverage ought to be considered in preference to raw numbers. Indeed, PR professionals are often dispatched to keep negative stories out of the public eye as much as they are tasked to promote positive coverage – which undermines the premise of a purely quantitative approach.

Equally, there is a raft of more useful measures available to lawyers and firms – and this will only increase as news content, and news readership, increasingly moves online. There are many sophisticated online media monitoring tools available, some of which include complex sentiment analytics – tools which are vastly more informative on issues of brand awareness and perception.

Similarly, thought should be given to client behaviour. A rudimentary – but informative – analysis can be conducted by keeping track of web traffic on a particular page or website if it has a correlation to newly generated news coverage. In the case of a prominently placed quote from a lawyer, who has been named in the reporting, you will typically see a spike in web traffic for that lawyer's personal web presence as interested readers turn to Google to learn more about the person quoted. Drawing a direct link between media relations and client behaviour is a compelling argument to maintain and bolster investment by firm management.

As with many things within media relations, measurement of this sort demands nuanced internal communications. It can be daunting to place hard, quantitative metrics on something as unpredictable and uncontrollable as media coverage – but ultimately, communications professionals within law firms should welcome the scrutiny as it is a means of demonstrating worth and, ultimately, learning from past experiences. The tactics and messages that resonate with the press evolve over time, so a rigorous measurement model compels practitioners to give thought to their own continuous improvement.

7.   Last-mover disadvantage: the flight to digital

There is a degree of irony in devoting analysis to the practice of media relations in that the media landscape has been in a state of constant flux for a decade, which shows no signs of abating. By and large, law has been slow to enter the media compared to other sectors, and now that it is fully embracing media relations, it has done so just in time to see disruptive technologies take hold and a diminished 'mainstream' media.

However, with the disrupted media landscape comes a convergence of other communications options – primary among them being online communication and the rise of social media.

While there is some truth to the stereotype that social and digital media are the purview of retail brands, as opposed to business-to-business advisers, it is far from exclusively so. Professional social network LinkedIn, for instance, is increasingly a source of business and driver of reputation for all manner of professional services companies. Clients are now regularly seeking out lawyers – particularly for highly niche advice – through this platform, often using no further research than the information provided on the lawyer's LinkedIn profile itself.

These platforms are fundamentally changing news consumption. The proliferation of mobile devices is building towards a tipping point, whereby mobile news consumption will exceed traditional news sources such as newspapers and television. What is more, the rise of tablets, improved video compression technologies, greater cellular bandwidths and expanding 'wi-fi' coverage means that it is easier than ever for mobile users to consume audio and video as much as they do the written word – in turn, demand for video comment is booming.

Legal and media relations professionals can take comfort from the fact that while the delivery and presentation of news continues to evolve, the fundamentals of media relations remain intact. The basic demand from likely legal buyers – genuinely insightful information from credible sources – is the same as it ever was. The change is for the most part limited to the composition of media and outlets that are the gatekeepers to readers.

Progressive lawyers and firms should look at this disruption as an opportunity to regain the ground that has been lost to other advisers in the past. The arrival of mainstream digital communications creates, in some sense, a 'reset' for the professional services sector and gives rise to new opportunities for experts in the legal sector to redefine themselves as experts in business. With this disruption, though, comes new onus on all lawyers to stay abreast of these new avenues of communication.

8.   Cutting through the noise

Communications – and particularly public relations – within law firms can seem like a rapidly moving target that never fully settles to a stop. However, the same impediments in this space – conflicts pressures, confidentiality concerns, a divergent media and troublesome measurement – are the same reasons that media relations is an opportunity that continues to exist for those lawyers and firms that take it seriously.

The world's largest law firms – companies with revenue in excess of US$1billion annually – for example, are not subject to the same marketing 'arms race' that characterise almost every other industry of the same size, where companies are forced to take on significant marketing spend merely to keep up with the competition. Law remains one of the very few realms of the commercial world where brand building largely remains a battle of ideas, of substance over style.

To that end, those lawyers and firms not yet seriously considering media relations as part of their broader marketing mix do themselves a great disservice. In some respects, law firms find themselves at an interesting crossroads – the rise of alternative business structures and disruptive law firm configurations will see a rise in innovative communication techniques from these new entrants. Incumbent firms would do well to choose to embrace the media now, rather than being compelled to do so in a more mature, and more fractured, legal marketplace and media landscape in the future.

Social media and business development in law firms

Rainer Kaspar
PHH Rechtsanwälte
Joanna Michaels
Beyond Social Buzz

1. The truth

Social media are here to stay. The profitable future for law firms will belong to those able to harness the power of social media while effectively managing the underlying risks. Such firms will thus establish a strong presence built on trust, compliance and quality service, while remaining approachable and open.

The sooner law firms understand and accept this new reality, the better the business results that social media can provide. Those which fail to adjust will be offering their portion of the market to digitally savvy competitors.

The benefits of using social media marketing for law firms are diverse and include:

- gaining access to the latest news and industry trends;
- increasing brand recognition;
- identifying new opportunities and prospects;
- limiting marketing expenditure when compared to traditional methods;
- providing opportunities to highlight the firm's values and extend the firm's brand online;
- establishing thought leadership by showcasing expertise and becoming a go-to expert in your area of law;
- humanising the brand (people hire lawyers, not law firms);
- networking and connecting with influencers and thought leaders in the field;
- differentiating your firm and making it stand out;
- positioning your firm as more competitive, attractive and profitable;
- extending the reach of your brand message – communicating with (potentially) millions rather than a few;
- building relationships and staying in touch with your clients, remaining at the forefront of their minds;
- limiting the barriers of traditional, lengthy and formal introductions;
- continuing conversations in between face-to-face meetings;
- missing no leads – social networks allow your firm to stay open beyond the usual office hours;
- increasing search engine rankings of the firm's website;
- building trust (potential clients are more likely to hire firms with lawyers whom they know, like and trust);
- gaining competitive intelligence – social media provide effective tools for monitoring and gathering information on competitors, clients and prospects;

- attracting top-tier talent by engaging with graduates; and
- gaining access to a younger audience, which increasingly perceive digital channels as the key mean of obtaining and sharing information.

2. Engage – developing a successful social media strategy

Is your firm ready to embrace social media? The following section considers how to use social media to your firm's benefit.

2.1 Make social media a part of the marketing mix

Social media do not exist in a vacuum. They should be seen as an integral part of your firm's wider marketing efforts to ensure that all your social activity is aligned with your overall business goals.

Consequently, social media should be treated as an essential part of the client's experience. When a client meets one of your partners in person and then checks your firm's website, blog and social channels, he should be presented with a consistent, seamless image of the firm. Brand consistency, whether online, in print or in person, builds trust, encourages engagement and ensures a positive customer experience.

While most corporate clients will rely on personal recommendations rather than Google when looking for a legal expert, they are still likely to perform some type of online search before making the initial contact with the firm. This is where social media can benefit your firm, by demonstrating your expertise and thought leadership, and increasing exposure of your brand, values and unique selling points.

Formulating a social media strategy is a key step in ensuring focus, brand consistency and results. Diving into social media without a thought-through strategy will make you vulnerable and directionless, unable to measure success or timely respond to risks and change. This means that you will always remain one step behind your more focused, strategic competitors. An *ad hoc* approach to social media will result in wasted time and resources.

A clearly defined social media strategy will help your firm to stay on track and align your activities with your business goals. That strategy should be refined based on regular analysis of results.

While there is no 'one size fits all' solution, a number of general principles and steps should be followed when planning the process.

2.2 Conduct a social media audit

The main objective of a social media audit is to establish how your firm is using social media and how this can be improved in order to connect with clients and prospects better and to maximise business results.

If your firm already has a social media presence, start with analysing your social activity up to that point in time by evaluating all your existing social media profiles. You should also check any 'unofficial' accounts for your firm, which could have been created by former employees or spammers.

Check whether all information displayed on your profiles is complete and up to date, and ensure brand consistency in terms of logos, imagery and the brand message across all platforms.

When evaluating your activity, remember to analyse web traffic data to find out which social channels drive the largest volumes of traffic. In addition, you should consider the visitors' behaviour – that is, how long are they visiting your website for and what specific links do they click on? You should also pay close attention to social media channels that drive less traffic but deliver higher quality visitors – those who stay longer on your site and 'convert' by taking a desired action, such as subscribe to your mailing list, fill out an enquiry form, etc.

Another factor to consider is the level of engagement with the firm received from social networks by analysing which channels generate the most 'likes', 'shares' and comments. Lastly, you should look at the overall 'conversation landscape' on social media channels and analyse trends and conversations about your firm and your lawyers. Each time that your firm or one of your lawyers is mentioned provides you with an opportunity to strengthen your brand. Listening tools that can be helpful in this respect are Google Analytics, Facebook Insights or Tweetreach. More advanced, paid-for tools include Synthesio or Radian6.

The next step is to compare your firm's social media presence with that of your competitors to indicate areas of improvement, growth opportunities and brand differentiation.

Analyse which social media channels your competitors use, what type of content they share and how much engagement is generated as a result of these actions. However, while these valuable insights will certainly help improve your own firms' strategy, remember that in order to succeed you must find the best way to use social media for you. This may be different from firms because of your unique strengths, personality, objectives, selling points and values.

2.3 Define your audience

To ensure success on social networks, your firm needs a crystal clear view about the audience that it is trying to reach.

This is because your chosen approach will differ depending on whether you seek to attract new recruits or target prospective clients within a specific niche. Defining your audience will help create highly relevant content that will instantly resonate with that audience, which will have a direct impact on engagement levels.

It will also enable you to position your firm as an expert, a go-to source within your field.

2.4 Select relevant social networks

If your firm has no social media presence, you should start by determining the most relevant channels.

Choosing the right social networks to connect with your audience is one of the key decisions when planning your social media strategy. Consider how your target audience use social media and how you can use this information to engage with that audience and build relationships.

Investing your valuable time in platforms that are unpopular with your target audience will only lead to wasted time and resources.

You need to follow your clients and prospects to ensure that you are establishing your firm's presence and networking on the right platforms.

It is worth mentioning here that while you may select only a couple of platforms to build your firm's social media presence, you should consider taking ownership of your firm's name across all social networks.

The general guideline is to build a social media presence on channels that:

- suit your firm's business strategy;
- suit the type of content that your firm creates (eg, if your firm does not produce highly visual content, a presence on Instagram, which relies on sharing images, may not be the best choice); and
- are popular among your clients and leads, as you otherwise run the risk of wasting time and resources on platforms whose audience will not be receptive to your message.

You should also recognise the differences between the various social media channels to ensure that the tone of your firm's profile is right for the network. Many law firms make the mistake of posting the same content across all their social platforms. This can damage chances for engagement as each platform has its own characteristic and your communications there should be tailored accordingly to ensure results. For example, Twitter users expect near-immediate responses, therefore you may need to consider whether your firm has the resources in place to deal with such a requirement.

It is also worth highlighting that different platforms might fulfil different purposes when supporting your firm's specific goals. Hence, it is advisable to establish a clear purpose for your presence on each chosen platform. For example, Facebook will be used to show the human side and the values of the firm in order to attract graduates.

Lastly, the question of channels' relevance is especially important when looking at business-to-customer (B2C) and business-to-business (B2B) platforms. Selection and prioritisation of social channels is crucial if your firm operates in a B2B market. Starting with a carefully planned LinkedIn activity would be a safe approach here, but being active on YouTube or Twitter may also be appropriate.

Remember that you do not need a presence on all social platforms. Choose relevant channels, start small and build from there.

2.5   Set objectives

Setting your social media goals and clarifying your expectations are of paramount importance. If you do not know what your aim is, you cannot move forward, measure your success or improve the process. This is not about getting 10,000 Twitter followers, but about aligning your social media goals with the overall business objectives of your firm.

It is important not to become preoccupied with the number of followers or fans, but to focus on steady, organic growth of an audience that genuinely listen and care about what you have to say.

Start with analysing your firm's overall needs and decide how social media can help in fulfilling those. Are you trying to raise awareness of your brand? Increase traffic to your firm's site? Establish your firm as a thought leader in your niche? Cross-sell your services? Or recruit, top young talent?

Whatever your goals, consider using a goal-setting framework such as SMART so that each of your objectives are:

- specific – target a specific area for improvement;
- measurable – quantify or at least suggest an indicator of progress;
- assignable – specify who will do it;
- realistic – state what results can realistically be achieved, given available resources; and
- time-bound – specify when the result(s) can be achieved.

2.6 Develop your content strategy – social media content calendar

The most successful brands on social media have mastered the art of creating customer loyalty and attracting new prospects through the power of their ideas and insights. Generating such relevant, high-quality content is time consuming, so it is important to have a plan in place to ensure productivity and efficiency.

Building your social media content in advance can make this task much less challenging. It will allow you to plan ahead, save time, allocate available resources and ensure consistency of posting and high quality of updates. It also enables you to think ahead and create content relating to events, seminars and conferences that your firm has planned for the year.

Do not forget to balance your pre-planned social media schedule with real-time updates and engagements. While planning ahead and scheduling some of your content in advance will ensure consistency and better time management, social media is about real-time conversations and interactions.

How to develop a content calendar for your firm is outlined below.

(a) Decide on themes

Decide on three to five main topics, most relevant for your firm and your target audience, that you would like to promote through your content. Think about relevant keywords and phrases, connected to these areas, for the purpose of search optimisation. When choosing main topics, analyse the performance of previously shared content (eg, using Google Analytics) to see what type of information resonates with your audience.

(b) Allocate resources

Consider who will be responsible for generating and creation of content. Will you do it in-house or outsource it? Also, decide how often you will create content in-house and how frequently you will share content from external sources.

Once you have selected the specific topics that you would like to focus on, the list can be passed over to the responsible team member. This advanced notice will give that person enough time to evaluate his expertise on the subject matter, as well as research, create and edit the copy of the blog post. The same applies to researching and generating relevant articles and publications, generated from external sources.

Advanced planning of content has another benefit – namely, of involving more team members into the content creation process. So you can showcase the diversity of knowledge and expertise available within your firm.

(c)   *Select social platforms*

Consider which social platforms you would like to use to promote your content, as well as how frequently would you like such posts to appear.

Make sure that you maximise the effect of each piece of content by sharing it via social media channels more than once. This tactic, also known as 'content repurposing' or 'recycling', is especially recommended for fast moving platforms, such as Twitter, where the lifecycle of updates is very short. The main aim of content repurposing is to ensure that more of your fans and followers will see your updates. Remember, however, not to share the exact post twice, as it may be perceived as spamming. Instead, vary headlines by pulling fragments of the blog post and including them into the post or adding thought-provoking questions before the link in the post.

(d)   *Choose the right format(s)*

Your content can be developed in a variety of forms such as blogs, videos, industry articles or downloadable ebooks.

Monitor what type of content performs best (ie, generates most engagement or drives most traffic) from your audience and focus your efforts there.

(e)   *Monitor and measure*

Although social media are more than a decade old, measuring return on investment in this area remains tricky. However, a number of metrics can be used to measure social media success, including engagement, subscriptions, clicks, downloads or conversions. It is advisable to set key performance indicators for each selected social media platform in order to evaluate their impact and performance.

For example, if your objective is to raise awareness of your brand, you will be checking how far the reach of your message is by analysing volume, reach and exposure.

If your objective is to boost traffic to your firm's website, you will be looking at your site's analytics to determine which social media channels are the major drivers of site visitors. Additionally, it is worth analysing which of the social media platforms sends valuable traffic. This can be done by looking at the visitors' behaviour on your site (ie, click-through rates, downloads or subscriptions). For the purpose of accurate analysing of social media leads, make sure that tracking codes are attached to the links promoted via social channels.

If your objective is to increase brand engagement, you will be evaluating the amount of people participating in interactions with your brand, by looking at likes, retweets, shares, comments and replies.

In any case you should analyse the results obtained from each social media channel and assess which platforms drive best results.

Monitoring and evaluating your social media performance should take place regularly. You may consider monthly or quarterly reporting.

Useful tools for social media monitoring and measuring include:

- Google Analytics, which allows you to set up links for specific campaigns and track results;
- Facebook Insights, which highlights user growth and demographics;
- Twitter Analytics, which has a detailed activity dashboard;
- Buffer, a scheduling platform that provides detailed analytics for all posts;
- Hootsuite, another scheduling tool that provides detailed metrics tracking;
- Klout, a free tool that measures your brand's overall influence on social media; and
- Social mention, which tracks brand mentions across all social networks.

(f) ***Refine your approach and repeat***
Always remember that no social media strategy is set in stone and in order to succeed one must constantly monitor and evaluate the performance of social campaigns, and tweak the chosen approach according to results. Only by refining your strategy will you ensure the future effectiveness of your social media marketing efforts.

3. Platforms' overview
Below is a review of some of the most popular and useful social media platforms that can be used by law firms for developing business.

3.1 LinkedIn
The 2015 Social Media Marketing Industry Report, by M Stelzner, named LinkedIn the best social media platform for B2B marketing.

Also, Google loves LinkedIn and links from this channel are included in Google's search rankings and the search engine optimisation algorithm. This means that your activity on this platform can directly affect the search engine's rankings for your firm's website.

(a) ***Key benefits***
Recruit new talent: LinkedIn is used by a lot of headhunting professionals to search for new talent. Do the same.

Refer high volumes of traffic to your corporate website: your company profile works as a gateway to your company website. Instil interest in your contacts and other visitors by posting information which requires to be linked to your website.

Establish thought leadership: choose an area of expertise and continually post information on such area. LinkedIn users do not necessarily expect this to be written by you, but will notice that you have an interest in, and understanding of, a certain practice area. This way you can stay at the forefront of your clients' thoughts.

Obtain direct access to decision makers: LinkedIn allows you to bypass gatekeepers and reach out directly to decision makers.

Maintain offline relationships: LinkedIn is a great tool for staying in touch with your clients and prospects. That way, when they have a need that you can fulfil, they will reach out to you and nobody else.

(b) *Top tips*

Be active: check who viewed your LinkedIn profile. This shows you who is interested in your company and enables you to make new connections. LinkedIn helps you to build new potential business relationships as it is solely used for professional purposes.

Get down to the nitty-gritty: optimise your LinkedIn company page by filling all necessary company data and hard facts. Use relevant phrases and keywords that you would like your firm to be found for.

Share your knowledge: share relevant business news, including updates that could be of interest to your target group. Publish posts containing company news and share it with your network.

Socialise: create your own LinkedIn group and join other relevant groups. By creating your own LinkedIn group you can demonstrate your skills and your practice areas.

3.2   Facebook

Faceook has approximately 1.49 billion active users – more than WhatsApp (500 million), Twitter (284 million) and Instagram (200 million) combined, with 968 million people logging onto Facebook and over 4.5 billion likes generated daily.

Facebook is moving into the B2B segment, although it is still regarded as mostly a personal network.

(a)   *Key benefits*

Build and sustain personal, rather than professional-only, relationships: this may help get closer to your business contacts.

Affordable advertising: it is worth considering Facebook advertising, due to the fact that the organic (unpaid) reach on the platform decreased dramatically over the past few years. This is due to the fact that Facebook has introduced changes to its news feed algorithm, prioritising paid posts in terms of visibility. This means that it is getting increasingly harder to get your unpaid posts in front of your audience. However, the good news is that Facebook advertising is very affordable compared to any other form of online advertising. What is more, the targeting of Facebook ads is exceptional. Facebook allows you to target your chosen audience using highly specific criteria like age, location, behaviours, interests and more.

Undisputed reach: as the largest social media platform, the reach of your marketing is also the most extensive.

(b)   *Top tips*

Prioritise your contacts: this will enable you to decide who will see what.

Use sparingly: studies have shown that Facebook users do not wish to read more than one or two news feed updates per week from each contact – do not become the annoying person who spams his contacts with several posts an hour.

Keep your posts short: use short headlines to promote your content. Social media users usually skim headlines and short summaries before they decide if they want to read the whole article.

Tag other organisation in your post: this will increase the range of your target audience.

Start a conversation: an effective way to get to know your audience better is to ask questions and carefully consider the answers. This helps you understand the specific needs of your target group and thus customise your content.

3.3   Twitter

With posts, known as 'tweets', limited to 140 characters, this platform has been described as a cocktail party full of trivial conversations, celebrities and self-serving narcissists. This explains why many lawyers approach this platform with reluctance. But while Twitter's ambience is far less formal than LinkedIn, it is a powerful information-sharing, networking and listening tool and should not be ignored.

(a)   *Key benefits*

Establish thought leadership: Twitter is a great tool for demonstrating your professional knowledge and positioning yourself as an expert and thought leader in your field.

Gather real-time competitive intelligence: it is one of the best social networks when it comes to listening. You are likely to get more legal and technical news from Twitter than from any other online source. This is because Twitter acts as a real-time search engine, allowing you to listen to conversations and gather intelligence, monitor your reputation, as well as obtain important insights into what your clients and competitors are doing.

Follow up: Twitter is the perfect tool for a post-meeting follow up and 'keeping in touch' interactions. It can help you to stay at the forefront of your contact's mind.

Network at live events: Twitter is also perfect for live events and meeting people, as it facilitates real-time conversations, as well as relationship building before, during and after the event. Tweeting from conferences and seminars, using relevant hashtags, is also a great way of sharing information and learning from other attendees.

Hashtags are an integral part of the Twitter experience. They facilitate conversations and help to navigate through the fast-paced and cluttered Twitter feed. Hashtags allow users to find content, activity or discussions focused on specific topics, and can be created by simply adding a hash sign in front of a word or a group of words. When searching for a chosen hashtag on Twitter, users receive a filtered list of all the posts and conversations mentioning the relevant hashtag.

Gain direct access to high-profile individuals: on Twitter you can engage with people that you would like to connect with, a simple mention can easily lead to a conversation. You can also gain access to people with whom you would not normally interact, due to geographical or other barriers.

(b)   *Top tips*
Align your firm's values with your voice on Twitter: this will enable your activity there to build a consistent reputation.

Listen to conversations: also analyse trends that affect your niche.

Be approachable: Twitter's tone is personable and light-hearted. The majority of professionals who have succeeded on this platform recommend finding a balance between sharing expertise and personality.

Initiate and join conversations with your connections: share your comments on relevant industry topics.

Choose your approach: Twitter is a public platform; a good idea may be to run two types of account – one connected to your work and a personal one (that can be protected). Many lawyers choose to have one account and post both personal and professional updates, balancing their professionalism and individualism. See what works for you.

Be creative: character restriction requires catchy headlines. Thus, if you publish a post on the new law of contracts, a headline such as "Why your contracts may be unenforceable from next week" is much more likely to grab attention than "Here is our new blog on the new law of contracts".

Add visual content: Twitter, like all other social networks, is increasingly visual. Research shows that visual content can significantly increase engagement on social media. You can obtain images from stock photography libraries such as Shutterstock, as well as other creative resources like Canva.

Remain professional: Twitter is a public platform and therefore all your posts are public. Consequently, your conversational footprint on Twitter is permanent.

3.4 YouTube

YouTube is a free, video-sharing website with over 1 billion users that dominates the visual-centric social networks. The platform was created in 2005 and purchased by Google in 2006. YouTube fans use this platform for research, learning and entertainment. According to a recent survey by Global Web Index, 85% of adult internet users identify themselves as regular YouTube users. YouTube accounts for over 28% of all Google searches.[1]

Video is considered one of the most powerful forms of online communication.

What does it mean for law firms? That ignoring these powerful figures would equal missing out on opportunities to get in front of a large, captive audience. (Note also that YouTube is the second-largest search engine, positioned right behind its parent company Google.)

(a) Key benefits

Humanise your brand: video allows law firms to present the personality and values of both the firm and the people.

Gain trust: video provides a great opportunity to share powerful content that can make more of your prospective clients know, like and trust you, so they are more inclined to hire you and recommend your services further.

Offer transparency: video can assist in explaining processes to prospective clients. Thus, Whatson Thomas, family law solicitors from Hampshire, United Kingdom, have used a YouTube video[2] to present their unique selling points, including personal service and fixed fees, in an engaging and transparent way.

Educate: your firm's YouTube channel can serve as an educational library that builds trust and authority in your practice area. DLA Piper maintains an active YouTube channel. One of its videos,[3] in the form of a fictional drama, explores the threats of cyber crime. Kingsley Napley LLP uses video to give practical advice on shared parental leave or challenging the validity of a will.[4]

Integrate your marketing: video is a highly shareable type of content for other social media channels such as Facebook or Google Plus. By distributing your YouTube videos on other platforms, you can instantly increase the exposure of your message.

(b) Top tips

Create a YouTube channel for your firm: to ensure brand consistency, add the firm logo, customise the colours and add relevant information and links. All your messages should be aligned with your firm's unique selling points and values.

---

1   Source: Comscore.
2   https://www.youtube.com/watch?v=-DOMxkBx4t0.
3   https://www.youtube.com/watch?v=TvhS_KLA6Nk.
4   https://www.youtube.com/watch?v=mgjJMHA91_w.

Monitor competition: this will help determine what type of video message best resonates with your target audience.

Solve problems and provide useful information: create videos that answer common clients' questions, such as "Three things you need to know before hiring a property lawyer".

Consider your audience: is your message aimed at graduates, current clients or prospects? Understanding your various audiences and their specific needs will help clarify your message.

Optimise your videos for online search: if your videos are invisible to your prospective clients, your message will not reach them. Make sure that you choose the right keywords to help YouTube determine the relevance of your content. Include them in your title, description and tags.

Create webinars: this will help connect better with your target audience, create a competitive edge and establish your firm as an authority in a specific niche. This will bring leads and business.

Be creative without losing professionalism and relevance: showing your team's personality and sense of humour will make your videos more appealing to viewers.

Never compromise on quality: if there is no in-house know-how, allocate a budget for hiring a professional production agency. The quality of your visual presentation is just as important as presenting valuable content.

3.5 Pinterest

Pinterest is a visual social network, based entirely on photo and video posts, with 25 million users. It is often described as a visual inspiration board.

Users can upload, save and manage images, known as pins, which are stored under specific boards (virtual albums). Boards are organised by category. Users can also browse content uploaded by others, as well as like and follow each other, and repin content shared by others.

Pinterest's audience is unique in that 83% of the platform's users are female.[5]

While primarily associated with do-it-yourself projects, beauty and interior design, Pinterest can also present opportunities for both B2C and B2B brands.

(a) Key benefits

Generate traffic: while it may be less powerful in terms of leads than other platforms, Pinterest is often described as the most powerful traffic referral tool (ie, sending traffic to your website and improving your search rankings).

---

5   Source: Engauge, 2012.

Drive away: Pinterest is the only social media channel that drives away traffic from the platform.

Promote your blog content: distinguish yourself from other users by creating a strong, optimised presence – think of keywords for your niche. Be specific when naming your boards – for example, instead of general terms like 'personal injury', use specific phrases and long-tail keywords, such as 'car incident compensation London', 'back injury claim London'. Terms that are too general should be avoided, though, as too many users are competing for those.

Increase your brand authority and build trust: do this by creating highly relevant, focused boards that provide detailed, up-to date information on your specific niche. Note that you can balance your own content with relevant resources from other industry experts. Thus, your account will become a go-to source for relevant information on your niche.

(b)   *Top tips*
Identify keywords: pin descriptions and board titles are searchable, so remember to use keywords that you want to be found for.

Stay relevant: keep your pins with specific boards relevant to your chosen name and subject.

Create the super pin: most popular pins combine appealing images with content that solves problems, inspires or educates. Or create relevant infographics based on interesting case studies or industry reports. Or get creative with images and think how best to tell the story of your brand, for instance by using 'behind-the-scenes' photos reflecting office culture and your firm's values.

Stay fresh: not everything has to be 'dry', you may want to lighten your presence on Pinterest, and show a glimpse of your personality. Some law firms add character to their Pinterest presence by creating less formal, yet still relevant boards like 'legal humour' or 'parenting on budget'.

3.6   Excursus – China

Social media usage continues to grow across the world, and China is no exception. But while China has admittedly and significantly opened up to the world over the past few years, the government still aims to control and censor the Internet where it believes that it could have a negative effect on its citizens. As a result, China has blocked access to most of western social networks. However, rather than to eliminate social media as a whole in China, the restriction has resulted in the Chinese creating and intensely using their own social networks.

User numbers are staggering and even exceed those in the United State and Europe. According to a report released by the China Internet Network Information Centre in 2014, there are 618 million internet users in China, a 45.8% internet penetration rate, of which 500 million are mobile users. And of all Chinese internet users, 58% use social networks.

The top websites include:

- QQ (830 milion users), a messaging platform also offering online games, music and shopping;
- QZone (755 million users), a social networking platform whose users can share photos, music and videos;
- Weibo (600 million users), a micro-blogging website that is a cross between Twitter and Facebook; and
- WeChat (468m users), a micro-messaging app similar to WhatsApp.

There is a lot to gain for those who understand China's social media platforms; and even more to lose for those that stay away from this development.

Business development in law firms of the future: focus and infrastructure

Norman Clark
Walker Clark LLC

Although predictions of the death of law firms might be exaggerated, they nonetheless contain a bitter kernel of truth: the law firm, as we have traditionally known it, is an endangered business species. To flourish, all law firms will need to refocus and redirect their priorities with respect to both the internal structures of the firm and the way in which they approach the market. The client-service orientation of today's successful law firms will thus continue to be a core element of law firms of the future.

Similarly, the emergence of 'Big Law' – that is, the multi-billion dollar global law firms – does not mean the end of smaller firms. With a well-developed sense of strategic alertness, exceptional client service and close attention to sustainable profitability, small and mid-size firms will continue to thrive and compete successfully with, and not necessarily against,[1] the global giants. However, all firms of all sizes might need to reconsider some of their traditional strategic assumptions and tactical priorities.

This chapter examines one such cluster of assumptions and priorities that law firms must reconsider today in order to improve their chances of survival: business development. Successful business development in the future will require clarity in at least three areas:

- an understanding of the fundamental nature of a law firm's practice and its desired client base;
- the selection of marketing or business development tactics that will address the unique needs of the firm; and
- for some law firms, a new infrastructure to support the retention of their best clients.

1. The future is already here

Any consideration of an issue as dynamic and multi-dimensional as the future of the legal profession inherently raises risks. Even the best-informed and logical predictions of today can be far off the mark 10 years from now.

---

[1] A central premise of this chapter is that, in the future, law firms must remain open to the possibilities of collaboration with other firms, even direct competitors, to improve the conditions in the legal market by delivering legal services and products more cost-effectively and with higher levels of client satisfaction. These efforts will include, most notably, collective action to use an improved legal services environment to build confidence by foreign investors in the stability of their national economies. In other words, you should market your jurisdiction to develop new business for your law firm.

To a great extent, the future is already here. The globalisation of business and, with it, the beginnings of at least a broad-based internationalisation of the legal services industry, have already been instructive. Barring major economic dislocations or social upheavals worldwide, recent experiences and observations suggest some general pathways into the future. We can expect, therefore, that the law firms of the future will face

- even more intense competition for high-value legal work;
- increased price sensitivity in practice areas that traditionally have been relatively price insensitive;
- the continuing consolidation of law firms;
- 'global vision' – that is better alertness to, and understanding of, political, economic and regulatory developments, especially in emerging and recently emerged legal markets;
- a shift in emphasis away from traditional marketing efforts to create general visibility to more highly personalised client services and ongoing relationships to improve client retention;
- ever-rising client expectations for availability, speed and economy in the delivery of legal services and products that traditionally have been viewed by lawyers as being customised or high value;
- an increased importance in being able to articulate compelling competitive advantages in terms that are relevant and important to the best clients, even as it becomes more intellectually challenging to do so;
- a dramatic expansion of, and increased demand for, legal services and products to include added-value elements that most law firms today consider to be outside the scope of their business;
- a shift from an obsession with short-term profits to a farther-focused investment mentality in order for the firm's fee earners to remain competitive and profitable;
- greater investment in, and reliance on, outside expertise to support better decision making and implementation in a constantly changing business environment; and
- the emergence of new non-traditional forms of legal service providers into prominent, if not dominant, positions in markets previously occupied only by traditional law firms.

1.1 Finding a way through the fog

This emerging evolution of the legal services industry has created a difficult paradox, which law firm leaders – especially those of traditionally structured firms – must resolve now. A 'wait and see' deferral of understanding and action will be fatal.

The first part of the paradox is that, as noted above, the big trends in business will continue to affect directly the way that law firms market themselves, develop and maintain client relationships, and generate new business from existing clients. The Internet long ago revolutionised the way that customers communicate and obtain information that previously commanded a high fee, if it were available at all in the public domain. It also has created a 'do it yourself' approach to problems that previously were the exclusive province of highly trained, expensive, professional service providers. As we saw in the period 1995–2010, law firms eventually went along with these trends, sometimes amid storms of scepticism from partners, creating websites and beginning to experiment with social media.

One of the results of this awareness of the trends in the business world has been a temptation simply to cut and paste what works in other industry sectors, assuming that it also will work well for law firms. Some lawyers and law firms invested substantial amounts of time and staff resources in maintaining Facebook pages, Twitter accounts and other social media, only to discover that their efforts produced no significant benefits. At the same time, other law firms have had reasonable success with these same tools.

It is easy to overreact, however. The new technology and communications media available to law firms are merely tools, not panaceas. As this chapter points out later, even the most powerful, imaginative and attractive technology is useless when the organisation lacks the basic infrastructure – systems, processes, commitment and resources – to support it. A firm's systems and processes drive and determine how the technology operates, not the reverse. For example, some law firms mistakenly assume that licensing and installing a sophisticated customer relations management system can serve, in effect, as their marketing and business development programmes. They forget that you cannot automate what is not there.

The second part of the paradox is that, notwithstanding the embrace by the business world of new modes of communication and more powerful technological tools, sophisticated consumers of legal services continue to make their engagement decisions in ways that differ significantly from their practice in other commercial transactions.

As one general counsel of a major multinational enterprise commented, "I love social media, but we don't buy legal services that way. And we probably never will."

The challenge for law firms, both now and into the future, will be to resolve this paradox by reconciling changing client expectations for communications and service delivery with the basic values that sophisticated clients continue to use to guide their decisions about which law firms to entrust with their most important legal matters. Finding the right path through this foggy landscape will be even more difficult as technological change in the business world continues to accelerate, and the response, as always, will be to stay one step ahead of the client, anticipating needs and pointing out risks even before the client is fully aware of them.

As we try to reconcile this dilemma, a few conceptual definitions can be reliable lighthouses to guide us past the indistinct shapes that emerge as we look into the future.

1.2 What kind of law firm are you?

Each law firm must develop and internally agree on a clear understanding of the fundamental nature of the services that are the core of its business and the clients that it wants in its client base. These decisions then guide each firm in the selection of the right blend of marketing and business development for its unique set of strategic objectives and business needs.

Although there are many exceptions and hybrids, most law firms worldwide are mainly influenced by one of two centres of gravity, which generally describe their most profitable services and client sectors: commercial law and retail law.[2] These differences will become more important in the future, in which – as a result of natural market processes in many parts of the world – the differences between commercial law firms and retail law firms will evolve into two distinct sectors in the legal services industry.

Commercial law firms generally offer sophisticated corporate and commercial services to corporations, government agencies and high net-worth individuals. Most large law firms and many mid-size firms today can be characterised as commercial law firms. They handle large, complex transactions and cases. Competition for these 'best' clients is intense; and client retention is essential to a commercial firm's market position and long-term financial success.

Retail law firms tend to be smaller practices, including most solo practices. They usually focus on a limited number of legal services and products delivered primarily to individual clients and small businesses. Examples include small firms specialising in personal injury, employee rights, criminal defence, estate planning, family law and personal taxation. Some mid-size retail law firms might include several of these practice areas. Their clients tend to be infrequent users of their services, most of them engaging the firm only once.

The determination of whether a firm is oriented primarily to commercial law or to retail law does not depend on size. Most large firms offer some services that might be considered to be retail law, and smaller law firms – particularly industry-sector specialists or boutique firms offering highly sophisticated services – compete very successfully for commercial law engagements. The important point, however, is that each firm should clearly understand which centre of gravity has the greater influence on its most profitable lines of business.

This determination is relatively easy for many large firms and most small firms. It can be challenging, however, for the one variety of traditional law firms that truly is threatened with extinction: the mid-size local firm that attempts to offer full service. Unless the mid-sized full service firm clarifies its priorities for service offerings and desired clients, it risks being picked apart competitively by large firms that can offer the same or better commercial law services at a competitive price and by smaller firms that can offer retail services more cost-effectively with equally good results.

1.3   Marketing or business development?

One of the central themes of this chapter is the need for clarity about the distinction between marketing and business development in law firms. Some law firms

---

2   Some observers might identify a third centre of gravity – namely, the organisation that delivers 'commodity' legal services and products, such as insured defence litigation, trademark registration and administration, or residential real estate conveyancing. Further analysis, however, usually results in such commodity firms gravitating more toward commercial law firms, for purposes of marketing and business development strategies, because of the importance of attracting and retaining large clients with repeated, high-volume business.

incorrectly use the two terms almost interchangeably, thereby thickening the fog that surrounds their determination of priorities and resource allocations.

As used in this chapter, 'marketing' refers to the process of establishing and promoting the visibility of a law firm in its selected markets. It is directed at the first two steps of the sales process for professional services: attracting attention and gaining interest.[3] 'Business development' consists of activities aimed at the retention of profitable or potentially profitable clients and the sale of additional legal services and products to those clients. This is an important distinction, because many law firms today waste vast amounts of money, partner time and management attention on marketing, while overlooking the much higher return-on-investment in business development.

2. Which strategy is better?

Most of this chapter explores basic strategic decisions that law firms should make now in order to be better prepared to respond to the challenges of the future. A clear understanding of the strategic foundations of a firm – what kind of firm it is and where it wants to go – will make the selection of the right bundle of marketing and business development tactics significantly easier and much more reliable.

As the markets for legal services and products continue to mature, every law firm will need to understand how to allocate resources between marketing and business development. A wrong decision, or no decision at all, will result in a wasted investment of a firm's resources, which, coupled with poor results, could plunge a firm into a death spiral.

The decision should be driven by a clear understanding of where a law firm is placed between the two centres of gravity: commercial law and retail law. For some firms, one strategy – marketing or business development – will clearly be the better choice. Other firms will need to strike the right balance, adopting tactics that address the unique characteristics of the firm's services and products, and the nature of its client base.

At the risk of oversimplifying complex strategic considerations, which will continue to vary substantially among different law firms, successful commercial law firms of the future will focus primarily on business development – keeping the good clients and getting more work from them – with very little effort being required in the area of basic marketing. Retail law firms, by contrast, will gain only marginal value in business development strategies and will concentrate instead on marketing and sales.

2.1 Client retention in increasingly competitive commercial law markets

Business development will be more important than marketing for most commercial

---

3   The five steps in the sales process for professional services are:
    • attract attention;
    • build interest;
    • establish rapport;
    • answer objections; and
    • close the deal.

practices, because one of their biggest challenges will be to retain, and to expand, the scope of profitable services that they deliver to their best clients.

(a) *The frustrating limits of a marketing-oriented strategy*

In mature legal markets, such as already exist in most developed jurisdictions, a relatively large number of service providers compete for a relatively smaller number of high-value clients. In these highly competitive environments, the opportunity to win new clients is limited by three factors.

The first limiting factor is that the number of desirable clients with profitable commercial law work is unlikely to increase significantly in many of the most dynamic industry sectors. Any growth in the population of new entrants into the client population will be offset to a great extent by corporate mergers.

The second factor is the growth of in-house law departments and the 'in-sourcing' of commercial legal work that used to be referred to outside law firms. This trend is almost certain to continue, as corporate boards and shareholders continue to demand, sometimes unrealistically, reductions in corporate legal spending. Competitive outsourcing of legal services, which became so popular in the 1990s and early 2000s, has been an incomplete solution, usually effective as a cost-saving tactic only with respect to matters, such as routine litigation,[4] in which the fees charged by outside firms are significantly lower than the fully loaded operating cost of having in-house lawyers do the work.

The third factor, ironically, is client satisfaction. Clients are generally satisfied with their law firms, notwithstanding their frequent grousing about high fees. Strategic business development surveys and confidential interviews conducted by Walker Clark LLC since 2002 confirm that clients generally have a very high level of overall satisfaction with their current providers of legal services.[5] The respondents also have clearly indicated, by a wide margin, that the most important factor in the decision to engage or retain a firm is the "prior relationship with the firm". Despite a possible trend toward decreased loyalty by some clients, these two factors mean that it is frustratingly difficult for most commercial law firms to win new clients, absent significant dissatisfaction with the services provided by a competitor.

(b) *Rethinking marketing tactics for commercial law firms*

This does not mean that a commercial law practice can ignore marketing. In the future, as today, it will remain important to establish visibility in the market, especially in industry sectors that are the most profitable and offer the greatest growth potential. However, the relatively secondary importance and limited return on investment for most traditional marketing activities suggest some major changes

---

4   For a brief discussion of one of the classic examples of the convergence of outside corporate legal services in the 1990s, see Gregory Bardnell, "The DuPont Convergence Program: How One Outside Service Provider Benefits", *The Metropolitan Corporate Counsel*, June 1996, p 53, reprinted at www.dupontlegalmodel.com/the-dupont-convergence-program-how-one-outside-service-provider-benefits/.

5   Since 2002 Walker Clark LLC has administered a strategic business development survey to more than 4,000 clients of commercial law firms. Approximately 77% of the respondents have reported that they are "very satisfied" overall with the services that they receive from their law firm; and a total of 92% state that they are either "very satisfied" or "satisfied." These numbers appear to be gradually increasing.

in marketing assumptions and tactics, which might be uncomfortable for some law firm partners and their marketing advisers. For example:

- Mass advertising, such as at airports and in business magazines, will probably have almost no return on investment, even in terms of new clients.
- As electronic information becomes even more available at little or no cost, 'pay to publish' articles in business and legal industry publications will have little, if any, impact on selection decisions by sophisticated clients. Most law firms will consider them to be a waste of a partner's time and the firm's money.
- The return on investment in attending international legal conferences and other networking opportunities to attract new clients will continue to decrease, compared to using those events to develop more business from existing or recent clients.
- Social media will have almost no value in attracting new clients, although they will become more important tools for demonstrating competitive advantages – especially responsive communications and availability – to existing clients.
- Seminars and similar events to demonstrate the firm's expertise will not produce a reasonable return in terms of new clients or improved visibility for the firm; but they will continue to be important in client retention and the development of new high-value commercial legal work from existing clients.
- Rankings in major legal directories will continue to be important channels for communicating the firm's expertise to the commercial legal market, but only to the extent that the rankings demonstrate significant, differentiating advantages over competitors, and only if the directory has an unquestionable reputation for integrity and transparency in the rankings process. Unfortunately, many law firm submissions and some rankings directories fall short of these basic criteria for credibility.[6]
- 'Law Firm of the Year' awards presented by legal publications will have almost no value in improving a firm's visibility, because these awards will continue to go to law firms that already are well known. Although deservedly gratifying to a law firm's partners, these awards will not add much value to the firm's visibility or market reputation among clients that it wants to attract.

This is not to say that any of these examples of traditional law firm marketing activities will be totally irrelevant or worthless to commercial law firms in the future; however, as is already the case, they will not produce the best return on investment – especially of partner time – and will not be high-priority activities. To the extent that successful commercial law firms of the future will engage in traditional marketing activities, they will be precisely tailored to specific prospective clients and industry sectors – in other words, personalised marketing.

---

6   Rankings for individual lawyers already might have less weight among potential clients than rankings for the firm, because there is little genuinely differentiating information in the published editorial comments about individual lawyers.

(c)   ***The shift from marketing tactics to client retention and business development***
Instead of investing time and resources in traditional marketing activities, many of which already have only limited value for most commercial law firms, the better strategy for commercial law firms of the future will be to focus on building client loyalty and engaging new profitable work from existing clients. Instead of working hard to try to attract new clients, the most successful firms will focus their efforts on cementing their relationships with their clients.

This shift will be difficult for many commercial law firms. This will require people, not high-tech glossy marketing tools. The firms that will make this transition from the visibility-oriented marketing of legal services to precisely targeted business development will have three characteristics infrequently observed in law firms today:

- cultural and intellectual diversity to relate better to an increasingly diverse global client base;
- well-developed business skills and emotional intelligence to focus legal knowledge on better understanding and meeting the expectations of clients; and
- a shift in focus and responsibility for business development from marketing staff to the lawyers, especially partners.

In short, not only must the law firms change, but so must individual lawyers.

The first step, of course, is to identify those clients that offer the best long-term return on investment, the clients that a firm wants to retain indefinitely while continuing to expand the scope of profitable legal services that it delivers to them. There are two simple but, if supported with adequate financial data, reliable ways to select these 'keepers'.

Analysing the client pyramid: Consider the extent to which a client contributes to your firm's total fee revenue. There is an 80/20 rule of law firm economics that describes how the structure of a commercial law firm's client base affects its financial performance, overall profitability and business development potential. In most law firms approximately 80% of the fee revenue is produced by only approximately 20% of the clients.[7] When the clients are sorted from largest to smallest, as measured by each one's fee revenue, sometimes in the shape of a pyramid, several distinct tiers of client productivity emerge.

The top-tier and second-tier clients in a typical commercial law firm usually total

---

7   This principle was first presented by Jay Curry in *The Customer Marketing Method* (Simon & Schuster, 2000). While Curry's research was conducted primarily among businesses other than professional services firms, it also included law firms. Curry observed that "[w]hile these companies have been wildly different in terms of size and types of businesses, their customer pyramids reflect remarkably similar patterns of customer behavior. And the ways in which all these companies interact with their customers also are remarkably similar". Client-base analyses that Walker Clark LLC has performed for its clients in the legal profession since 2002 likewise demonstrates great similarities among law firms and validate the general 80/20 rule. There appears to be no correlation between the 80/20 rule and the size or geographic location of the firm. The phenomenon can be observed in firms of all sizes and in all legal markets. However, retail law firms and firms with high-volume commodity practices tend to have less concentration of fee revenues from a relatively small number of clients. For those firms 70/30 and 65/35 ratios (ie, 70% of the fee revenue produced by 30% of the clients, or 65% of the revenue produced 35% of the clients) frequently appear.

less than 20% of the total number of clients, but together they produce at least approximately 80% of the fee revenue. These clients are the ones that also produce a disproportionately large share of the firm's profits. They are clients that most commercial law firms want to keep. They also are the clients that most commercial law firms need to keep in order to sustain and improve their profitability and market position. Although there might be opportunities to obtain more work from the top clients, many of them have already given to the firm all of the profitable legal work that they have available.

With future significant growth unlikely, the major direction of business development among these clients should be:

- to retain the clients; and
- to encourage these usually highly satisfied clients to act as a secondary marketing force for the firm by referring the firm to potential clients with similar possibilities for highly profitable legal work.

Identifying the top clients does not end the analysis, however. An examination of the fee performance history of the clients in the middle tiers, usually the second quartile of the client base, often suggests a small number of clients with good growth potential. The primary goal of business development efforts among these clients should be to obtain more profitable legal work through vigorous cross-selling of the firm's full range of services.

Assessing current profitability and long-term growth potential: A second reliable way for a commercial law firm to identify its best opportunities for business development is to evaluate the relative current profitability and growth potential of each major client sector or industry sector that the firm currently serves. This analysis consists of two basic questions. First, which client sectors have the relatively highest levels of current profitability? The issue is actual profitability for the law firm now, not how profitable the client sector could be in the future or how profitable it might be for other law firms. Second, what is the relative growth potential of each client sector? In other words, to what extent could your firm substantially improve its market share of the commercial legal services and products that you offer to that client sector?

As with the client pyramid, this analysis usually will highlight two types of highly desirable client:

- high profitability and low growth potential – these are sometimes called 'cash cows' and frequently are among commercial law firm's largest clients. Although relatively profitable, there is little opportunity to develop a larger market share in these client sectors. As with the top clients in the client pyramid analysis, these clients are the targets for intense client retention efforts through close and frequent communications, strong client relations and thoroughly outstanding service – completely meeting or exceeding the client's needs and expectations the first time and every time; and
- high profitability and high growth potential – clients in these sectors usually respond positively to an 'added value' approach to legal services, coupled

with demonstrated abilities to integrate multidisciplinary legal teams to provide a broad range of high-value services for each client.

As the expectations of sophisticated commercial law clients continue to expand, added-value tactics will include:

- the anticipation of client needs for legal services before the client requests them;
- a broad range of ancillary and other services and products traditionally characterised as 'non-legal';
- a practical, in-depth understanding of each client's business objectives; and
- close, frequent communications between lawyers and clients.

This level of client care will not only make the switching costs to another firm unacceptably high, but will also present a compelling case for converging as much high-value work on the firm as it is able to handle competently.

In other words, treat each client as if it were the firm's only client.

2.2   Keeping retail law firms competitive

The same trend toward consolidation, through mergers, strategic alliances and affiliations with specialised networks, that will restructure much of the legal services industry over the next 15 years, will also be felt in the retail legal services markets. Retail law firms will be larger and more geographically dispersed in order to capitalise on broader visibility and name recognition, as well as to take advantage of economies of scale stemming from more robust knowledge management systems.

Because of the inherent nature of retail legal services – predominantly relatively uncomplicated one-time cases and transactions for individuals and small businesses – retail law firms should not expect a high return from ongoing client relations and client retention tactics. Although client pyramids and the analysis of a firm's client sectors by reference to relative profitability and growth potential, as described above, might help to identify special opportunities, they will not be major foundations of a retail law firm's strategy. Repeat engagements, although welcome, will continue to be relatively rare, which will sharply limit the potential return on investment from business development strategies that will be so important to commercial legal services providers. The primary benefit of the fairly low levels of investment in client relations will be indirect marketing – that is, developing satisfied recent clients into referral sources, thereby improving and sustaining the visibility of the firm.

Where permitted by local bar regulations, marketing by successful retail law firms of the future will focus primarily on visibility and name recognition. The most effective marketing strategies of retail law firms will also articulate a limited number of demonstrable competitive advantages that deliver clear, relevant benefits to retail clients.

The media that currently produce only limited benefits for commercial law firms will by contrast become even more important marketing tools for retail firms. Most of the sophisticated consumers of legal services that go to commercial law firms will still be unlikely to be influenced by a posting on social media. However, individuals and small businesses, many of which do not have established, trusted relationships with partners in major commercial law firms, will rely even more heavily on social media to identify and, at least preliminarily, screen law firms that they want to consider for retail legal services and products.

The same need to provide basic information about retail legal services and providers will continue to support advertising through a variety of media ranging from television advertising, to ads in telephone directories, to displaying a firm's name, logo and "drink responsibly" message on plastic beer cups sold at sporting events. These tactics are, and will continue to be, relatively worthless efforts by commercial law firms; but they will continue to be vitally important in marketing a retail law firm in the hyper-competitive environments in which most of them will operate in the future.

3. Building a marketing and business development infrastructure for the future

For law firms of the future, the marketing message will be much less important than the demonstrated ability to deliver on its promises. Clients in both the commercial and retail subsectors of the legal services market will be even more knowledgeable than they are now about the growing range of options that are available to them; and they will be even more perceptive at spotting empty promises.

Delivery, not catchy tag lines and beautiful brochures, will be what matters. A failure to deliver high quality and added value consistently will be the great sword that will cut away unsuccessful providers of legal services, regardless of whether they focus on marketing, business development, or both.

We cannot predict with certainty all of the tools, techniques and tactics that will be available, nor how quickly they will become a part of everyday operations, both in the business world and in the legal profession. However, all law firms of the future, whether traditional survivors or cutting-edge alternative business structures, will need common infrastructure elements to ensure the best results at a reasonable investment of time and money, both of which will be even scarcer resources in most firms than they are today.

These five essential elements are:

- market intelligence;
- constant communication with the client;
- universal participation in marketing and business development;
- investment in skills development; and
- quality assurance.

To be sure, these are not the only aspects of an infrastructure to support business development; but they will be among the most important ones in most law firms in the future. A weakness in any of these five areas could undermine the smartest strategies and the most earnest efforts of an otherwise well-managed law firm.

3.1 Market intelligence

The role and functions of marketing departments are changing in law firms. Traditionally, marketing staff worked on the dissemination of information about the firm into the market. This role will continue in the future, especially in retail law firms; however, the law firm marketing departments will evolve into market intelligence departments, collecting information and analysing trends in the market, as well as in the client sectors that are the focal points of the firm's marketing and business development strategies.

This will be a critical component of the business development structure in commercial law firms. The communication flow from law firm marketing departments will be different. Instead of broadcasting information out into the market, the marketing staff will communicate it to the leaders and lawyers in client sector and industry sector practice teams.

This market intelligence will produce two substantial competitive advantages. First, it will give the firm's lawyers the information that they need to communicate more relevantly with both existing and prospective clients. Nothing demonstrates a thorough understanding of a client's business more persuasively than being able to discuss its future challenges and opportunities fluently and in depth.

Second, the communication of market intelligence to a client, pointing out imminent opportunities and risks that the client might not have spotted yet, is an outstanding example of delivering added value. It differentiates the lawyer who is also a trusted business adviser from an ordinary legal technician.

In the future, as client expectations for legal services and products expand, market intelligence will be the fuel that powers successful business development. It will demonstrate that the law firm offers more than slogans.

3.2 Constant communication with the client

"I want to feel like my lawyer is always by my side, no matter when or where." This comment by a general counsel in the telecommunications industry summarises the importance of communications as a basic component of a successful business development strategy. It applies not only to the availability and responsiveness of the lawyer who works directly with the client, but also to the entire support structure of the firm: non-lawyer fee earners, administrative staff and technological capabilities. All of these should be walking alongside the client.

Clients today expect constant availability from their lawyers. Clients frequently say that it is one of the key indicators of quality in the legal services that they receive. Most clients consider availability to be a decisive factor; they will not engage a law firm that fails to deliver it.[8] Availability is going to be even more important[9] as communications technology becomes even faster, cheaper and accessible anywhere on earth (or while flying above it).

---

8   In surveys administered by Walker Clark LLC for its law firm clients since 2002, availability – defined as "a partner is available to advise me when I need one" – has consistently ranked as one of the top five or 20 standard quality indicators, although its specific ranking in individual surveys has varied within the top five.

9   Since 2002 Walker Clark LLC has observed the average score for availability steadily move up among the top five quality indicators, from fourth place to third place, along with "prior experience with the firm", "responsiveness", "practical advice" and "understands my business".

Frequent communication with clients is the best way to demonstrate that a law firm understands client needs and expectations and, even more importantly, how those needs and expectations may be changing. By communicating often and in depth with clients, lawyers can detect the early signs of client dissatisfaction before it turns into a client retention crisis. Thus, constant communication with the client can also support quality assurance, another basic element of a successful marketing or business development strategy.

Responsiveness also can differentiate any law firm from its competitors, provided that the firm can consistently demonstrate this service quality.

3.3   Universal commitment

In successful law firms of the future, every lawyer – not just one or two rainmakers – will have a well-defined, accountable role in marketing and business development. The legal markets will be too competitive to permit most law firms the luxury of lawyers who do not contribute directly to attracting new clients or to retaining and expanding the relationship with existing ones.

The cult of the rainmaker, which is an anachronistic business development model left over from the early 20th century, will die out in all but the most traditional law firms.

Market forces will force reliance on rainmakers to become obsolete. All but the largest law firms will discover that the 'finder-minder-grinder' myth[10] that was so popular in the late 20th century is a costly waste of human capital and prevents a law firm from achieving its full potential. In the successful law firm of the future each partner, with enhanced market intelligence, will perform all three roles; and everyone in the firm, lawyer and non-lawyer alike, will understand how he contributes to advancing the reputation of the firm, both in the market and in its client base.

3.4   Investment in skills development

There is a direct, substantial return on a law firm's investment in the development of professional and business skills in its lawyers and staff.[11] Effectiveness in marketing and business development is the product of well-defined skills and behaviours, which anyone can learn. Instead of searching for rainmakers and ignoring everyone else, successful law firms of the future will focus on building these skills across the firm.

Some of these are basic sales and client relations skills. Additional skills involve

---

10   This model asserts that some law firm partners are natural producers of new clients and new business (the finders), some are good at client relations (the minders) and others are good only at producing large volumes of high-quality legal work (the grinders). Law firms that followed this model usually would rely almost entirely on the finders to develop business for the firm and would therefore see no need to invest in marketing and business development skills for other lawyers.
11   Analyses that Walker Clark LLC has conducted for its clients, especially in the commercial law sector, have shown a direct correlation between the amount of a firm's investment in professional and business skills development and measures including average revenue per lawyer, median value of new client origination and percentage of formal proposals resulting in engagements. Lawyers in firms that invest significantly in professional and business skills development also anecdotally report higher levels of morale and job satisfaction, and a greater level of long-term commitment to a career in the firm.

areas of emotional intelligence, such as empathy.[12] Every skill and behaviour that produces good business development results can be measured and improved.

Because of their different personalities, backgrounds and experience, some people feel more comfortable with some marketing and business development activities than others. The goal should be to create consistent basic marketing and business development skills at two levels:

- individually among all partners and senior lawyers in the firm; and
- as a group among teams supporting client relationships, especially when individual strengths can be applied to different aspects of business development.

This will produce much better, more sustainable results than continuing to rely on a very small number of lawyers to bring in most of the high-value legal work. It also creates a ready structure to support the cross-selling of new products and services to current clients, something which most law firms lack today.

3.5   Quality assurance

Quality assurance systems and procedures constitute the most reliable way to ensure that a law firm can deliver on its claims and promises. Quality assurance delivers several strong advantages to marketing and business development strategies:

- Quality is defined by the client, in terms of specific needs and expectations. A quality assurance system includes frequent feedback from clients about their needs and expectations, as well as how completely the firm is meeting them. The fact that a law firm invests in quality assurance and asks clients about their perceptions of the firm's quality can, by itself, create a positive impression of the firm. The existence of a quality assurance system also can make clients more tolerant of occasional lapses by the law firm, because they know that the firm has a system in place to identify the causes of substandard work and to reduce the probability of future mistakes.
- Unlike quality control measures, such as proofreading,[13] which correct mistakes only after they are discovered, quality assurance is a systematic method to identify and quantify the causes of errors, so that they can be prevented in the future.
- The existence of a serious, functioning quality assurance system – something more than a slogan on the website – can by itself create a differentiating competitive advantage for both commercial and retail law firms.

Notwithstanding the fundamental importance of each of the five elements outlined in sections 3.1 to 3.5 above, very few small and mid-size firms have ever

---

12   There is a high correlation between emotional intelligence and success in business development. Skills of emotional intelligence include, for example, transparency, self-confidence, influencing others, listening, self-awareness, flexibility, developing others, managing conflict, being a change agent, optimism and inspiring others.

13   This is not intended to suggest that proofreading is not an important procedure in law firms. However, even the most attentive proofreading is itself subject to errors and inconsistencies. Therefore, a law firm should not rely on proofreading or any other after-the-fact inspections of work product as its only quality assurance measures.

invested the time and resources to conduct even a cursory evaluation of them; and in some firms some of these elements do not appear to exist at all. Moreover, successful quality assurance requires fundamental cultural changes that are uncomfortable for most traditional law firms. For example, the leaders of a firm with a serious, functioning quality assurance system dislike mistakes as much as anyone; but they also welcome them as information that suggests areas for improvement.

By contrast, the traditional habits, in most law firms, of covering up mistakes, shifting blame and not learning from the experience will drag down business development efforts in the more demanding legal markets of the future. A firm that relies on after-the-fact fixes, unbillable rework, damage control and witch hunts – all of which will become increasingly unprofitable in a more price-sensitive environment – will never produce any significant and sustainable improvements in client service and satisfaction.

4.   Managing change in fast-moving blurry world

As Thomas Friedman said, the world is, indeed, getting flat,[14] as traditional assumptions and boundaries that used to protect the legal profession have been trampled by the conversion to a legal services industry that began at the end of the 20th century. It also is getting blurry as forces and trends emerge and move so quickly that many of us have difficulty even seeing them, much less comprehending their full impact on our professional lives as lawyers.

It also is a world that has been turned somewhat upside down for some lawyers. Even with respect to relatively simple retail legal services, the client, not the lawyer, now drives the relationship: effectively setting the price, demanding more value for money and expecting levels of personal attention unknown outside, perhaps, the medical profession.

Although we can identify some trends that could affect law firm strategy and tactics, their force and direction is hard to forecast in the complex, fast-moving environment in which all law firms, commercial and retail alike, will be asked to deliver legal services and products, in new ways, faster, less expensively, and with added-value components that only 20 years ago were almost never imagined as part of a law firm's line of business.

Because we cannot always be sure or even bravely confident about how innovations will continue to change the legal services industry, we need to be sure, more than ever before, that our basic strategic decisions and directions are solid ones, based on facts, not aspirations, but flexible enough to enable us to respond quickly and appropriately to change. One of the most important parts of a firm's business development infrastructure will be difficult to observe:[15] the skill with which it manages change.

---

14   Thomas L Friedman, *The World is Flat: A Brief History of the Twenty-First Century* (Farrar, Straus and Giroux, 2007).
15   Good change management is not completely invisible, however. Its positive effects on business performance, especially in terms of the return on investment in strategic marketing initiatives and innovative business development tactics, can be observed in the firm's financial performance, especially when compared to law firms that do not manage change in any systematic way.

Good decisions will not be enough. Probably the most important change that we will see in successful law firms of the future will be the firm-wide mastery of the skills of change management. Even now, change management is emerging as an essential set of tools and methods for the implementation of any worthwhile business strategy. As the pace of change continues to accelerate, six key elements of change management will be critical in the planning and operation of successful market and business development efforts:[16]

- committed leadership, which communicates four clear leadership messages to the entire firm:
  - The change will be reinforced and rewarded;
  - The change will improve the strength and profitability of the firm;
  - The change will make everyone's professional lives more satisfying and financially rewarding;
  - The change will be achieved only through collective firm-wide commitment and actions;
- data and evidence, which are critical to well-informed decisions about what changes are necessary, how to implement them and the ability to spot implementation issues before they become a crisis;
- a compelling business case with financial markers, which include an honest assessment of the value of partner time and any opportunity costs;
- a well-informed process that maintains a steady reference to the firm's strategic priorities;
- alternate actions and solutions that fit the unique characteristics of the firm; and
- shared measured results.

The right blend of these six elements can be highly firm-specific, but a thoughtful examination of the presence or absence of these is essential to ensure that great strategies and brilliant plans do not become dusty binders on a managing partner's bookshelf. In the blurry future world of law firm business development, the firm that does not master change management will find it increasingly hard to survive.

---

16   See Lisa Walker Johnson, "Managing Change" in *Good Governance in Law Firms: A Strategic Approach to Executive Decision Making and Management Structures* (Globe Law & Business, 2014), pp 203–229. Walker Johnson urges law firms to develop "continuous change capacity" in order to improve alertness to strategically significant changes and to implement effective responses.

The 10 fundamental elements of business development

Stephen Revell
Freshfields Bruckhaus Deringer

Competitive pressures mean that clients demand more from their lawyers. Simply doing good work is no longer enough. At its core, business development is about building relationships and winning work – it is about chasing opportunities for new instructions without being too pushy or in any way unprofessional. Firms which stay close to their clients and build deep, long-term relationships with these clients are more likely to be successful. This concluding chapter offers some practical 'how to' points on good business development from the perspective of both the lawyer and the law firm. These points are not some sort of magic formula nor do they amount to rocket science. They are largely drawn from the various chapters in this book and the conversations that I have had with the contributors and others in the bringing together of this volume.

I strongly encourage lawyers and law firms to consider which 10 elements are fundamental to their firm's approach – business development has to be moulded to suit the clients, the target clients, individual lawyers and different law firms.

1. Ten things that lawyers should know about good business development

1.1 Know your own firm – understand both the basics and the big picture
The starting point for lawyers is to understand what the firm does and has done, the firm's strategy and the type of business that the firm wants to build. This knowledge is mission critical and will inform the lawyer's business development activities. It is important to be fluent on the firm's key facts and figures – for example, to be able to name the practices, the main products and services that the firm is known for, the office locations, the number of lawyers, the names of the firm's market-leading experts and senior management.

1.2 Know your clients – focus on the priority group
Familiarity with the firm's priority and target clients avoids wasted time and effort. In particular, lawyers should know the identity of the firm's 'super clients' (those representing the largest proportion of revenues) so that these relationships can be actively protected and supported. Plus, get to know the names of the lead partners for the key client relationships. It is essential to run a conflicts check before chasing a new client – you will have wasted your time if you cannot act for them. Also remember that it is easier to get more work from existing clients than new work from new clients.

1.3   **Know your market – stay tuned in to the firm's position**

Lawyers need to understand the firm's position in the market, its differentiation from the competition and the buying priorities of clients for different legal services. Being conversant with a firm's market profile through award wins and rankings, website and press commentary stories ensure that the lawyers are tuned in to the firm's public and market position. Be aware of what other law firms in your market are doing.

1.4   **Build your network and profile – stand out from the crowd. Law is a personal service and the individual lawyer is a big part of that service.**

What will make a client choose you instead of another lawyer? What is your personal brand? A lawyer can take deliberate steps to build a wide personal network and profile – for example, go to networking events and actively follow up afterwards, use online sites like LinkedIn to have an appropriate social media presence, keep in touch with referrers of work, publish articles and comments, use travel opportunities to meet connections, think laterally and make introductions.

1.5   **Be curious and cross-sell**

Lawyers who are curious about their clients' business, network outside the firm, ask questions and think laterally about potential new business opportunities are often natural cross-sellers and, as a result, build a deep understanding of a client's needs. Successful cross-selling is based on personal knowledge about your firm and its services. Never assume that a client knows everything that a firm can offer.

1.6   **Create a personal business development plan – good business development requires a shift in mindset**

Putting some achievable business development goals in writing (ie, things over which the lawyer has control) – a form of business development to-do list – is an excellent way to make a start on business development activities. Break down the tasks into specific doable actions and set a deadline. Factor this into your performance appraisal discussions.

1.7   **Think like a client – show empathy**

Clients want their lawyers to anticipate their questions and think about the legal difficulties that they face from a business perspective with solutions and ideas to tackle the issues. Using simple language when writing helps readability and clarity of advice. Keep asking yourself: what will the client think?

1.8   **Talk to your clients – become the trusted adviser**

Clients expect active relationship management from their law firms. This means that lawyers must stay close to their clients and look for opportunities to keep in touch – whether through formal client feedback programmes or informally through conversations – as well as stay close to what is going on in the client's world.

1.9 Know your firm's systems – know where to get the information

A firm will normally have a range of tools and systems to help lawyers in business development activities and will often be supported by business development professionals. Lawyers need to be familiar with, and know how to access, client and matter data, financial reports, pitch toolkits and templates, and marketing materials to deliver on the business development work.

1.10 Think value and innovation – clients like new ideas

Consider whether you can develop a thought piece about a new issue or a new way of carrying out routine legal work for a particular client. Share ideas with clients in a personal way, not just as a mailshot; when you talk to clients, speak about helping the client whilst identifying if there is an opportunity to win work.

2. Ten things that law firms should know about good business development

2.1 Prioritise your clients – strategically segment your clients

Use robust criteria to segment the client base (eg, a value potential versus effort to grow analysis) and identify which clients form the priority group for client relationship management (CRM) efforts.

2.2 Train and educate your lawyers about business development

Help your lawyers understand that business development skills are integral to both personal success and the success of the firm. Run formal training and awareness sessions to develop lawyers' confidence and competencies

2.3 Map your clients – get under their skin as part of a good CRM programme

For priority clients, a client map helps a firm really understand a client and which individuals to target for work. The map can be used to support efforts to build deeper connections and track progress of expanding existing relationships with the client's organisation.

2.4 Reward and recognise good cross-sellers

Encourage and reward good cross-selling behaviour. Cross-selling is an excellent way to build client retention, and develop relationships and new business opportunities. Teach your lawyers about the firm so they are equipped to cross-sell.

2.5 Support your lead client partners

Partners with a lead role for specific client relationships need support and encouragement to be accountable for the progress of the client relationship.

2.6 Showcase the firm's services and expertise with campaigns – but not too many!

Campaigns can raise the profile and general awareness of the firm, position the firm's lawyers as experts, and develop and maintain relationships. Invest in a small number of well-structured campaigns with clear goals, a target audience, core messages and reporting measures. Seek to personalise the client contact.

2.7   Get the right business development infrastructure in place

Employ business development professionals and invest in the right CRM and business development infrastructure, resources and practices – tools, templates, checklists, databases, IT software and systems.

2.8   Senior management engagement drives buy-in

Visible senior management leadership and engagement is critical to the success of business devolvement and CRM programmes. They can communicate on the importance of the activities and spell out what is expected from the lawyers.

2.9   Hear the client's voice – run a formal client feedback programme

Clients are generally positive about being approached for feedback and like to know that the firm values their opinions and that they are being listened to. Having a regular client dialogue offers opportunities to cross-sell, to introduce more partners to the client and to build trust – as well as improve and make more effective the firm's business development activities.

2.10   Track progress and success

Ensure that business development and marketing activity have clear measurable goals which can be reviewed and reported on at regular intervals to assess the return on investment.

About the authors

André Andersson
Partner, Mannheimer Swartling
andre.andersson@msa.se

André Andersson is a partner of Mannheimer Swartling where he chairs the firm's banking and finance group. He is also the firm's global relationship partner. He has previously been on the firm's management board and was for several years responsible for legal recruitment and employer branding. Currently he is responsible for the firm's alumni programme.

Mr Andersson is a member of the board of the Stockholm Centre for Commercial Law and the education committee at the Stockholm Law Faculty. He has degrees in law and business administration from the universities of Lund and Oxford.

Mr Andersson works in particular with the structuring of different types of financial transaction, but his work also includes insolvency-related advice and debt restructuring. In 2011 he received the *Chambers* European Award for Outstanding Contribution to the Legal Profession – the first lawyer in the Nordic region to do so.

Mannheimer Swartling has been the most popular firm among Swedish law graduates for the past 13 years.

Hugo T Berkemeyer
Managing partner, Berkemeyer Attorneys and Counselors
hugo.tberkemeyer@berke.com.py

Hugo T Berkemeyer is managing partner of Berkemeyer Attorneys and Counselors in Asuncion, Paraguay. His general practice includes corporate law, mergers and acquisitions, financial and banking law, foreign investment, commercial transactions, project finance, infrastructure and public-private partnerships. His IP practice covers trademarks, patents, enforcement, franchising, licensing, agency and distribution law. He is a member of the International Bar Association, the American Bar Association, State Capital Group, Alfa International, the Paraguayan Association of Industrial Trademark Agents and the Paraguayan Bar Association.

Tom Bird
Partner, Møller Professional Services Firms Group
Tom.Bird@mollerpsfg.com

Tom Bird is a founding partner of the Møller Professional Services Firms Group. Located at the Møller Centre, Churchill College, in the University of Cambridge, the group brings together professional service firms experts who focus on leadership, strategy, business development, talent management and coaching issues within the professional service firm market.

Mr Bird focuses on developing business development, influencing and pitching skills with partners in professional firms in the United Kingdom, Middle East and Far East as part of the Møller business development practice group. He works extensively with a number of major law firms and accounting practices to deliver high-impact and pragmatic training and development. He is also a conference speaker and co-author of *Brilliant Selling* (published by Pearsons) and *The*

Financial Times Guide to Business Training. His next book, *The Leaders Guide to Presenting*, will be published in 2016.

Tracey Calvert

Director, Oakalls Consultancy Limited
tcalvert@oakallsconsultancy.co.uk

Tracey Calvert is a lawyer and the director and owner of Oakalls Consultancy Limited. Her legal experience is extensive and varied, having worked both in private practice and in local government before joining the Law Society of England and Wales. She was a senior ethics adviser and, when representation and regulation split, became part of the Solicitors Regulation Authority where she was a policy executive and part of the team which drafted the *SRA Handbook* launched in 2011. She now runs her own business providing regulatory compliance services to lawyers and prospective alternative business structures. She lectures nationally and internationally and has written numerous books and articles on her areas of expertise.

Daniela Christovão

Head of business development and corporate communications, TozziniFreire Advogados
dchristovao@tozzinifreire.com.br

Daniela Christovão has been the head of the business development and corporate communications department of TozziniFreire Advogados since the end of 2014. She has over 10 years' experience in heading corporate communications and institutional relations departments in Brazilian public companies and large law firms. She is an experienced professional in crisis management and reputation matters.

She began her career in 1998 as a journalist specialised in legal matters and was editor of the most important Brazilian business daily from 2000 until 2004. She is co-author of *Guia Valor Econômico de Tributos*, a guide to the Brazilian tax system.

Ms Christovão holds an undergraduate degree in law from the University of São Paulo, a specialised degree in leadership from *Escola de Governo* (Government School) and a law business master's degree from the University of São Paulo.

Norman Clark

Managing principal, Walker Clark LLC
norman.clark@walkerclark.com

Norman Clark is a co-founder and managing principal of Walker Clark LLC, a global legal management consultancy based in the United States. He is a past chair (2009–2010) of the Law Firm Management Committee of the International Bar Association, and teaches law firm management in the LLM programme of the International Institute of Law and Business in Panama City, Panama, and Miami, Florida.

For the past 20 years he has led international project teams advising law firms on business development strategy and tactics, governance, and mergers and acquisitions, with particular experience in emerging and recently emerged legal markets.

His recent publications include chapters in *The Business of Law: Strategies for Success* (Globe Law and Business, 2012) and *Good Governance in Law Firms: A Strategic Approach to Executive Decision Making and Management Structures* (Globe Law and Business, 2014).

Murray M Coffey

Chief marketing officer, Haynes and Boone LLP
Murray.Coffey@haynesboone.com

Murray M Coffey began practising law almost 26 years ago. For the past 15 years he has focused solely on business development at *AmLaw* 100 firms.

Mr Coffey joined Haynes and Boone in 2012 as the firm's chief marketing officer. He works directly with the firm's management in developing go-to market strategies and business development goals for the firm.

Prior to joining Haynes and Boone, Mr Coffey

was the second full-time marketing professional hired at the firm of Jenner & Block LLP in Chicago. While at Jenner & Block, he had roles of progressively greater responsibility, starting as a manager and culminating in being named chief marketing officer in 2009.

He is an avid reader and writer, enjoys live music and hiking with his family, and has come to love the mild Dallas winters.

Emily Cunningham Rushing
Director of competitive intelligence, Haynes and Boone LLP
Emily.Rushing@haynesboone.com

Emily Cunningham Rushing is the director of competitive intelligence for Haynes and Boone LLP. Her work involves leading a research, analysis and technologies group for the firm, which is based in Texas and ranked among the top-100 US firms by *The American Lawyer*.

Ms Cunningham Rushing frequently writes and presents on competitive intelligence and innovation for law firms.

Chris Davis
Senior media relations manager, Freshfields Bruckhaus Deringer
chris.davis@freshfields.com

Chris Davis is the senior media relations manager in Asia for global law firm Freshfields Bruckhaus Deringer. He is principally responsible for the firm's external communications throughout the Asia-Pacific region – including traditional, digital and social media – and is part of the firm's global media relations and thought leadership apparatus.

In addition to Freshfields, he has advised various law firms in Australia and Hong Kong on their media relations, including international plaintiff law firm Slater & Gordon.

Prior to his time in law firms, Mr Davis spent nearly a decade in various communications functions for one of Australia's two major political parties.

He has an MA in communications with a specialisation in public relations and a political science degree.

Shelley Dunstone
Principal, Legal Circles
shelley@shelleydunstone.com

Shelley Dunstone is the principal of Legal Circles, an Australian-based consultancy practice that helps lawyers to have better businesses and more satisfying careers. Ms Dunstone assists lawyers build their profiles and attract clients by focusing on thought leadership. She was admitted to legal practice in 1981 and is a former law firm partner. She also holds qualifications in marketing. She provides professional development for lawyers throughout Australia and internationally.

Akil Hirani
Managing partner, Majmudar & Partners
akil@majmudarindia.com

Akil Hirani is one of India's leading lawyers with over 22 years' experience. He is the managing partner at Majmudar & Partners, and also heads the firm's transactions practice. Mr Hirani has been ranked as one of the most in-demand lawyers in India by *Chambers Asia*. He is qualified to practise law in India, California, and England and Wales, although he is currently on inactive status in the latter two jurisdictions. Mr Hirani graduated with a BA in psychology from St Xavier's College, University of Mumbai, in 1989, and obtained his LLB (Hons) from the Government Law College, University of Mumbai, in 1992, having specialised in private international law. He has worked in California and London. Mr Hirani's particular areas of expertise include structuring investments of foreign companies and financial institutions into India, tax and regulatory advice, mergers and acquisitions, joint ventures and private equity.

Silvia Hodges Silverstein

Executive director, Buying Legal Council;
Fordham Law School; Columbia Law School
silvia@buyinglegal.com

Silvia Hodges Silverstein researches, teaches and speaks on purchasing decisions and metrics in the legal industry. She is executive director of the Buying Legal Council, the organisation for professionals tasked with sourcing legal services and managing legal services supplier relationships.

Dr Hodges Silverstein co-authored the Harvard Business School case studies "GlaxoSmithKline: Sourcing Complex Professional Services" on the company's legal procurement initiative and "Riverview Law: Applying Business Sense to the Legal Market" on the new model law firm.

She authored many articles on law firm management, including "I didn't go to law school to become a salesperson" (*The Georgetown Journal of Legal Ethics*), and is the author/editor of several books, including *Legal Procurement Handbook* and *Buying Legal: Procurement Insights and Practice*.

She earned her PhD at Nottingham Law School (United Kingdom), holds a master's degree in business from Universität Bayreuth (Germany) and Warwick Business School (United Kingdom) and an undergraduate degree (economics) from Universität Bayreuth.

Rainer Kaspar

Partner, PHH Rechtsanwälte
kaspar@phh.at

Rainer Kaspar is a partner in the corporate/mergers and acquisitions (M&A) department of PHH Rechtsanwälte. He advises private and corporate clients, private equity firms and financial institutions on a wide range of matters, with a particular focus on cross-border M&As, financing and capital markets transactions.

Mr Kaspar is a frequent speaker at seminars and conferences, including those sponsored by the International Bar Association and AIJA (the International Association of Young lawyers). He speaks German, English and French.

Martin E Kovnats

Partner, Aird & Berlis LLP
mkovnats@airdberlis.com

Martin E Kovnats is chair of the Aird & Berlis LLP's (Toronto, Canada) mergers and acquisitions team, co-chair of the international team and member of the firm's corporate finance and mining groups, private equity and venture capital team, and technology and communications groups. Mr Kovnats practises primarily in the areas of mergers and acquisitions, capital markets matters such as takeover bids, public and private debt and equity financings and other corporate commercial matters. He has extensive experience in cross-border and multinational matters abroad (principally in the United States and United Kingdom), advising clients on various mergers and acquisitions, corporate finance and corporate governance matters. He has extensive experience in advising participants in mid-market activities, as well as mines and mineral finance and acquisition. He is also the vice-chair of the International Bar Association's Professional Ethics Committee and is a member of Aird & Berlis LLP's Conflicts Committee.

Szymon Kubiak

Partner, Wardyński & Partners
szymon.kubiak@wardynski.com.pl

Szymon Kubiak has been practising law since 2000 – mainly in individual and collective Polish and European labour law and outsourcing. He has extensive experience in restructurings, covering outsourcing and group dismissals, cross-border business transfers and advice on atypical/flexible forms of employment, among other things.

He graduated with distinction from the Faculty of Law and Administration (Jagiellonian University) in Kraków (2001), where he completed his doctorate (2005). He earned an LLM at Harvard

Law School (2002). He has authored numerous publications on employment and European law and business development in law firms, and lectures at Jagiellonian University. He is a co-chair of the European Regional Forum of the International Bar Association and member of the European Employment Lawyers Association.

Over the past three years he has helped design and implement several internal programmes aimed at increasing external activities at Wardyński & Partners.

Camila Kutz
Associate, Prieto y Cía
ckutz@prieto.cl

Camila Kutz is an associate lawyer of Prieto y Cía. She is part of the firm's corporate team, specialising in mining law, energy and natural resources, construction projects, and mergers and acquisitions. Ms Kutz earned her law degree from the Pontificia Universidad Católica de Chile in 2009. She also obtained a diploma in natural resources/water rights from that university's law school in 2013. Before joining the firm, she worked at Cariola Diez Pérez-Cotapos y Cía.

Christine Liæker Lindberg
Director of marketing and communication,
Wiersholm
cli@wiersholm.no

Christine Liæker Lindberg is head of marketing and communication at Wiersholm. She has been with the firm for over 10 years. She holds a master of business economics and a master of commerce in business from Macquarie University in Sydney. She is an adviser and discussion partner for the firm's managing partner, partners and lawyers. She also works closely with the chief financial officer on business development initiatives. Her team handles external communications, marketing activities and events, as well as internal communication and cultural initiatives.

David W Marks
Barrister
dmarks@qldbar.asn.au

David W Marks QC is an Australian commercial barrister, specialising in tax. He has a traditional Chancery practice involving tax advice, tax appeals, companies, trusts, equity, insolvency, property and estates.

Rachel T McGuckian
Principal, Miles & Stockbridge PC
rmcguckian@milesstockbridge.com

Rachel T McGuckian is a principal and member of the board of directors of Miles & Stockbridge PC, a US law firm with offices in Washington, DC, Maryland and Virginia. Ms McGuckian has a diverse trial and appellate litigation and arbitration practice. She represents businesses ranging from listed public companies to real estate developers, from government contractors to family enterprises in all aspects of their dealings, internal and external, defends lawyers against legal malpractice claims, and also represents private clients in complex divorce, Hague and contested estate matters.

Ms McGuckian has been named one of the Top 100 *Super Lawyers* in both Washington, DC and Maryland, was appointed by Maryland's governor to both Maryland's State Ethics Commission and its State Board of Elections, is a lieutenant colonel in the JAG unit of the Maryland Defense Force, and serves as co-vice chair of the Professional Ethics Committee of the International Bar Association.

Joanna Michaels
Founder, Beyond Social Buzz
joanna@beyondsocialbuzz.co.uk

Joanna Michaels, founder of Beyond Social Buzz, is a digital marketer specialising in social media marketing for forward-thinking businesses and professional firms, looking for a differentiation in today's competitive marketplace. An engaging speaker and in-demand consultant, Ms Michaels has spent the past four years assisting small and mid-sized enterprises and professional firms developing their social media marketing strategies. She provides easy to implement, tried and tested techniques, and empowers firms to use social media to maximise their marketing impact.

Joram Moyal
MMS-Avocats
j.moyal@mms-legal.com

Joram Moyal specialises in corporate law, mergers and acquisitions (M&A) and banking at MMS-Avocats in Luxembourg. His practice also involves civil and administrative law litigation, labour law, immigration law and debt collection matters. Before co-founding MMS, Mr Moyal had been a sole practitioner, an associate in the corporate department of a well-established Luxembourg business law firm, legal counsel of a Luxembourg trust company and manager of a boutique law firm specialising in corporate and tax law. Mr Moyal has represented *Fortune 500* companies and private clients with respect to M&A transactions. He has also advised international businesses on corporate restructuring, partnerships, internal financing and international sale of shares, and has acquired significant experience in commercial litigation and labour and immigration law.

Alberto Navarro
Senior partner, NAVARRO CASTEX Abogados
anavarro@navarrolaw.com.ar

Alberto Navarro is senior partner at NAVARRO CASTEX Abogados, Buenos Aires, Argentina. Mr Navarro was previously the majority equity partner of G Breuer, before leaving the firm in 2008 with a group of partners and associates following a 45% firm split. Before going into private practice, he had served as in-house legal and general counsel at Acindar Industria Argentina de Aceros – a leading non-flat Argentine

steel producer and exporter – and prior to that as in-house lawyer at Cargill – a leading US commodities trader.

Mr Navarro is the founder of the department on legal issues in doing business at IAE (the management and business school of the Universidad Austral), where he has been teaching part time since 1992, giving lectures and seminars in corporate finance. He is also a professor of corporate law at Universidad Austral Graduate School of Law.

Seiichi Okazaki
Partner, Mori Hamada & Matsumoto
seiichi.okazaki@mhmjapan.com

Seiichi Okazaki, admitted to practise in Japan (1995) and New York (2000), is a partner in the corporate and mergers and acquisitions (M&A) practice group of Mori Hamada & Matsumoto. His main practice areas include M&A and cross-border corporate and finance transactions. He has extensive experience in advising non-Japanese clients doing and expanding business or making investments in Japan, and also has represented a variety of Japanese and foreign financial institutions, private equity funds and corporations with business operations in Japan. He joined Mori Hamada & Matsumoto in 1995, attained his LLM in 1999 from Columbia Law School and worked as a visiting attorney at Simpson Thacher & Bartlett LLP in New York from 1999 to 2000.

Julia Randell-Khan
Consultant
Juliarandellkhan@gmail.com

Julia Randell-Khan is the former head of marketing and business development, global markets, at international law firm Freshfields Bruckhaus Deringer where she worked for over 20 years in legal, marketing and business development and knowledge management roles.

Ms Randell-Khan joined Freshfields as the first knowledge management lawyer for the global finance practice, to develop the knowledge management function across the firm's international offices. She was involved in reshaping the firm's strategic approach to knowledge management and marketing and business development, devising the relationship programme with leading law firms in countries where the firm had no office and consulting with clients.

For over 10 years her roles included leading the marketing and business development activities for the firm's industry sectors and geographical regions, and client relationship management for international clients.

Stephen Revell
Partner, Freshfields Bruckhaus Deringer
stephen.revell@freshfields.com

Stephen Revell is a long-time partner of Freshfields and is currently head of the firm's corporate practice in Asia and managing partner of Freshfields Singapore. He also has responsibility for the StrongerTogether initiative, a network of relationship firms around the world that supports Freshfields' global approach to advising clients. Mr Revell was educated at Christ's College, Cambridge. He joined Freshfields from university and became a partner in 1987; he was the firm's US managing partner from 1998 to 2002.

Mr Revell works on all types of corporate transaction – from mergers and acquisitions and joint ventures to initial public offerings, equity offerings and debt offerings, many with a cross-border element and often involving emerging markets. He has broad sector experience and as a hands-on partner gets fully involved in all drafting and negotiations.

He also has extensive hands-on experience of business development, as well as of giving talks about the subject, and of creating and embedding business development systems. Having practised in the United States and the United Kingdom, across Europe and the Commonwealth of Independent States and, more recently,

throughout Asia, he has interacted with an extraordinary range of clients, which makes him extremely well qualified to edit a book on business development for lawyers.

Mr Revell is very active in the International Bar Association and has been and is involved in a wide array of projects, activities and committees. He is presently a council member of the Section on Public and Professional Interest.

Steven M Richman
Partner, Clark Hill PLC
srichman@clarkhill.com

Steven M Richman is a partner in the Princeton, New Jersey office of Clark Hill PLC. His national practice includes representation of foreign and domestic companies in commercial litigation and arbitration. His areas of practice include international and domestic contract law, copyright and trademarks, and appellate work, as well as counselling in supply chain and distribution issues. He is a graduate of Drew University and New York University School of Law. He is the author of *The ABA Photography Law Handbook*, and has written extensively in the areas of international law and professional responsibility. He is a member of the National District Export Council, serving from New Jersey, as well as holding leadership positions within the American Bar Association (ABA) and International Bar Association. He is vice chair of the ABA's Section of International Law and a member of the ABA House of Delegates.

Steven Stevens
Principal, Stenas Legal
steven.stevens@stenaslegal.com

Steven Stevens is co-chair of the International Bar Association's Professional Ethics Committee and chair of the Law Council of Australia Professional Ethics Committee. He is a member of the Legal Services Council in Australia and the Legal Services Board in the state of Victoria. He is a past president of the Law Institute of Victoria and former director of the Law Council of Australia; he has also represented the legal profession on a number of external bodies, including the Australasian Institute of Judicial Administration and on consultative fora of the Australian Taxation Office. Mr Stevens is a tax practitioner and principal of Stenas Legal in Melbourne. He practised as an economist before being admitted to legal practice in 1988. Between 1993 and 2011 he was a tax partner in the Australian office of Herbert Smith Freehills.

Paul P Subramaniam

Chief risk officer and head of knowledge management and training, ZICO Holdings Inc

paul.p.subramaniam@zicoholdings.com

Paul P Subramaniam is responsible for the overall risk management and mitigation for ZICO Holdings Inc, an integrated network of professional service firms focused on southeast Asia. He is also responsible for developing and implementing knowledge management and training initiatives for the group and the ZICO Law Network. He was a practising lawyer for over 28 years prior to joining the group.

Mr Subramaniam now keeps the clients of ZICO Holdings updated as to changes in the law and industry which would affect them. He also serves as editor of the group's clients publications. In his role as head of knowledge management and training, he arranges training sessions for law firms to equip them not just with the law, but also the skills necessary to serve their client's interests. He is in frequent demand as a speaker, presenter or panellist on a range of topics both legal and non-legal.

Angela Swan

Counsel, Aird & Berlis LLP

aswan@airdberlis.com

Angela Swan is counsel to Aird & Berlis LLP in Toronto, Canada, as well as a member of the corporate/commercial group and the legal education department. She was previously a partner at the firm and an associate at a national firm in Montreal. She is particularly experienced in contract law and statutory interpretation, and consults with members of the firm on many legal issues, including corporate transactions and civil and commercial litigation. Ms Swan stays involved with the firm's practice groups in order to provide topical information on recent case law. She has written numerous papers, reviews, books, case comments and annotations in regard to matters such as contract law, civil litigation and conflict of laws. She is frequently retained by other law firms as an expert witness in connection with matters pertaining to the law in Ontario.

Liam Tracey-Raymont

Articled clerk

ltracey-raymont@airdberlis.com

Liam Tracey-Raymont is an articling student at Aird & Berlis LLP (Toronto, Canada) who recently graduated from law school at Queen's University in Kingston, Ontario where he focused on business and corporate law. He earned his BA (Hons) from McGill University, majoring in political science and was a member of the International Relations Student Association. After finishing his undergraduate studies, Mr Tracey-Raymont spent a summer interning at the International Criminal Court in The Hague, Netherlands, where he worked in the prosecutor's office alongside other interns from around the world. As a first year law student at Queen's, he spent a semester working with undergraduate students as a full-time teaching assistant in the school's political science department. He was also a member of the Corporate Law and Investment Club at Queen's and was a co-recipient of the David Sabbath Prize in first year tort law.

Claudio Undurraga
Partner, Prieto y Cía
cundurraga@prieto.cl

Claudio Undurraga earned his law degree from Pontificia Universidad Católica de Chile. His wide legal experience covers energy, natural resources, transportation and telecommunication, as well as project finance, banking and corporate matters. He also handles litigation related to electricity, telecommunications, and gas and oil. He has acted as arbitrator and is a member of the Superior Council of the *Centro Nacional de Arbitrajes*. He has been a board member of blue-chip telecommunication companies. He specialises in mergers and acquisitions, energy and natural resources, litigation and arbitration.

Carlos Valls Martinez
Partner, Fornesa Abogaos
c.valls@fornesaabogados.com

Carlos Valls Martinez practises in intellectual property, litigation and arbitration at Fornesa Abogaos, in Barcelona, Spain. He specialises in advice on and protection of intellectual property, unfair competition, fundamental rights and data protection matters. He started his career at Clifford Chance (1989), becoming a partner and founding the Barcelona office in 1993 before becoming managing partner. In 2002 he left Clifford Chance to found his own firm, Iuris Valls Abogados (2003–2013). He is a regular speaker at conferences organised by the International Bar Association (IBA), the Barcelona Bar Association, the *Centro de Patentes* and the International Association of Lawyers. He is treasurer of the IBA International Sales Committee and founding member and present vice president of *Associació pel Foment de l'Arbitratge* (Association for the Promotion of Arbitration) (secretary 2010–2011).

Patricia Villanueva
Partner, López, Villanueva & Heurtematte – Lovill LatamLex
pvillanueva@latam-lex.com

Patricia Villanueva is founding partner of López, Villanueva & Heurtematte – Lovill LatamLex, where she heads the real estate law department and provides legal advice to local and international companies developing real estate projects in Panama. Ms Villanueva has a master's in business administration from the University of Louisville, a *juris doctor*'s degree from the School of Law, Loyola University New Orleans and a bachelor of arts (political science) from Loyola University New Orleans. She is also a licensed real estate broker and a licensed translator (English/Spanish). She was named 'Outstanding Practitioner' in the areas of real estate and corporate law by *Chambers & Partners Latin America* in 2011, 2012, 2013, 2014 and 2015.

Tomasz Wardyński
Partner, Wardyński & Partners
tomasz.wardynski@wardynski.com.pl

Tomasz Wardyński is an adwokat (lawyer) and founding partner of Wardyński & Partners.

His career spans over 40 years. His main expertise is in the field of arbitration, but he has also practised in civil, commercial and competition law. He was one of the first lawyers in Poland to develop a practice in EU and competition law.

Tomasz Wardyński holds degrees from the University of Warsaw (1970). He also studied at the College of Europe, Bruges (1973) and at the Institute of European Studies at the University of Strasbourg (1975). He is an honorary legal adviser to the UK ambassador in Poland. In 2001 he was appointed Honorary Commander of the British Empire by Queen Elizabeth II.

He is a member of the International Chamber of Commerce's (ICC) Commission on Arbitration and Alternative Dispute Resolution, and also serves as a member of the ICC International Court of Arbitration in Paris.

Dariusz Wasylkowski
Partner, Wardyński & Partners
dariusz.wasylkowski@wardynski.com.pl

Dariusz Wasylkowski has been practising law since graduating from the University of Warsaw in 1993. He also studied at the University of Copenhagen (1991) and obtained a joint MBA from the University of Warsaw and University of Illinois at Urbana Champaign (1993–1994). He continued his education at the International Bureau of Fiscal Documentation in Amsterdam (1996–1997) and in two executive education programmes at Harvard University (2010 and 2012). His main areas of practice are tax law, state aid law and penal fiscal law. He is a member of the Tax Consultation Board to the Minister of Finance and a member of the Permanent Scientific Committee of the International Fiscal Association.

Over the past three years he has helped design and implement several internal programmes aimed at boosting the firm's external activities.

Eduardo M Zobaran
Partner, Mundie Advogados
emz@mundie.com.br

Eduardo M Zobaran co-heads the corporate department of Brazilian law firm Mundie Advogados, which has offices in São Paulo, Rio de Janeiro and Brasília. He is a graduate of Universidade do Estado do Rio de Janeiro (LLB) and has an LLM from Johann Wolfgang Goethe Universität, Frankfurt-am-Main, Germany.

Thorsten Zulauf
Consultant, Law Firm Change Consultants
thz@lawfirmchange.com

Thorsten Zulauf is a law firm consultant specialised in the economic operations of law firms. Coming from an education in business administration, he has worked in leading professional services firms such as Accenture and Linklaters, where he held the positions of business manager for the commercial practice groups and head of finance and controlling.

His strengths lie in supporting partnerships in all business development-related matters, providing financial/business analysis, as well as expertise in the implementation of professional financial management and business support functions within large law firms.

Mr Zulauf was a speaker and moderator at a seminar on successful pitching and for the AIJA (the International Association of Young Lawyers) German Speaking Regional Meeting on the theme "Where the money is (and the associated risk)".